HOW TO cheat IN PHOTOSHOP
Elements 10

Release your imagination

David Asch and Steve Caplin

ELSEVIER

AMSTERDAM • BOSTON • HEIDELBERG • LONDON • NEW YORK • OXFORD
PARIS • SAN DIEGO • SAN FRANCISCO • SINGAPORE • SYDNEY • TOKYO
Focal Press is an imprint of Elsevier

Focal
Press

Focal Press is an imprint of Elsevier
The Boulevard, Langford Lane, Kidlington, Oxford, OX5 1GB, UK
225 Wyman Street, Waltham, MA 02451, USA

First edition 2012

British Library Cataloguing in Publication Data
A catalogue record for this book is available from the British Library

Library of Congress Cataloguing in Publication Data
A catalog record for this book is available from the Library of Congress

ISBN: 978-0-240-82047-7

For information on all Focal Press publications visit our website at www.focalpress.com

Book design and cover by Steve Caplin

Printed and bound in Canada

12 13 14 15 10 9 8 7 6 5 4 3 2 1

Contents

Contents

How to cheat, and why

The truth about cheating

We've used the word 'cheating' in the title of this book in two ways. The most obvious is that we're describing how to make images look like photographs, when they're not. In this sense, it simply means creating photographic work without the need for a studio.

The other sense of 'cheating' is finding shortcuts to help you work more quickly and more economically. Wherever possible, we've used the quickest solutions we can find to achieve the results.

Each workthrough in this book is designed as a double-page spread. That way, you can prop the book up behind your keyboard while following along with the associated image.

At the end of each chapter you'll find an Interlude, in which we discuss an issue of relevance to the Elements artist. Some cover essential information about file sizes and types, color mode, and so on; others take a broader view. Think of them as light relief, and read them to save eye strain from staring at the screen for too long.

Who is the book for?

As the 'baby brother' to the full Photoshop CS5, Photoshop Elements has long suffered the stigma of being a cheap, unprofessional product. Cheap it may be, but it contains 90% of the features found in the full Photoshop and, as we've seen from user-created artwork, it's anything but unprofessional.

It's true that Elements is rarely used in a graphics studio or publishing company. But this is mainly because it doesn't include the high-end prepress features found in Photoshop: using Elements doesn't mean that you're working with a substandard application.

Some Elements users simply want to enhance their digital captures, perhaps adding a caption or two. But there are also those who want to take their work further: to explore the field of photomontage, and to make reality from the dreams locked in their heads. It's for these users that *How to Cheat in Photoshop Elements 10* will be of most benefit, helping them to release that potential and get their ideas out of their heads and onto the screen.

As a montage application, Elements is only as limited as your imagination. It can realize any montage you can conceive, as long as you have the technical skill required. We aim to provide you with that skill set, enabling you to unleash your creativity. Whether you're montaging missing family members into a group portrait, or creating a complex work of art, Elements can help you achieve your goal.

Where do I access the images and other files?

Simply point your web browser to the following address:

http://www.howtocheatinphotoshopelements.com/resources/

You will be asked to supply login details: the username is htcie, the password is takemethere. Both must be in lower case.

A new page will open. All the photographic images from the workthroughs in this book are available to download, so that after reading about them you can open up the original files and experiment with them for yourself. There are also a number of QuickTime movies showing specific techniques in action.

The online content also includes a set of layer styles and custom shapes that we've created in Photoshop. Although you can't create these effects in Elements, you can import them and apply them to your own artwork – and modify them to quite a large degree.

Many things have changed in Elements since we started writing this series and some of its features have been removed or replaced. We do, however, want to keep the book as compatible with older versions as possible. To avoid confusion, we have moved old projects and those that refer to these features to the download area as PDF files.

Going further

As well as the dowloadable content on the website, you'll find the Readers' Forum. This is where you can post questions or problems, and exchange ideas with other readers: we'll also do our best to solve any Elements-related issues that may be troubling you. If you get stuck, either on a tutorial in the book or elsewhere in Elements, this is your first place to look for a solution.

David Asch and Steve Caplin
London and Brighton, 2011

How to use this book

We doubt if any readers of this book are going to start at the beginning and work their way diligently through to the end. In fact, you're probably only reading this section because your computer's just crashed and you can't follow any more of the workthroughs until it's booted up again. This is the kind of book you should be able to just dip into and extract the information you need.

But we'd like to make a couple of recommendations. The first four chapters deal with the basics of photomontage: making selections, working with layers, masks and distortion techniques. There are many Elements users who have never learnt how to make layer masks, or picked up the essential keyboard shortcuts. Because we talk about these techniques throughout the book, we need to bring everyone up to speed before we get to the harder stuff.

Although the book is designed for users of Elements 10, most of the tutorials will apply to those who have earlier versions of the program as well. We've indicated on each page where Elements 10 is specifically required to perform the task in hand.

The techniques in each chapter build up as you progress through the workthroughs. Frequently, we'll use a technique that's been discussed in more detail earlier in the same chapter, so it may be worth going through the pages in each chapter in order, even if you don't read every chapter in the book.

The downloadable content icon on each tutorial page indicates that the source file for that tutorial is on the website, so you can open it up and try it out for yourself. The movie icon indicates that there's an associated QuickTime movie, also available to view or download online.

If you get stuck anywhere in the book, or in Elements generally, visit the Reader Forum, accessed through the main website or directly via this address:

www.howtocheatinphotoshopelements.com/forum

This is where you can post queries and suggestions. We visit the forum every day, and will always respond directly to questions from readers. But expect other forum members to weigh in with their opinions as well!

Using keyboard shortcuts

Throughout the book we use the built-in keyboard shortcuts in Elements and it's really worth learning at least the most frequently used ones; they are there to help you work more efficiently. Not only is it far quicker to press a key to choose a particular tool or function, it also helps to save your aching wrists by avoiding the need for unnecessary mouse or pen movement. You can switch from tool to tool without leaving the area of the image you're currently working on, which also keeps your workflow more streamlined.

The Toolbox items all use a single letter for the shortcut, some correspond to the initial letter of their names, for example: T selects the Type tool, M selects the Marquee Selection tools; others are a little more obscure – J, for instance, selects the Healing Brush tools and F gives us the Smart Brush.

Given that we only have a relatively small amount of keys on the keyboard compared with the vast amount of commands in Elements, many features are accessed by adding what is known as a modifier key (or keys); these are pressed in conjunction with the letter or symbol key, giving each one the potential to have up to four different functions. Because the book is designed for users of both Mac and Windows and the modifier keys are slightly different on each platform, we list them color-coded: red for Mac and blue for Windows, along with their names: *ctrl* (control) and *alt* (alt), or in the case of the Mac, their symbols: ⌘ (command or Apple) and ⌥ (option or alt).

So, to demonstrate: if we want to open the Levels dialog we would first hold down ⌘ or *ctrl* then press the L key. We show this in the book as follows: ⌘*L* *ctrl**L*. There are also combinations of modifier keys: the shortcut for Remove Color, for example, is *Shift*⌘*U* *Shift**ctrl**U* and for the Magic Extractor it's the finger-twisting ⌥*Shift*⌘*V* *alt**Shift**ctrl**V*!

Although the Shift key is the same for both Mac and Windows, we keep it in the relevant color when it's part of a multiple sequence, as in the above example, to avoid confusion. On their own, keys like this and also the Toolbox shortcuts are shown in black: *Shift*, *Enter*, *T*, *M*, *J*, *F* and so on.

Getting up to speed

REGARDLESS OF YOUR SKILL LEVEL it's always useful to have a refresher on the basics. We've used these two pages to not only document some of Elements' standard features but also to illustrate how they are used and referred to throughout the book.

The Layers panel

We use the Layers panel all the time when we're editing images in Elements. It displays all sorts of information about how layers interact with each other. It's worth taking the time to get to know how it works, and how to use the icons and settings to make our layers behave as we want them to.

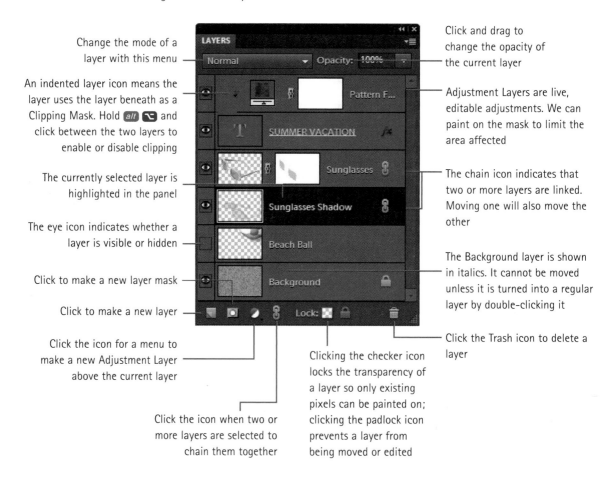

Change the mode of a layer with this menu

An indented layer icon means the layer uses the layer beneath as a Clipping Mask. Hold *alt* ⌥ and click between the two layers to enable or disable clipping

The currently selected layer is highlighted in the panel

The eye icon indicates whether a layer is visible or hidden

Click to make a new layer mask

Click to make a new layer

Click the icon for a menu to make a new Adjustment Layer above the current layer

Click the icon when two or more layers are selected to chain them together

Click and drag to change the opacity of the current layer

Adjustment Layers are live, editable adjustments. We can paint on the mask to limit the area affected

The chain icon indicates that two or more layers are linked. Moving one will also move the other

The Background layer is shown in italics. It cannot be moved unless it is turned into a regular layer by double-clicking it

Click the Trash icon to delete a layer

Clicking the checker icon locks the transparency of a layer so only existing pixels can be painted on; clicking the padlock icon prevents a layer from being moved or edited

The Toolbox

The Toolbox is the most important part of the Elements editor. Tools can be selected by either clicking their icons or pressing their corresponding keyboard shortcut.

Many of the tools have two or more options – denoted by a small black triangle next to its icon. These can be selected by clicking and holding the mouse to display the sub-menu or by pressing the shortcut key repeatedly to cycle through them.

The various settings for each tool appear in the Options bar. This is found at the top of the Elements window under the menus.

Here is a list of the tools along with their shortcuts. These are mainly the same for both the Windows and Mac versions – differences are shown in color.

Move tool **V** (or hold down **ctrl ⌘** to access temporarily)

Hand **H** (or hold down the Spacebar to access temporarily)

Rectangular/Elliptical Marquee **M**

Magic Wand **W**

Horizontal Type/Vertical Type/ Horizontal Type Mask/ Vertical Type Mask / Text on path tools **T**

Cookie Cutter **Q**

Red-eye Removal Tool **Y**

Clone Stamp/Pattern Stamp **S**

Brush/Impressionist Brush/ Color Replacement **B** & Pencil **N**

Paint Bucket **K**

Rectangle/Rounded Rectangle/ Ellipse/Polygon/Line/Custom Shape/ Shape Selection Tool **U**

Sponge/Dodge/Burn **O**

Set to default colors **D**

Foreground/Background Color

Zoom tool **Z** (or hold down **ctrl ⌘** and the Spacebar to access temporarily)

Eye-dropper tool **I**

Freehand Lasso/Magnetic Lasso/Polygonal Lasso **L**

Quick Selection Tool/ Selection Brush **A**

Crop/Recompose tool **C**

Straighten Tool **P**

Spot Healing Brush/ Healing Brush **J**

Eraser/Background Eraser/ Magic Eraser **E**

Smart Brush/ Detail Smart Brush **F**

Gradient tool **G**

Blur/Sharpen/Smudge **R**

Swap Foreground & Background colors **X**

3

■ The photograph of a woman in Ecuador, above, shows a strong face, brightly colored clothes and a neatly incongruous hat. But that background is just confusing: how much better it is when we change it for the view across the street. Removing the woman from her background is easier than you might think!

1

Selection techniques

WORKING IN PHOTOSHOP ELEMENTS almost always involves making selections. Whether you're combining images from several sources into a single montage, or simply replacing an overcast sky with a bright sunny one, you need to make selections within your image.

Elements offers a range of tools for the purpose. Some are automatic, and will find areas of similar color; some involve tracing around an object's edge; some combine the two methods, making complex selections easy to do.

Whether you're new to Elements, or an old hand, it's worth your while going through this chapter to make sure you're up to speed on the selection methods that are available to you.

Marquee selections

THE MARQUEE TOOL is the basic tool for making selections in Elements. Pressing **M** is the keyboard shortcut for this tool: pressing the key again will toggle between the standard Rectangular Marquee tool, and the Elliptical Marquee tool.

Every Elements user should be aware of the ability to hold the **Shift** key to draw a square or a circle, rather than a rectangle and an ellipse, and to hold **alt** **⌥** to draw a selection from the center out.

We're not limited to just one selection at a time, however; by holding combinations of the **alt** **⌥** and **Shift** keys, we're able to add and subtract additional selections – and we can even create intersections between the old and the new.

1 The default method of drawing out a marquee selection, either rectangular or elliptical, is from corner to corner. In the above example we've positioned the cursor in the top-left corner of the document, then clicked and dragged with the mouse to the opposite corner.

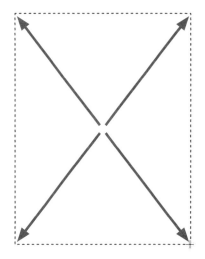

2 If we begin to draw out our selection as before and then hold down **⌥** **alt**, the selection expands out from the original cursor position. This is especially useful when making selections with the Elliptical Marquee as it's much easier to judge the positioning from the center point.

3 So far we've seen how to draw freeform selections. If, however, we start to draw out a selection and then hold down **Shift**, the selection becomes constrained to form a perfect square (or circle). If we hold **⌥** **alt** as well, it will expand from the original cursor position as before.

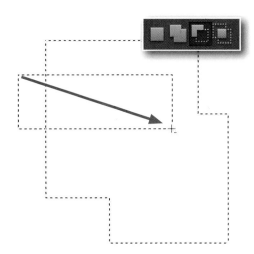

4 Selections can also be made to interact with each other: if we hold down *Shift* *before* drawing a new selection, it will combine the two to create a single selection. We can also set this in the Options bar (see the inset). Notice how the cursor gains a small + to indicate it's in add mode.

5 Here are the two previous selections joined together. If we hold down ⌥ *alt*, again before we start to draw, we see a small – (minus) sign next to the cursor. This denotes that we are in subtract mode. This time the rectangle we are drawing here will be cut away from the shape.

6 The final selection mode is called intersect. This is invoked by holding ⌥ *Shift* *alt* *Shift* before drawing the selection; our cursor gains an x symbol this time. This has the effect of only leaving the portion of the previous selection where it falls within the new one.

7 Here's the end result of drawing with all the different selection modes. We've filled the shape with color to make it easier to see what's left. These modes are available to use with almost all the selection tools in Elements. We'll see them in action throughout the rest of the book.

HOT TIP

The order in which you press the keys and the mouse button makes a difference to the result. Holding the keys shown here before pressing the mouse button will affect how the selections interact; pressing them afterwards will make a square or a circle, or draw from the center out.

One additional tip is to hold the Spacebar as you're drawing a selection. This will allow you to move the selection around while you're still drawing it; release the Spacebar (but not the mouse button) to continue.

SHORTCUTS
MAC WIN BOTH

7

More selection tools

WE LOOKED AT the Marquee tools on the previous pages – but what if you want to make a selection that isn't rectangular or round? There are several other tools we can use for this purpose.

Here, we'll look at the Lasso, Magic Wand, and Selection Brush tools. While the Magic Wand selects a range of colors, the other two select only those regions you trace. They're three quite different tools, but they each have their uses, as we'll see here.

We're going to use all these tools to remove the sky from this photograph of the Statue of Liberty, beginning with the Magic Wand to select the bulk of the sky.

1 To select all the sky in this image, first use the Magic Wand tool **W**. You can change the tolerance to select a smaller or wider range of colors: a setting of 32 works well. Click once to the left of Liberty's body, and you'll see a selection something like this.

2 The top right and bottom right corners weren't included in the selection, as the color there is just outside the range. To add to the selection, hold **Shift** and click with the Magic Wand in the top right corner. These colors are now added.

3 We can see a few stray pixels – most probably dirt on the lens – above the book, and to the left. Rather than use the Magic Wand, switch to the Lasso tool **L**. Hold **Shift** once more and draw a loop around the stray dots to add them to the selection.

4 We can add the sky between the crown and the shoulder with the Magic Wand, holding **Shift** as before. Now that we're zoomed in, we can see a problem: part of the pale green statue has inadvertently been selected along with the sky.

5 Here we'll switch to the Selection Brush Ⓐ, which we can use like a paint brush. Since we want to subtract from the sky selection, hold *alt* � as you drag over the area: everywhere within the radius of the tool will be removed from the selection.

6 There's a problem with 'leakage' on the other shoulder as well, and we can use the Selection Brush to fix that. The book, however, has straight edges to it; even if we made the Selection Brush really tiny, we'd find it hard to trace those straight lines.

7 Instead, let's go back to the Lasso tool: this time, we'll use the Polygonal Lasso instead. Holding *alt* ⎘ before we drag once more, click from inside the body onto each corner of the book to add it with a straight line selection.

HOT TIP

You can make the radius of the Selection Brush bigger and smaller without opening a panel or dialog: use the square bracket keys *[* and *]* to make the radius smaller and larger in stages.

8 Once we've done a little further tidying up, our statue is selected. Except, of course, that it's the sky that we've selected rather than Liberty herself. We need to inverse that selection, by pressing *ctrl Shift I* *⌘ Shift I*.

9 With Liberty now properly selected, we can make a new layer from her by pressing *ctrl J* *⌘ J*. When we hide the original layer by clicking on the eye icon in the Layers panel, we see Liberty just cut out against a checkerboard background.

10 Once the original background has gone, we can replace it with anything we choose – such as this more appealing sky, for example. See the following chapter for more about working with layers.

In step 7 here, we use the Polygonal Lasso tool, which you can choose from the toolbar when you pick the regular Lasso. As a shortcut, though, you can make the regular Lasso work like the Polygonal Lasso (tracing straight lines between click points) by holding *alt* as you use it.

SHORTCUTS
MAC **WIN** **BOTH**

The Magnetic Lasso tool

ALTHOUGH THE LASSO TOOL is useful for tracing outlines, it can be tricky to draw accurately with it. There is another method: the Magnetic Lasso is a variant. As its name implies, this tool sticks to the edges of shapes as you draw around them, making the process of cutting objects or people from their backgrounds very much simpler.

The tool isn't perfect, by any means; it's almost impossible for any computer program to figure out the difference between foreground and background objects with any degree of accuracy. But it's a real time-saver, and can be used to make quick selections with ease.

To choose the tool, click on its icon in the Options bar when the Lasso tool is selected, or simply select it from the fly-out Lasso choices in the Toolbox.

1 Start in one corner of the statue and trace along the edge of the object, sticking as close as you can to it. We've zoomed in here and enhanced the Magnetic Lasso edge to show it more clearly. The tool places square 'anchor points' each time it marks a change in direction.

2 Right away, we hit a problem: when we get to the shoulder, the Magnetic Lasso wants to follow the gold bar, rather than the paler white cloth. No need to start again; simply press **Backspace** to remove the last placed points, backtracking along the traced line.

3 We can now force the tool to go in the direction we want. Drag a little way up the perimeter, and before Elements places another point, get in first by clicking the mouse button to place one of your own. Continue doing this until the tool recognizes the direction in which you're going.

4 We'll hit a few more of these snags as we work our way around the figure; they occur each time Elements finds a strong line to follow. Once again, it's not a problem; simply delete the misplaced points, and then click the mouse button to add your own.

5 To make it easier to trace the outline, press the *Caps Lock* key on your keyboard. This will change the Magnetic Lasso cursor to a circle, which shows the perimeter of the area in which it searches for boundaries.

6 When you get to the end of the object – in this case, the bottom right corner – it can be tricky to trace back along the bottom to the start, as the tool will think you're still looking for edges. Rather than get this wiggly line, press *Enter* to turn the path you've drawn into a selection.

HOT TIP

In step 5, we change the icon from a standard Magnetic Lasso to a circle showing the radius. You can make this larger and smaller using the Width setting on the Options bar; make it bigger for straightforward images, smaller for lots of fiddly edges.

The Edge Contrast and Frequency settings determine how much variation the tool looks for, and how often points are added to the path. In practice, you'll rarely need to change these from their default values.

SHORTCUTS
MAC WIN BOTH

The Quick Selection tool

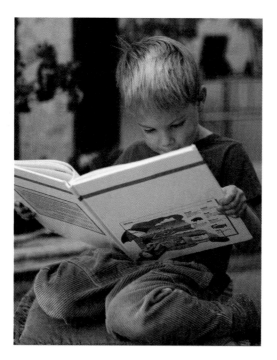

THE Quick Selection tool may well be the fastest method yet for cutting a person or object away from the background.

We've seen several selection methods already in this chapter, but they all involve a fair amount of work on the part of the user. The Quick Selection tool can help the process of lifting a complex subject from a complex background, quickly and painlessly.

The image we'll work with here is of a boy reading in his living room. It's a tricky selection to make: both the boy and his surroundings include a range of colors and tones, making it harder for automatic selection to take place. But even in cases like this, we can perform the function with ease.

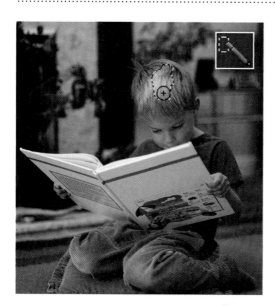

1 Begin by switching to the Quick Selection tool **A**. We'll see the cursor change to a circle with a cross in the center. We'll start by making a small selection on the boy's head. This only needs to be a single click at the moment, just to set the process off. We're going to be doing something slightly different to begin with.

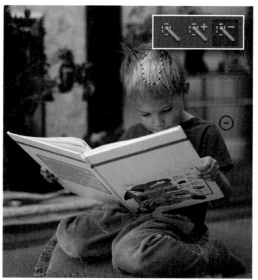

2 The Quick Selection tool learns about the image whilst you're using it. So to begin with, we'll tell it about the areas we don't want selected. First switch to subtract mode by selecting it in the Options bar. Using a small brush, paint around the outside of the boy; keep close to the edges but don't touch them. We don't see any difference yet.

3 Although there's no obvious change, we should see better initial results when we select the boy. Make sure you're back in add mode. Start to select the boy by painting loosely over his body and his book. As before, we don't need to go too close to the edges as the tool will find them itself. It's not a bad start, with only a couple of missed areas.

4 With our initial selection made, we can start to sort out the problem areas. Most are spilling away from the boy, so before we continue, we need to switch back to subtract mode. Make the brush small enough to fit comfortably into the missed sections. Now make small strokes to snap the selection back into place, varying the brush size accordingly.

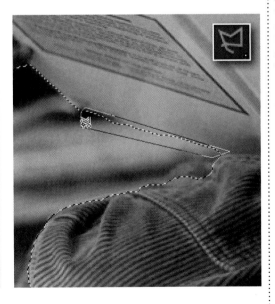

5 There are occasions where the tool will simply refuse to make the selection properly. This generally happens in areas of very low contrast: the shadows where the boy's leg meets the cushion, for example. If it becomes too fiddly it's better to switch to the Selection Brush **A** and add or subtract the areas manually..

6 We can also combine other selection tools to finesse the selection. Here, for example, we can see a problem with the edge of the book. To remedy this, select the Polygonal Lasso **L**. Set it to subtract mode. Now mark out an area that follows the edge of the book. When we complete the selection it will give us a nice straight edge.

SHORTCUTS
MAC WIN BOTH

Fine-tuning with Refine Edge

W HEN SELECTIONS ARE MADE, especially with the intelligent tools such as the Magnetic Lasso or the Quick Selection tool, the resulting cut-out of the person or object can be disappointing when viewed close-up and can leave our montage looking unrealistic. The biggest problems are harsh jagged edges, or a halo where the selection has taken in part of the background.

We've always had the ability to address these issues with the selection adjustment tools; it can be hit-and-miss getting it right. Instead, we now have the Refine Edge command. As we'll see, this clever tool gives us the ability to see at a glance areas we might have missed and then adjust our selection visually before we cut our object away from the background.

1 Start by using the Quick Selection tool **A** to select the guitar. Being on a white background this is an easy task, taking only a few strokes to catch everything. Sometimes, however, we miss areas without realizing; this can result in holes in the image when it's pasted into a montage.

2 Open up the Refine Edge dialog; when using the Quick Selection tool, there's a button on the Options bar, otherwise it's accessed via the Select menu. By default it opens with suggested settings; we need to set these all to 0 as we're only checking for potential problems at the moment.

3 There are five viewing modes: first is the standard selection view. Next we have a semi-transparent overlay (shown here). The next two hide the image background and replace it with plain black or white. Finally, we have the mask view, which is generally the best for error checking.

4 In mask mode we can clearly see our problem areas: a part of the body is missing, and we need to sort out the sections of the tuning head at the top. We'll cancel the dialog for now and use the Lasso tool and the Magic Wand to fix the problems.

5 Having addressed the problems we can fine-tune the selection. Open the Refine Edge dialog again. We'll keep the default settings this time. Switch to the black background view. As our image was originally against white this will clearly show us where the selection needs attention.

6 Most of the problem area seems to be on the head so we'll zoom in on that. We can see there's a white halo around it. We'll begin by reducing the smoothing as it's a little too high for this size of image. We can also reduce the feathering for the same reason.

7 That's starting to look better. To finish our example off we'll tighten up the selection by dragging the Contract/Expand control to the left. Around 30% works well here. Any more and we might start losing too much detail around the rest of the guitar.

HOT TIP

Each setting has a helpful description that appears at the bottom of the dialog as you hover over them; this tells you how it affects the selection. It's worth reading them but if you find they become distracting, you can always hide them by clicking the double arrow icon next to the word 'descripton'.

We can cycle through the different display modes by pressing **F**, toggle the before and after preview with **P**, and switch between the current display mode and the standard image preview with **X**.

SHORTCUTS
MAC WIN BOTH

Magic extraction

1 Use the Foreground Brush **B** to drag within the area you want to keep. Make sure the brush touches areas like the hair, which could be mistaken for background.

SOME TYPES OF IMAGE are just too complex to cut out with the Quick Selection tool, or the Magic Wand; photographs such as this accordionist, with his complex instrument photographed against a busy background, would be tricky to trace with the Lasso or Selection Brush.

The Magic Extractor, however, offers a relatively quick and painless solution to this problem. It works within its own dialog, using a range of tools that combine to make difficult object selection far easier.

The precise order in which you use the tools depends on the image you want to cut out, but you always start with the Foreground and Background Brush tools, before moving on to fine-tuning.

Begin by choosing Magic Extractor from the Image menu or by pressing `alt` `Shift` `ctrl` `V` `⌥` `Shift` `⌘` `V` on the keyboard.

2 Switch to the Background Brush **P** and drag in areas you want removed. This brush paints a blue stroke, in contrast with the red of the Foreground Brush.

3 Now hit the Preview button to see how the extraction looks so far. There are some problems – pieces of stray background, and the keyboard is missing – which we can fix.

4 Use the Foreground Brush once more to drag a line over the keyboard, and the Background Brush to drag over those extra background elements.

5 When we press Preview again, we can see a much better result. This is also a good time to change the preview background from None to Black, so we can see it clearly.

You can view the entire photo at any point by choosing Original Photo from the Display pop-up. The Touch Up section of the dialog includes useful tools: Feather will soften the edge of the whole image; Fill Holes will make sure there are no stray pieces missing by accident; and Defringe will smudge the colors at the edge of the selection to make the edges crisper.

6 One or two stray background elements remain. We can remove these with the Remove From Selection tool **D**, which works like an eraser.

7 The Add To Selection tool **A** is used to paint missing parts back in. Use a very small brush for fiddly areas, such as the edge of the accordion's bellows.

8 The extraction process does leave some ragged edges. Trace over the edge with the Smoothing Brush **J** to soften out the jaggies; hit OK when you're done.

17

Working with selections 1

S O FAR IN THIS CHAPTER we've looked at how to make selections using a variety of methods. Here, we'll look at what we can do with those selections when we've made them.

As well as being used to extract areas of an image from their background, selections can be used to contain, isolate and protect an area; for painting and filling localized parts of the image with color, for example. They can also be used in conjunction with filters and other effects.

Note: each of the steps on these pages are individual actions to demonstrate the different methods of filling the selections. After trying each one, go to Edit > Revert to restore the example image back to its default state.

1 We'll work mainly with circular selections here, for clarity – although any selection will work. To fill a selection with the current foreground color, press *alt* ⌥ *Backspace*; to fill it with the current background color, press *ctrl* ⌘ *Backspace*.

2 If you hold down *Shift* along with either of the keys we used in step 1, it will fill with color but preserve the transparency of the current layer – as we can see here with this palmistry hand, which is on a layer of its own. Only the areas that already contain pixels are affected.

3 Pressing **Shift Backspace** will open the Fill dialog. There are several options: here, we're filling the circle with a pattern, as chosen from the 'Use' pop-up menu. Press OK to complete the fill process. The Preserve Transparency feature would have the same function as holding **Shift** in step 2.

4 We can also change the blend mode of the fill (more on these in Chapter 2). One of the more useful ones, shown at the bottom of the dialog, is Behind. This fills the selected area behind the pixels already present on the current layer: the hand here remains fully visible.

5 We can also vary the opacity, or the strength of the fill. Here, we're filling with the current foreground color, but we're choosing to fill with an opacity of just 50%, so we can still see the hand through the filled circle. The lower the percentage, the more we see through the filled area.

6 We can also use the selection to contain filter effects. Here we've used the Mosaic Tile filter; it only affects the pixels within the selection. If we wanted to apply the filter to the area of the hand outside of the circle, we would inverse the selection first by pressing **ctrl Shift I** **⌘ Shift I**.

HOT TIP

The Revert command is Elements' panic button; it does need to be used with caution of course, as it resets the image to its last saved state. It is a handy thing to fall back on if something has gone horribly wrong and you find you have run out of undo steps. You can, however, undo and redo the Revert command itself, which is a quick way of seeing the image in its before and after states.

SHORTCUTS

19

Working with selections 2

WE EXPLORED THE MANY WAYS to fill areas using selections on the previous pages. In this project we'll put them to practical use and create a shadow that's directly attached to an object. We'll also look at another feature of selections: the ability to duplicate the selected object on the same layer.

This technique is great for creating repeating patterns and effects and keeps the document tidier than if you were to create the objects on separate layers; particularly useful if you know that you won't need to edit the individual copies at a later date.

1 This key has previously been selected and placed on a separate layer. We can recall its selection by holding *ctrl* ⌘ and clicking its thumbnail in the Layers panel. This is known as 'loading up' the selection and we'll be referring to this in the techniques throughout the book.

2 Make sure you have one of the selection tools active. Using the cursor keys, tap three or four times to the right and down to nudge the selection away from the key slightly; we could have also dragged the selection with the mouse but it's far more accurate this way.

Feather Selection

Learn more about: Feather Selection

OK

Cancel

Feather Radius: [4] pixels

Fill Layer

Learn more about: Fill Layer

OK

Cancel

Contents

Use: Black

Custom Pattern:

Blending

Mode: Behind

Opacity: 60 %

Preserve Transparency

HOT TIP

When we reload the selection in step 5 it appears that the shadow area is not included. This is because Elements does not visually include pixels below a certain opacity in the selection boundary. They will still be present when copied or moved, of course.

3 We'll need to soften the outline a little. Go to Select > Feather, or press *ctrl* *alt* *D* / ⌘ ⌥ *F*, and choose a fairly low value. A radius of around 4 pixels is sufficient here. This will vary depending on the size of the image you are working on. We don't see any difference yet, of course.

4 Now we have the selection in place, we can create the shadow. Press *Shift* *Backspace* to open the Fill dialog. We'll set the Contents to Black and the Blending mode to Behind; this will only fill the empty pixels within the selection. Lower the Opacity to around 60% and click OK.

5 We now have a soft shadow. Before we start making our duplicates, however, we will need to reload the selection as it's still offset; otherwise the left edge of the key will be feathered and cut off. Press *ctrl* *D* / ⌘ *D* to deselect, then load it up again to surround the entire object.

6 Hold down *ctrl* *alt* / ⌘ ⌥. Click and drag inside the selection. This will create a copy on the same layer; if the selection wasn't active it would create a new layer each time. Release the mouse but keep the keyboard shortcuts held. Click and drag again to make another copy.

SHORTCUTS

MAC WIN BOTH

Setting up Elements

WHEN YOU BUY MOST APPLICATIONS, you can just install them and run them straight out of the box. (Or out of the zip archive in which you downloaded them, if you prefer.) And so, to some extent, you can with Elements; but there are a few tricks you can do to make the experience more comfortable.

It isn't that Elements is a particularly awkward program, but that since it involves working with images, it's memory hungry. It will happily gobble up all the RAM (memory) you allocate to it, and then sit panting for more. If it can't find any more real memory, it will settle for virtual memory, using vast chunks of your hard disk to store temporary files while you're working. These 'scratch' files, as they're called, are slotted in around the other files on your hard disk, and are then deleted when you quit Elements. The more fragmented your hard disk, the more pieces these files will end up in, and the slower Elements will run. In the Interlude following Chapter 2, we'll look at the best way of coping with scratch files.

The Elements interface can be customized in a number of ways. Normally, you probably wouldn't bother to mess around with the interface of your applications – after all, the people who designed the program probably know it better than you do, so why not just trust their judgment and leave things as they are? Well, believe it or not, the people who designed Elements don't seem to spend that much time actually working in it. If they did, they wouldn't have the Project Bin turned on by default. Sure, it gives you access to all your currently open files, but it uses up an inch or more of valuable real estate. And that's an inch you could be using to view your pictures that much larger. Turn it off: you don't need to have it permanently on view. You can always pop it open when you need it.

The Palette Bin, down the right-hand side of the screen, contains your most frequently used panels. Store your favorites here, but collapse them to just their title bars when you're not using them: they take up a lot of space, and you want to give the maximum amount of space to the Layers panel. When you have a document with a lot of layers in it, consider reducing the size of the thumbnails (using the pop-up menu at the top of the panel) to fit more in.

Auto Select Layer
to activate a layer
when you click it

Tabbed windows
give extra space
for the image

Show Highlight on
Rollover: helps to
identify layers·

Tabbed Panel Bin
lets you stack your
most used panels
for quick access

Open panels when
you need them

Give as much space
as you can to your
Layers panel

The Project Bin takes up valuable
space: hide it away

When the Move tool is active, the Options bar will display a number of choices. Checking Auto Select Layer will mean that a layer is activated when you click on it, but this can happen by accident; when this is unchecked, you need to hold the Ctrl/ Cmd key when clicking on a layer to select it. You can also check the Show Highlight on Rollover box, which will pop up a blue rectangle surrounding each layer as you roll over it. This can help to identify layers, but can quickly become irritating. If you don't find the feature useful, turn it off. Similarly, the Show Bounding Box option will place handles around each selected layer. Again, this prevents you from seeing the image clearly; don't use it unless you find it helpful.

The tabbed window view is a great space-saver, giving you as much viewing area as possible. If, however, you prefer to work with the classic floating window setup, you will need to initially enable it in Preferences. This is found under General > Allow Floating Documents in Full Edit Mode.

23

■ This little chap seems overwhelmed by all the gifts. If they had all been placed directly onto the photo, it would be stuck like that. Using layers in our image means we can freely move them around. Now we can clearly see that, like most children, he's not really interested in the gifts at all; he's perfectly happy playing with one of his balloons.

2 Working with Layers

WHEN CREATING A MONTAGE, layers are probably the most important part of the process. Aside from the design itself, of course. Without them, creating complex composite images would be a slow and difficult process. Think of layers as individual celluloid sheets: each one can be laid on top of (or beneath) another to build up the artwork. These can be manipulated independently without affecting the rest of the picture. There are many different types of layer, too, as we'll see.

We'll be exploring techniques that demonstrate the many functions and abilities of the main layer types. Beginning with the basics and on through to more advanced concepts, we'll see how layers are created, controlled and can be made to interact with each other in a variety of different ways.

Importing images as layers

BEFORE WE CAN START CREATING our masterpieces, we need to know how to add more than one image into a document. There are several ways to do this; we'll be going through the most frequently used methods here to create a simple montage.

It's worth mentioning here that when in the book we discuss opening image files to use in the projects, we assume to do this through the File menu in the Editor, rather than using the Organizer (or Bridge, in earlier Mac editions). There is no right or wrong method, of course, it's just easier to describe and hopefully less confusing this way.

1 Here we have all the images for our montage open in the Editor workspace. We've arranged their windows for clarity, keeping the wood texture as the main image; this can be done using the presets in the Arrange menu (just to the right of Help). If the menu is unavailable, you will need to open the program preferences dialog *ctrl* *K* *⌘* *K* and enable the option Allow Floating Documents in Full Edit Mode. We also have the Project Bin open at the bottom; this also shows all our open files and allows us to switch between them by double-clicking their thumbnails.

2 The first and probably easiest method of adding an image to our main document is to drag it from the Project Bin. Simply click and drag the thumbnail onto the main window. Note: using this method always results in the image we add being centered on the document.

3 We can also drag an image from the Layers panel. First, click on the scissors window on the right of the workspace to make it the active image. Go to the Layers panel then click and drag the thumbnail over to the main document. We can position the image on the document with the cursor; it will appear once we release the mouse. If we wanted to center the image as we imported it, we could hold **Shift** as we drag it across.

4 The next method is to use the Move tool **V**. Remember to select the correct image first. This time we'll click and drag from its window across to the main document. As we do this, notice that it's also moved across in its window; it will snap back into position once we drop it onto our montage. As before, we can position the new layer with the cursor and it will appear when we release the mouse.

5 The final method we'll use is to copy and paste from one image to another. Select the string image window. Press *ctrl* **A** ⌘ **A** to make a selection of the whole image. Next, press *ctrl* **C** ⌘ **C** to copy it to the clipboard. Now switch back to the main image and press *ctrl* **V** ⌘ **V** to paste a copy. As we can see, creating layers in this way also positions the new image in the center of the document; it's now on top of the eraser. None of this is fixed permanently, of course; we'll be exploring how layers interact with each other in greater detail throughout this chapter.

HOT TIP

In the last step, we use copy and paste to import the image as a layer. This is a handy technique to know as using this method does not limit our source image to the confines of Elements. We could just as easily copy an image to the clipboard in another program: Microsoft Word or Internet Explorer, for example.

SHORTCUTS

MAC WIN BOTH

27

How layers interact

1 In our example image we have a document containing four separate layers – the background and three playing cards. If we look at the order and position of the cards' layers in the Layers panel we can see how this relates to their appearance in the image.

O N THE PREVIOUS PAGES, we saw how we can import and combine images from separate files as individual layers, to create a simple montage on a single document. Here we'll examine the concept of layers in more detail. We'll see how they interact with each other; by changing the order in which they appear, we can place them in front of, or behind other layers in the document. We can also make layers translucent, hide them, or delete them from the document completely.

2 The order of the layers is not fixed, of course. Click and hold the queen layer's thumbnail in the Layers panel. Now drag it up above the king's layer. An indicator line will appear over its thumbnail. Release the mouse. The queen is now sitting on top of the other two cards.

3 Although we've moved the queen to the top of the stack, both literally and visually, her position in the image relative to the other cards remains the same. To alter this, we can use the Move tool **V**. Simply click and drag the card to move it around the document.

4 We can also move more than one layer at a time: currently the queen is the active layer. If we hold *ctrl* ⌘ and click the king's layer (not the thumbnail) in the Layers panel, both layers become selected. We can now move them both around the document together.

5 If we want to make sure the postiton of the layer cannot be changed, we can lock it. To do this select one of the layers in the Layers panel, the queen in this case, then click the padlock icon at the bottom of the panel. We'll now receive a warning message if we attempt to move the layer.

Although it's easy to see which layers are which in a simple montage such as this, it's always good practice to give your layers meaningful names as they are added: Finding *Jack of Hearts* will be far easier than *Layer XX* when working on a complex piece of artwork with dozens of layers. Simply double-click the layer's label and replace it with your own.

6 The solidity of a layer can also be adjusted. Unlock the queen by clicking the padlock icon again. Click the arrow next to the Opacity value at the top of the panel. Dragging the slider to the left makes the layer increasingly more transparent. At 0% it will be completely invisible.

7 If we want to hide a layer, perhaps to remove some clutter while we work on the image, we can do so by clicking its visibility (eyeball) icon to the left of its thumbnail in the Layers panel. Here we've hidden the jack. To make it visible, we just need to click the icon again.

8 If we want to see a particular layer on its own we can hold *alt* ⌥ and click the layer's visibility icon. This hides every layer except the current one; doing the same to reverse the view. We can also click and drag up or down the column of eyeballs to hide or show the layers sequentially.

9 Finally, if we want to delete a layer completely we can either select its entry in the Layers panel, then click the Trash icon at the bottom, or alternatively click and drag the layer onto the trash icon. Remember, this is final, once you have saved and closed the file, that layer is gone for good.

29

Divide and multiply

S O FAR WE'VE SEEN how to add layers to a document and adjust their position, order and visibility. In the following tutorial we'll go a stage further; using the Move tool and a combination of keyboard shortcuts we'll reposition and duplicate a single layer to quickly create multiple copies of the same object. This is similar to the technique we used in Chapter 1, except when we duplicate the objects here, they are placed on a new layer.

In the most recent versions of Elements, multiple layers can be selected to form a temporary group, allowing us to manipulate them as a single item. This is a much better way of working as there is no need to merge the layers into one before duplicating them, as was the case with earlier revisions of the program.

1 Here's our single plate. Its shadow has been created using a layer style; we'll be covering these later in the chapter. Notice how the shadow from the shelf falls across the plate. This is because both the shelves and their shadows are on a separate layer in front of the rest.

2 Make sure the plate layer is active by clicking its thumbnail in the Layers panel. Select the Move tool **V**. Click and hold the cursor over the plate. Now drag it across to the left edge of the shelf. Additionally, you can hold **Shift** to constrain the movement.

3 Holding *alt Shift* ⌥ *Shift*, click and drag the plate over to the right. Instead of simply moving it, this action has created a copy of the plate on a new layer. Release the mouse but keep the keys held. Now click on the new plate and drag once more to create the third.

4 Go to the Layers panel. Hold *Shift* and click the first plate layer. This will highlight all three layers and in doing so temporarily group them together. Use the same keyboard shortcut as before; this time, drag the cursor straight down to create a copy of the entire row.

5 Leave the previous grouping enabled. Create a duplicate set for the final row. If you need to retain the group on a more permanent basis, click the chain icon at the top of the Layers panel. An icon will appear to the right of each layer denoting that it is part of a linked set.

6 Currently there are nine separate plate layers. If you don't intend to make changes on an individual basis, you can flatten them into three rows or even one single layer. To do this, use the multiple select method to group the layers together. Finally, press *ctrl E* ⌘ *E* to merge them.

HOT TIP

Make sure the Move tool's Auto Select Layer option is disabled in the Options bar. Whilst this feature can be useful for finding a layer buried deep in your artwork, it can also cause chaos. You may find yourself moving or copying the wrong part of your image if you accidentally click another layer instead of your intended target. You can mimic this function at any time by holding *ctrl* ⌘ and clicking the layer in the document.

SHORTCUTS
MAC WIN BOTH

Adding a little style

1 Styles can be added to a layer by double-clicking their thumbnail in the Effects panel, dragging their thumbnail across to the layer itself, or by highlighting them and clicking Apply. In the example, we've added the Simple Sharp Inner Bevel and Low Drop Shadow presets to our text object.

LAYER STYLES ARE VERSATILE, REUSABLE effects. With them you can quickly place shadows under objects, create metal textures, add embossing and much more. Unlike filters, however, they are non-destructive; once applied, they can be altered, added to or removed without the need to undo previous changes or recreate parts of the artwork. Styles are not limited to regular image layers either; in fact, they show their worth far better when applied to objects which themselves are changeable, such as shape or text layers.

From version 6 and later the program comes with a much better Settings dialog with which to fine-tune the styles. Previous editions still gave you control over the attributes but these were fairly rudimentary in comparison. If you're using an older version, you will, of course, still be able to follow the majority of this tutorial.

2 The default settings of the styles may not always be right for the image you are working on. Double-click the *fx* icon to the far right of the layer thumbnail to open the Style Settings dialog. Here you'll see the adjustments that can be made to the style's attributes.

3 We'll start by making the bevel a little smaller to fit the text better. Use the slider to lower the value; you'll see the effect change as you do so. Bring it down enough to make the bevel's ridges straight with a slight flatness on top. Here a value of around 12 pixels is sufficient.

STYLE STYLE

HOT TIP

Although styles are normally cumulative, you can force the current effect to be replaced outright by holding *Shift* when applying the new style. Be aware that many of the more complex built-in presets will override your effects as they already contain compound settings. It's also worth noting that patterned styles on surfaces in perspective may not look right, particularly those which contain strong horizontal or vertical lines. Such effects are generally designed to be applied to flat objects. You'll need to simplify (flatten) the style, then create the distortion on the object.

4 We'll adjust the shadow next. Start by lowering the size. This makes it sharper, as though the light source were closer to the text. Increasing the Distance value gives the appearance of the text being further from the background. You can also lower the opacity if required.

5 The Lighting Angle controls the highlight and shadow of the bevel effects as well as the direction of the drop shadow. The default is top-left. This can be changed within the dialog. You can also click and drag within the document itself. This allows you to set the angle visually.

STYLE STYLE
GRACE VOGUE

6 We can also copy styles: right-click the Layer Style icon and select Copy Style. Now when we right-click on another layer's label we can paste a copy. The text adopts the exact same effect. This is useful when you have customized the style and want to match it across the artwork.

7 Because the style affects the layer as a whole, you have the ability to change the content of the layer without the need to apply the style again. In the example, the color and wording of the text has been changed; the style is added as we type. This even works when painting on a layer.

STYLE STYLE
VOGUE VOGUE

8 The effects can also operate independently to the layer. Here both layers have been flipped vertically. You'd expect the bevels and shadows to follow suit. Instead, they retain their original direction. We can, of course, use the Lighting Angle to alter all the effects on the layer together.

9 Now you've set up your styles, what if you want to remove them? You can hide/show all styles from the Layer Styles sub-menu under the main Layer menu. You can also clear them from there (the same as deleting); this is also available from the More fly-out in the Layers panel.

SHORTCUTS

MAC WIN BOTH

Protect your work

I F YOU'RE PLANNING on putting your images up for sale online or sending them somewhere for evaluation, the last thing you want is for some unscrupulous person to stroll in and steal them for themselves.

One of the most common ways to prevent this is to add a watermark to the image; this will often be your website address or logo because they also serve as good advertising. The problem we can have is knowing where to place it: if we put it along the edges, it could easily be cropped or cloned away, and having something that covers up too much of the image is defeating the purpose.

There is a compromise, of course: we'll be using a shape layer and layer styles to create a way of protecting the image quickly and effectively by filling the document whilst leaving it almost completely visible beneath.

1 First of all, we need to decide what to use as our watermark: for simplicity, we'll use the copyright symbol. Select the Custom Shape tool **U**. From the Options toolbar open the Shape Picker; our shape isn't in the default set so go to the fly-out menu and choose Symbols from the list.

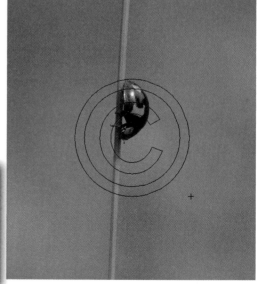

2 Holding **Shift** to retain the shape's proportions, click and drag out the shape. Make sure as much of the important detail is covered; if we also hold the Spacebar, we can move it into the correct position. Here, it's just the insect that matters so we've scaled the symbol down to suit.

3 Don't worry about the color as it will be removed later. We'll give it some styling: from the Effects panel, select Layer Styles and choose Bevels. Double-click Simple Sharp Outer. It's too large so we'll double-click the Layer Style icon to open the settings and reduce the size slightly.

4 We can't use the Opacity control to remove the color as we'd have to drop it to 0%, which would also remove the bevel. Instead, go back to the Styles panel and choose Visibility from the Layer Styles menu. From the three available options, double-click Hide.

5 We've removed all the color but kept the layer style. This lets us see the image without too much obstruction but also makes sure we protect it from being used without our consent. It would be difficult and time-consuming to restore the image convincingly, and more-so on a complex image.

6 We're not restricted to simple shapes, of course. We can also use text: here we've used the company name and its website address. Now it becomes a passive advertisement as well as preventing theft. As it's using live text and styles, it can easily be altered, too.

HOT TIP

Once we've set up our watermark we can save a file containing just its layer, or perhaps a whole range of versions for different situations. When we want to add it to another image we can simply open it up and drag it into the document.

SHORTCUTS
MAC | WIN | BOTH

The power of adjustment

WHEN YOU APPLY AN ADJUSTMENT such as Levels to an image, the affected pixels are permanently altered. If at a later stage you decide you no longer want that effect, unless you made a backup, you have a problem. With Adjustment Layers you apply the effect in the same way but it's non-destructive. Anything beneath them in the layer stack will be affected unless, of course, you don't want it to be. They are just like regular layers. You can alter their opacity and change the blend mode. Most importantly, however, they can be toggled on and off, disabling the effect.

1 Our image comprises two layers: the garden background and the man watering the plant. Make sure the gardener's layer is active by clicking its thumbnail. Click the split circle icon at the bottom of the Layers panel and select Hue/Saturation from the Adjustments menu.

2 Drag the Saturation slider to 0 in the Adjustments panel. This has removed all the color from both the gardener and the background as it sits above both layers. As we can see from their thumbnails, the layers beneath are physically unaffected and still have their color.

3 If we wanted the adjustment to only affect the gardener, we can create what is known as a 'clipping group' (more about these in Chapter 4). Make sure the Adjustment Layer is highlighted. Now press *ctrl* *G* *⌘* *G*. The background is now unaffected and its color has returned.

4 If we wanted to reverse the effect, having the gardener in color and the background in black and white, we simply need to drag the Adjustment Layer down between the two layers. The color is restored to the gardener's layer as it is now above the Adjustment Layer.

You can use Adjustment Layers to make temporary alterations to an image. For example, you may be having difficulty selecting and separating your subject from its background because there are areas of low contrast or it's simply too dark in places. Create a Brightness/ Contrast Adjustment Layer above it. You can take the values to their extremes for the duration of the task. Afterwards, you can simply turn the layer off or discard it completely.

5 We can add more Adjustment Layers to our image, of course. Here, for example, we've added a pattern fill layer that gives us a black and white grid. It's still beneath the gardener's layer so he appears above it. Being a solid layer, it covers up the original background.

6 We can change the blend mode of the Adjustment Layer. We've set the pattern layer's mode to Multiply which makes the white areas transparent, allowing us to see through to the background. We've also edited the original Hue/Saturation layer, setting it to Colorize with a green hue.

Exploring blend modes

EVEN IF YOU'VE NEVER USED THEM you
will no doubt be familiar with the term
'blend modes'. These determine how layers
interact with the other layers in the artwork.
In our example, we'll change the graffiti layer's
mode, which will affect the way it blends with
the wall, our background layer. There isn't space
to show every mode but the examples should
serve as a guide; the results you get will vary
greatly depending on the colors and tones of
the component layers in your image.

1 The default is Normal. Technically this isn't really a blend
mode at all as the top layer does not interact with the
base layer, apart from its transparency. Almost all layer types
can use blend modes. Individual tools such as the Brush and
Gradient use them as well.

2 This is Dissolve. On a crisp, fully opaque image this
mode has no effect. However, when you add some blur
or start to lower the opacity, random pixels will start to
disappear. The more the image is blurred, the stronger the
effect becomes. You can see this on the sprayed green edge.

3 On the left we have Darken. This blends any pixels that
are lighter than the wall: white becomes transparent.
There's little change in the color. On the right is its
counterpart, Lighten. This has the opposite effect, blending
where the wall is darker. The color is a little washed out.

4 Here we have Multiply on the left and Screen on the
right. Multiply produces rich, darker tones. Again, white
has no effect and is cancelled out. The opposite, Screen,
produces a much brighter blend. White is completely opaque.
Any black in the image has no effect and is not displayed.

5 Color Burn (left) and Color Dodge (right) produce similar
results to Multiply and Screen. The colors, however,
appear far more exaggerated using these modes. Following
on from these are Linear Burn and Linear Dodge (not shown).
These produce slightly stronger results.

6 This is Overlay. It's a combination of Multiply and Screen. It darkens lighter pixels and vice versa. In areas of midtones there is little or no effect, 50% gray being completely invisible. The highlight and shadows are retained, giving it a slightly blown out appearance.

7 Soft Light operates in a similar way to Overlay. The difference being it combines Darken and Lighten. As you can see, this produces a somewhat muted blend. This mode is often used for creating reflections because of its already slightly translucent qualities.

8 Hard Light, Vivid Light (shown here on the left) and Linear Light all produce strong color tones, Linear being the deepest. Pin Light (right) uses the tones of the base image to shift the color of the top layer, depending on lightness. 50% gray is invisible in all of these modes.

9 Hard Mix limits the blending image to eight colors – white, black, red, green, blue, yellow, cyan, and magenta; the mix depends on the blending colors of both layers. This produces a result similar to that of the Posterize filter. It is a brash, aliased effect and therefore has limited use.

10 In Difference mode color is subtracted from either the base layer or the blend layer, depending on brightness. Pure white inverts the blending colors; black has no effect. This can be used for comparing images for slight changes. Exclusion (not shown) gives a less contrasted effect.

11 The four remaining modes: Hue, Saturation, Color, and Luminosity, work by combining the named attribute of the top layer with the remaining two attributes (excluding Color) from the base layer. Here we have Luminosity, which discards the color, leaving only the layer's brightness values.

HOT TIP

Because using blend modes can produce very different results depending on the number of blended layers, their tonal values and many other factors, it's often easier to cycle through the individual modes until you find one that fits the effect you're looking for. There's a keyboard shortcut for this: press _Shift_ + to drill down the list and _Shift_ − to drill up. Make sure you're not in one of the painting modes as that will result in changing the mode for that tool, rather than the layer.

SHORTCUTS
MAC WIN BOTH

39

Banqueting arrangements

A FEATURE INTRODUCED in Elements 5 was the ability to automatically align and distribute layers within the document. In earlier versions, this would have needed to be done by hand, either by sight alone or by setting up and aligning to a grid – a somewhat messy business. Now you can accurately space out and arrange components evenly across your artwork with just a few clicks of the mouse. This is great for making precise designs such as navigation bars on web pages or for laying out and ordering text and images for scrapbook pages.

1 Here we have all the pieces of our place setting on separate layers. We could, of course, select and position each individual layer manually, but this is time-consuming and not altogether accurate. Instead, let's make use of

Elements' ability to select and work with multiple layers simultaneously. By grouping the sets of cutlery together we can then use the new Align/ Distribute feature of the Move tool to space them out neatly either side of the plate.

2 The first task is to bring the plate into the center of the canvas. Select the Move tool (**V**). Click the background layer in the Layers panel to make it active. Now hold **ctrl** **⌘**. Click on the plate layer's name (not the thumbnail) to

group the two layers. Start by selecting Horizontal Centers from the Align menu in the Options toolbar. This will shift the plate across to the middle. Now use the Vertical Centers option to move it down.

3 Now we can space the cutlery out. The Distribute function works by spacing the central layer(s) evenly between the two outer ones. Start by arranging the knives and forks into two rough groups. The forks have already been tidied in the example. Select all the knives by holding *ctrl* ⌘ and clicking on their name labels. Now click the Horizontal Centers option in the Distribution menu. They will now all be evenly spaced out.

4 Press *ctrl* ⌘ and click the plate layer's thumbnail to load its selection. Now group all the cutlery layers together. You can do this by holding *ctrl* ⌘ and dragging a bounding box across the document to encompass the knives.

You'll see the layers highlighted in the panel. Release the mouse and do the same for the forks. Go back to the Align menu. This time select Bottom Edges. All the cutlery will move down to align with the bottom of the plate.

HOT TIP

You can also align layers to selections. We've used this method in the final step to match the cutlery to the baseline of the plate. If we had only used a layer group, everything would have been aligned to the base of the entire document.

SHORTCUTS
MAC WIN BOTH

41

Keep up, no slacking

THERE'S ONLY ONE THING FASTER than the speed of light: the computer industry. It seems that no sooner do you remove the shrink-wrap from your software or prize the new PC from its snug Styrofoam packaging, than you expect to see a little fortune cookie-style note congratulating you on your purchase being out of date. That groaning, creaking sound you hear becoming progressively louder is not your antiquated computer about to keel over in a spectacular shower of sparks, but the heavy cogs of the corporate machine trundling toward you, decimating all but the newest of technologies in its path.

As with the fashion industry, it seems you're nobody unless you're first in line for this season's must have accessory. As the glossy adverts in magazines will imply and the even glossier sales people in computer stores will tell you (the prospect of a sales commission instantly makes you an expert, of course), your current system is already half way to the scrap heap and not fit for anything other than being the basis for a retro art statement.

You should not be too despairing of the seemingly decrepit piece of hardware chugging away beneath your desk, or that your copy of Whizz-Bang 3000 Professional Gold Edition SP5 is now 'so last Tuesday'. Before you rush out to part with a month's salary, you have to ask yourself: *is it good enough for my purposes and, if it lacks a certain area of functionality, can I achieve the same thing in a different way?* Unless the latest hardware or software is offering something completely revolutionary, the answer will almost certainly be yes.

There will, of course, come the time where an upgrade is necessary. Perhaps support for your current operating system is being dropped and its replacement will not run efficiently on your computer. It may also be that certain components, such as graphics cards, need replacing. This doesn't involve replacing the whole system.

Ask anybody in the world of digital imaging – unless they're trying to sell you a completely new computer – what, above all, are the most important system components and you'll generally get the same answer: memory and hard disk space. Even if you have the latest AMTEL liquid-cooled, 50 megagiga-googleplex processor, it is still very much at the mercy of these two commodities. The computer needs memory to run the graphics program itself and store the image(s) you are currently working on, not to mention everything else that's going on in the background. Adobe recommends 1Gb+ for the current version of Elements to run smoothly. The more complex the document becomes, however, the more memory it needs to use to hold that information. Images can often bloat out to hundreds of megabytes in size, especially when you start creating multiple layers. Add to that the history (undo) states and the space used by copying and pasting to the clipboard and you'll soon be pushing the resources to their limits.

There's no way to second-guess how much memory you will need. Presently the average PC comes with around 1–2 Gb, which is ample for most tasks. When the system starts running low on physical memory, it starts to free it up by using virtual memory, referred to as 'scratch' space in Elements. This is a temporary area on the hard disk set aside for storing the overflow. Think of it as writing things down on a scrap of paper when you begin to become overwhelmed with information. This is where you need to make sure you have a large enough hard disk. Remember, the operating system, programs and your data all share this space. If it's full to bursting, trying to cram in this transient file will at best slow things down to a crawl; at worst it can cause the program (or the entire system) to crash, taking whatever you are working on with it.

Enhancing your system needn't be expensive. A large external hard drive will set you back around $100–200; you just plug them in and they're ready to go with no fuss. An internal drive could be half that amount. You can add an extra gigabyte of memory for less than $50. If you're not technically minded and unwilling to delve into the arcane world that is the inside of your computer, there will usually be someone you know who can help. If not, there will be no shortage of people advertising in the classified section of the newspaper who will be able to do the work – usually for a reasonable price, too. If it keeps you up and running for a year or two more, it's certainly money well spent.

Making cards, notices and invitations is an enjoyable hobby in Elements. But why settle for a standard, head-on view of the text when we could show it on a billboard? It's easy to distort any text or images so they appear to be viewed in perspective, giving the design far more impact.

Transformation and distortion

COMPOSING MULTIPLE IMAGES into a single montage almost always involves scaling, rotating and moving the elements around. In this chapter, we'll look at the basics of using that most powerful tool, Free Transform: with its multiple keyboard modifiers, it's capable of producing good results.

There's more to distortion than simply scaling and rotation, though. In this chapter we'll explore how to make an image fit a flag, a mug and a computer screen, as well as several other surfaces, showing how to use Elements' tools and filters to match an image to just about any surface.

The science of transformation

WHEN PUTTING A MONTAGE TOGETHER, you'll almost certainly need to resize one or more of its components to fit the scene. You may also want to distort an image for a particular effect: to give it a 3D appearance such as photos scattered on a surface or placed on a virtual gallery wall, for example.

Free Transform allows you to move, rotate, scale and distort your image in real time so you can compare and position it in place to match the rest of the artwork. You can perform this on an individual layer or, if you have grouped multiple layers together, alter them in unison.

1 Press *ctrl* *T* *⌘* *T* to enter Free Transform mode. Its bounding box will appear, surrounding the layer content. The *Enter* key applies the transformation, *esc* cancels it.

2 Click and drag within the box to move the layer around the document. Placing the cursor outside the boundary and dragging will rotate the layer around the center point.

3 By grabbing and dragging a corner handle you can scale the layer up or down freely. This, by default, is relative to the opposite corner, which remains anchored in place.

4 By holding the *Shift* key whilst dragging a corner, the layer will be scaled in proportion to its original size. This option can be used when you need to ensure the shape remains constant.

5 Use the left or right center handles to adjust the width of the image. The top and bottom handles, as you might expect, scale it vertically.

6 Hold *ctrl* ⌘ while dragging a center handle to skew the image. Additionally, if the *Shift* key is also held, the skew is constrained to horizontal or vertical movement.

7 Press *ctrl* *alt* *Shift* ⌘ ⌥ *Shift* when dragging a corner to distort the image in perspective. This can be both horizontal and vertical, depending on the direction you move the cursor.

HOT TIP

You'll need to be a little cautious if you intend to increase the size of the image. Too much will result in noticeable degradation, especially with photographs, as Elements has to add pixels to compensate. Wherever possible it's better to start with a larger image and reduce it to fit.

8 You can distort the image freely by holding *ctrl* ⌘ when dragging a corner handle. This can be used to accurately match an existing part of the artwork: a billboard, for example.

9 Use the *alt* ⌘ key to force the image to scale around the center point, rather than the opposite corner. This works with most of the transformation modes.

10 You can change the reference point to one of nine positions from the Options toolbar. This allows you to rotate the image using a different pivotal point.

SHORTCUTS
MAC **WIN** **BOTH**

Think Smart!

WE'VE SEEN HOW LAYERS can be scaled and distorted to enable them to fit into another image. This versatility can come at a price, though. Scaling the image much larger or smaller than its original size, or repeatedly distorting it, will eventually result in its quality degrading, as Elements has to stretch or remove the pixels each time. This can be a problem if we're trying different layouts in our montage.

There is an answer to this problem. There are special types of layers called Smart Objects. These are created when you import an image file into a document using the Place command. Outwardly, they are no different. They do have one special feature, however: they can be scaled and distorted indefinitely without them ever losing their original image quality.

1 Opening our example image, we have two seemingly identical photos of some kids; apart from their tops, which we've recolored to make it easier to tell the difference. If we examine their layers in the Layers panel, we see that the photo

on the right has a small icon in the corner of its thumbnail. This tells us that it's a Smart Object. As far as outward appearances go, this is the only sign that it's different. Only when we start transforming the two, do we see any difference.

2 Here we've shrunk both versions down to around a tenth of their original size using Free Transform *ctrl* **T** ⌘ **T**. As we can see, both versions remain identical and have kept their quality, relative to their new size, of course.

3 When we scale the two images back to their original size, there's an obvious problem: the normal layer is now horribly blurred, whilst the Smart Object version has returned to the same state as it was before we transformed it.

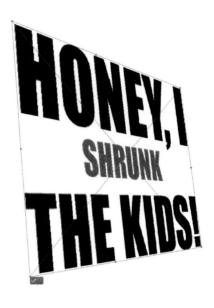

4 Another special feature of Smart Objects is they allow text to be fully distorted without the need to simplify it (convert it to pixels) first. Unfortunately, we can't convert layers to Smart Objects directly within Elements. There is a workaround though: we need to first create a new document with a single layer containing our text. This is saved as a separate Photoshop (.PSD) file. We then use the Place command from the File menu to import it into our image as a Smart Object. We can now scale and distort the text to fit in with the rest of our montage.

5 It is worth noting that, despite their usefulness, Smart Object layers are not without some restrictions: the content cannot be altered and we cannot paint directly onto them or apply filters. We can, however, perform every other action we would normally use on regular layers. We can change the opacity and blend mode, Layer masks can be added to hide areas of the image. Layer styles can be applied just as you would do normally; here we've added a stroke to the text. All this, of course, with the added bonus of being able to change the size and shape and never lose the quality.

49

Distorted field of vision

1 Here's our field with a single sunflower. We'll start by duplicating the flower. Make sure it's the active layer. Press `ctrl J` `⌘ J`. This is normally used to create a layer from a selection; as there isn't one defined here, it simply copies the entire image.

BY MIMICKING PHOTOGRAPHIC EFFECTS we can fool the viewer into believing an image is real, if only temporarily. This technique has been used frequently in the movies, television and other media – especially before digital technology was accessible. Indoor sets would have lavishly painted backdrops to give the impression they were shot on location. The scenery would be out of focus and not instantly recognized as fake.

We'll use this trick here to create a field of sunflowers using just a single object duplicated and scaled down many times. One larger flower is kept in the foreground, drawing focus away from the rest. The copies are all partially covered by one another; this prevents the viewer making an instant comparison. By blurring the rear rows and background, we are fooled into believing they extend far into the distance; we are accustomed to seeing photographs taken with a shallow depth of field so we don't question it.

2 Click the original flower layer's thumbnail. Press `ctrl T` `⌘ T`. Make sure Constrain Proportions is checked. Click and drag the top-right handle to scale the flower down. Click and drag inside the box to offset it from the original. Keep it a little lower than the foreground flower.

3 Now we'll complete the initial row. Repeat the first two steps to create three or four new flowers. Adjust the size and position slightly each time. Make sure you keep them fairly evenly spaced; they wouldn't be growing too close together in real life.

4 We can make some adjustments to the row. We'll begin by swapping some of the layers around. This gives us a more uneven appearance. To do this, click and drag the thumbnails above or below one another in the Layers panel. Keep them behind the original flower, of course.

5 Now we'll start adding the rows behind. Group all four flower layers by multi-selecting them in the Layers panel. Press *ctrl* *alt* **E** ⌘ ⌥ **E** to stamp them onto a new layer. This will be created above the group so drag it down the stack so it sits behind the others.

6 We'll fill that empty ground space behind the front row. Flip the layer horizontally via the Image > Rotate menu. Use Free Transform to scale and position the layer so its stalks are staggered behind the front row. Because they're hidden we can distort them a little more than before.

7 Press *ctrl* **J** ⌘ **J** to duplicate the current layer. Select the layer behind. Scale it down quite a way. Now duplicate it. Move them both to create a long row. Press *ctrl* **E** ⌘ **E** to merge them. Repeat this a couple more times until the foreground is more or less hidden.

8 To create the impression of depth we'll add some Gaussian Blur. Start with the first merged group. Add a small amount of blur, enough to knock the focus out. Move to the next adding a little more. When you've finished with the flowers you can blur the background to match.

9 The ground beneath the flowers is still visible and noticeably blurred. Grab the Burn Tool **O**. Set the mode to Highlights. Now use a large soft brush to paint in shadow over the grass. Finally, select the foremost flower rows. Add some shadow to their stems to complete the effect.

HOT TIP

If you're using a version of Elements which doesn't support layer grouping, you'll need to create the merged layers in a slightly different way. Start by creating a new layer above the layers you want to merge. Link the images together by clicking the empty box to the left of their thumbnails in the Layers panel. Using the keyboard shortcut *ctrl* *alt* **E** ⌘ ⌥ **E** will duplicate and stamp the layers down to the new empty one.

SHORTCUTS
MAC WIN BOTH

Simple perspective distortion

ONE OF THE MOST USED distortion techniques in photomontage is to add or replace an image where it will be viewed in perspective. This could be anything from a photo lying on a table to a billboard in a street scene.

As we'll discover in the following tutorial, this effect can be achieved quickly and simply using the Free Transform tool. The task is made easier still if we already have a basis for our distortion: the laptop's screen in our example. We'll also see how the effect can be made more realistic by blending the images to retain the original highlights of the screen.

1 Here we have our laptop along with the image we want placed on its screen. We'll use the screen's existing perspective as our guideline. Firstly, make sure the flower is the currently active layer by clicking its thumbnail in the Layers panel. Now enter Free Transform mode by pressing `ctrl` `T` `⌘` `T`. We'll begin by moving the image roughly into position. Click and hold within the bounding box. Now drag the photo across so it's covering the laptop's screen.

2 Press and hold `ctrl` `⌘`. This puts us into Distort mode, allowing the individual control points to be freely manipulated. Start by clicking and dragging one of the corners to the corresponding corner of the laptop's screen. Try to leave a little space between the new image and the bezel of the laptop. This adds a bit more realism as displays generally don't extend right up to the edges. Repeat the process for the remaining three corners.

HOT TIP

It can be tricky aligning the new image if you can't see the target layer below. To make the process easier, simply lower the layer's opacity enough for the base layer to show through. Once you've applied the transformation, you can bring the opacity back to 100%. In the latest versions you can do this whilst in Free Transform mode. For previous versions you would have to set it beforehand.

3 The image is now more or less in place. Check to see if any fine-tuning is needed. It's best to do this before you commit the transformation. This is mainly to avoid further quality loss but also because subsequent editing will result in the Transform tool's bounding box being squared off to the document, rather than conforming to the image as it is now, making it very awkward to align the image. Simply grab and adjust any of the point(s) as before.

4 With the distortion applied, the photo of the flower looks much more a part of the whole image. It's still not completely convincing, though. Adding the new layer has hidden the reflection and shading on the original screen. This has made the display seem a little flat. We'll fix this by changing the photo layer's blend mode, in this instance using the aptly named Screen. As the base layer is black, the two images blend, allowing the highlights to appear over the photo.

SHORTCUTS
MAC WIN BOTH

53

Tricky selections

EVEN WITH A WELL-STOCKED ARSENAL of selection tools at our disposal, there will be times when it seems we have been defeated. The locket in the example is a case in point: it's been photographed at an angle but the Elliptical Marquee cannot be tilted to match, so try as we might, we cannot make a selection of the window inside.

In Elements 8 and above we have the Transform Selection feature that allows us to distort a selection in the same way that we would an image layer; this is a bit cumbersome and in some cases it's difficult to see what you're doing. Instead, we prefer to use the Ellipse Shape tool. We can distort it to fit and also, if we need to, use its fill color as a visual aid for trickier subjects.

1 As we can see here, because the Elliptical Marquee can only be scaled horizontally and vertically, we simply cannot match the perspective. As soon as we get one part of the selection to match, the rest falls out of line. Wrestling with it is just an exercise in futility.

2 Select the Ellipse Shape tool **U**. We don't need to be too precise to begin with so draw out a shape roughly the same size as the aperture of the locket. It will be filled with color initially but that's not important as we only want to use its outline, which we'll deal with next.

3 Lower the shape layer's opacity to 0%. This removes the color fill, leaving us with an unobtrusive outline to work with. Enter Free Transform *ctrl* T ⌘ T, now rotate and scale the shape; we can get a better match than with the Marquee tool but it will need adjusting slightly.

4 Staying in Free Transform, hold *ctrl* ⌘ to switch to Distort mode. Now we can manipulate each of the handles individually to get a precise match with the locket's edge. It can be a little fiddly getting it just right but the result will definitely be worth the additional time spent.

Make Selection

Rendering

Feather Radius: 0 pixels

✓ Anti-aliased

OK

Cancel

Operation

● New Selection

○ Add to Selection

○ Subtract from Selection

○ Intersect with Selection

5 With our shape in position we can create the selection. Right-click on the document and choose Make Selection from the Context menu. This gives us more control over its attributes. Click Anti-aliased and hit OK. If we didn't set this, the selection would be too jagged.

6 The left-hand part of the locket is a little different as the clasp breaks up part of the oval. The technique is still the same but after we've created the selection we just need to remove the area around the clasp using the Polygonal Lasso, remembering to hold *alt* ⌥, of course.

Locket and load

FOLLOWING STRAIGHT ON from the previous technique, we'll be putting the selections we made to use. We'll add photos into the the locket with a little-used function called Paste into selection. This acts like a window; when we paste the images in, only the area within the selection can be seen. We can still scale, rotate and distort the image to get it looking the way we want. Once we've positioned the images as we want them, they become a part of the original image.

1 First we need to open our source image. For ease, we've saved it as a layer in the project file. Make it visible and active then select the whole document *ctrl* A ⌘ A. Now press *ctrl* C ⌘ C to copy the image to the clipboard. Once done, we can hide the layer again.

2 The selections have also been saved with the file so we can go straight to Select > Load Selection and choose Right Window. Make sure you're on the background layer then press *Shift* *ctrl* V *Shift* ⌘ V to paste the clipboard image into the selection.

3 It doesn't look like much at the moment because it's been pasted in at full size and we can only see a small portion. Enter Free Transform *ctrl* *T* *⌘* *T* and scale the photo down so we can see the girl's face. We'll stay in Free Transform so we can adjust the perspective.

4 Now hold *ctrl* *⌘* and drag the control handles to distort the image so it follows the perspective of the locket. Press *Enter* to commit the changes. At this stage we can still move the selection or go back into Free Transform if needs be. Finally, deselect to fix it in place permanently.

5 To add the image into the left window we can load up the other saved selection and simply use the Paste into command again, as it will still be retained in memory. Then it's just a matter of scaling it down and distorting to show the boy.

6 We've created a new layer above the locket and loaded up both window selections. These have been filled with 50% gray and the blend mode changed to Hard Light. We've used a soft white brush to add some highlights and an Inner Shadow layer style to give the impression of glass inserts.

Wrapping around surfaces

ADDING ARTWORK TO CURVED SURFACES can present the montage artist with all manner of problems to overcome. The most awkward are objects such as cylinders. When they are viewed at an angle the perspective effect causes not only the width to recede as it moves further from the camera, but the depth of the curves become considerably different between the top and the base.

In these situations, applying a uniform distortion to the artwork simply won't do the trick. The result will be confusing and look unrealistic. There is, of course, a solution, demonstrated here by placing a graphic around the surface of a plain coffee mug.

1 Although it's not obvious at this stage, as a result of the perspective effect, the slight angle at which this mug has been photographed causes the depth of the curves at the top and bottom to be different depths. This will be far more noticeable when the artwork is applied and initially distorted.

2 The artwork has been imported from a separate file. Press *ctrl* T ⌘ T to enter Free Transform. Make sure Constrain Proportions is checked. Now hold *alt* ⌥ and scale the artwork down to the appropriate size. Using the modifier key ensures it's scaled around the center.

3 Before we can apply the distortion, the artwork must be rotated by 90°. The Shear filter only operates on the horizontal axis. This can be achieved with Free Transform (hold *Shift* to constrain to 45° increments) or from the menu: Image > Rotate > Layer 90° Right.

4 Open the Shear filter dialog. By default, there is no distortion. Control points can be added by clicking and dragging on the line. It's better to create these towards the edge, rather than a single point in the center. This gives a smoother curve. You can see the effect in the preview.

5 The artwork has been rotated back to the correct orientation. As you can see, the top is true to the curve of the mug but the bottom is far too shallow. Firstly, enter Free Transform mode. Holding `ctrl` ⌘, drag the bottom corners in to match the perspective of the mug's edges.

6 Open up the Liquify filter (under Distort in the Filters menu). Select the Warp tool. Using a large brush, drag out the lower part of the artwork to increase the curve's depth. Try to use as few strokes as possible to avoid the edge becoming uneven.

7 Our artwork now fits the shape perfectly. It still looks a little out of place, though. The problem is that the mug has shadows and reflections whereas the artwork appears flat. This is easily solved. Set the layer's blend mode to Multiply. Finally, lower the opacity a little.

HOT TIP

The display in the Liquify dialog only shows the active layer. This makes it difficult to match up with the existing image. Before you open the filter, move the document window over to one side. You can then resize the filter's window and place it next to the original for reference.

SHORTCUTS
MAC WIN BOTH

Making curls and folds

PAPER TENDS TO HOLD ITS SHAPE after being folded or rolled up for any length of time. This can be a bit of an annoyance in everyday life. In the controllable world of digital montage, however, we can use these traits to our advantage, giving character and substance to an object.

Here we'll see how distortion and shading can transform a piece of flat artwork into a convincing three-dimensional map; one that has been rolled and folded many times.

1 The first thing we'll do is create some guides to divide the map into three sections. This will help us later on in the technique. Go to View > New Guide. Leave the Orientation as Vertical. Enter 33% as the position and click OK. Repeat this once more; this time set the position to 66%.

2 We need to make the document larger to allow for the distortions on the map. Open the Canvas Size dialog *ctrl* *alt* *C* ⌘ ⌥ *C*. Make sure the Relative box is checked. Change the measurement units to Percent. Now enter a value of 30 for the Width and Height, then click OK.

3 We'll be using the Shear filter to distort the map. Since this only works on the horizontal axis, we need to rotate the document. Go to Image > Rotate > 90° Left. Our document is now displayed vertically. Notice how the guides have also changed their orientation.

4 We need to isolate the three fold sections in turn and apply the filter separately to each. Grab the Rectangular Marquee tool *M*. Using the guide as a baseline, draw a selection over the first section. Drag it out to the edges of the document; the filter needs the extra space to work with.

5 Go to Filter > Distort and select the Shear filter. We want our edges to be curling upwards from the surface, so the bend needs to go to the left. Click the center of the guide and drag it a little to the right. It only needs to be a shallow curve; the end result will appear more exaggerated.

6 We need to repeat the same effect on the remaining sections of the map. Create a new selection for the middle section; again, use the guides to line it up. Now press *ctrl F* ⌘ *F* to apply the Shear filter again with the previous settings. Repeat this once more for the final section.

7 Create a new layer above the map. Hold *ctrl* ⌘ and click the map's thumbnail to load its selection. Go to Edit > Fill Selection. Set the Contents to 50% Gray and click OK. Now go to the Layers panel and set the blend mode to Hard Light. Finally, press *ctrl D* ⌘ *D* to deselect.

8 Select one of the map panels as we did earlier. Grab the Burn tool *O*. Set the Range to Highlights and an Exposure of around 70%. Using a large soft brush tip, paint one or two strokes across the map, over the selection where the fold would be. Repeat this for the two remaining panels.

9 Go to Image > Rotate > 90° Right to restore it to its correct orientation. Press *ctrl E* ⌘ *E* to merge the shading layer with the map. Now enter Free Transform *ctrl T* ⌘ *T*. Holding *ctrl* ⌘ drag the corner handles to distort the map into perspective. Press *Enter* to commit.

10 Create a new layer beneath the map. Load the map's selection. Now go back to the Fill dialog. This time, fill the selection with black. Press *ctrl D* ⌘ *D* to deselect. Go to Filter > Blur > Gaussian Blur. We want to create a soft shadow so an amount of around 5 pixels works well here.

11 Go to Image > Rotate > Flip Layer Vertical. Press *ctrl T* ⌘ *T* to enter Free Transform. Now distort the shadow into place. We should only see the shadow under the map at the front so tuck it in under the layer at the back. Finally, lower the shadow's opacity to around 50%.

The ripple effect

ESPECT WHERE IT'S DUE to the photographers with the skill and, more importantly, the patience to capture the ubiquitous image of a leaf or other such object causing delicate ripples as it lands on water. As pretty and serene as this all is, many of us simply don't have the time to wait for that perfect moment. We don't need to, of course. The effect can be recreated quickly with neither a tree nor a lake to be seen.

We photographed the leaf at a suitable angle to avoid the need to make excessive changes to fit in with the rest of the scene. We'll use a few different distortion techniques here. The main effect is creating the ripples; we'll use the rather misleadingly named ZigZag filter to create this.

1 We've already cut the leave out from its background and placed it on a new layer. The background has been filled with 50% gray. This will allow us to fine-tune the effect once everything is in place. We'll hide the leaf layer for the time being whilst we create the water texture.

2 Create a new layer. Press **D** to ensure you're using the default black and white palette. Fill the layer with the Clouds filter. We want a good spread of tones here. You can rerun the filter a few times by pressing *ctrl* **F** ⌘ **F** until you're happy with the result.

3 Now to make the ripples. Select the ZigZag filter from the Distort sub-menu. Select Pond Ripples as the style. We're creating a close-up image so we only need a small amount of ridges but a large amount of distortion. The exact settings will vary from image to image, of course.

4 Enter Free Transform *ctrl* *T* *⌘* *T*. Holding *ctrl* *alt* *Shift* *⌘* *⌥* *Shift*, drag one of the bottom corner handles out to alter the perspective. Release the keys. Hold *Shift* to constrain the dimensions and drag a corner point again to scale the image up to the required size.

5 We'll add some highlights using the Plastic Wrap filter (found under the Artistic sub-menu). Keep the effect subtle: overdoing it will leave us with syrup rather than water. Apply the filter. Lastly, press *ctrl* *Shift* *L* *⌘* *Shift* *L* to boost the contrast with Auto Levels.

6 With the ripples in place we can make the leaf layer visible again. Make sure it's the top-most layer. Drag it to the top of the stack in the Layers panel if necessary. We'll use Free Transform to alter its size and adjust the perspective slightly.

7 The leaf looks too flat on the surface as it has no reflection. Duplicate the layer *ctrl* *J* *⌘* *J*. Switch back to the original by clicking its thumbnail. Set the blend mode to Multiply. Now use Free Transform to distort the copy and give the leaf some depth.

8 We'll add a sense of movement by distorting the reflection. Open the Ripple filter. Set the size to Medium. Increase the amount gradually to give it a slight distortion. Soften it down by applying a small amount of Gaussian Blur. Lastly, lower the opacity a little.

9 Set the water layer's blend mode to Overlay. Switch to the Background layer. Open the Hue/Saturation dialog *ctrl* *U* *⌘* *U*. Check the Colorize box. Now adjust the hue and saturation to suit the image. Finally, drop the water layer's opacity to soften the effect.

63

A flag for all nations

1 Here's our flag artwork. This is a rasterized vector image. Graphic objects such as this work really well in this format. They can be rendered at any size and will never lose their quality. We've added some space around the image to allow for the distortion effects.

COMPONENTS OF A MONTAGE OR EFFECT are often created from the most unlikely of sources. The above image for instance: just a photo of an old bedsheet hanging up? Well yes, it is, but for the resourceful and imaginative artist, it can be a whole lot more!

We'll be using the image with the Displace filter to transform a two-dimensional graphic of the Stars and Stripes into a realistic flag blowing in the breeze. The technique is versatile too. As well as fabrics, it can be used with many other types of texture; almost anything which has a raised pattern such as rock, tiles or even the bark of a tree. In our example, the image can be saved as a template which can be reused with different nationality images or patterns.

2 Open the sheet image with the Place command. Rotate and scale it to match the flag graphic. Remember to uncheck Constrain Proportions in the Options bar. Press *Enter* to fix it down. It's still a Smart Object so right-click on the layer's thumbnail and click Simplify Layer.

3 Press *ctrl* *Shift* *U* *⌘* *Shift* *U* to desaturate the new layer. We don't need the color, just the tones of the folds. Add some more contrast by tightening up the highlights and shadows using Levels. This will give a much stronger effect on the texture map and overlay.

4 The Displace filter uses a separate texture map document to apply its distortion effect. Select Duplicate Layer from the Layer menu. Choose New for the destination. You'll need to give it a name. This will create a new copy of our grayscale sheet.

5 Load the layer's selection. Apply a Crop from the Image menu to remove the excess areas. Press *ctrl* D ⌘ D to deselect. Now apply some Gaussian Blur to soften the harsher edges. Finally, save the image as a new file on the hard drive in Photoshop format.

6 Go back to the flag document. Turn off the sheet layer for now and make the flag layer active. Open the Displace filter dialog. Use the default settings and click OK. A file dialog will appear. Browse to where you saved the texture map. Double-click the file to apply the filter.

7 Turn the sheet layer back on. Set its blend mode to Multiply. The effect is taking shape but there's a bit of a problem. The two layers no longer match; as yet only the flag has been distorted. Press *ctrl* F ⌘ F to reapply the filter using the same settings, without opening the dialog again.

HOT TIP

There will be occasions where you find the filter has caused areas of unwanted distortion, as with some of the stars on the flag. This is largely unavoidable as the image has been stretched too far over an area of strong contrast. You can often disguise the problem with a carefully placed foreground object or perhaps, as with our final image, some blur, if the context allows. You could, of course, use the Liquify filter to reposition the stars, too.

8 We'll add a shallow wave to the flag. Group the two layers. Press *ctrl alt* E ⌘ ⌥ E to create a merged copy. Hide the original layers. Now rotate the image 90° left. Open the Shear filter. Apply a very slight S curve. Click OK and rotate the layer back to its correct angle.

9 Here's our final image. A small amount of Motion Blur has been added to give a greater sense of movement. The addition of the flagpole and background boosts the realism of the scene. Save as a Photoshop document; you can always return to the image to change the nationality.

SHORTCUTS

65

Not so extreme close-up

FILTERS OFTEN SUFFER FROM ABUSE and consequently can quickly achieve cliché status. Even though their effects can be gradually increased, there is too much of a temptation to take it straight to the extreme. Spherize is one such casualty. Because of its potential for caricature, it rarely sees anything between -100% and 100%. It can, however, be used for much more subtle duties.

The following example uses the filter in moderation to create the illusion of an image being enlarged through a magnifying glass, in this instance on a collection of postage stamps. You'll also see how glass can be replaced using layer styles and blend modes. This is a great effect for drawing attention to something in your artwork or simply as a realistic component.

1 To save time, we've already cut away the original glass from the frame. Make a selection around the inside edge of the frame with the Elliptical Marquee **M**. Create a new layer between the magnifier frame and the background layer. We'll call it Glass. Fill the selection with 50% gray.

2 Deselect *ctrl* **D** ⌘ **D**. Select the Dodge tool **O**. Set the Mode to Highlights. Use a large soft brush to paint in a large area of highlight. Use a low exposure, building the effect up with several strokes. Reduce the brush size and add a couple of random spot effects for good measure.

3 We'll use layer styles to give our glass some substance. Begin by applying the Scalloped Edge Bevel preset. Now add a High Inner Shadow. Set the layer's blend mode to Hard Light. The gray becomes invisible, leaving us with just our highlights and styles showing. Lower the opacity slightly.

4 We'll create a shadow to add depth. Create a new layer above the background layer. Load the magnifier frame's selection and fill it with black. Now load the glass layer's selection; this time fill it with a light gray. Press *ctrl* *D* ⌘ *D* to deselect. Apply some Gaussian Blur to soften it.

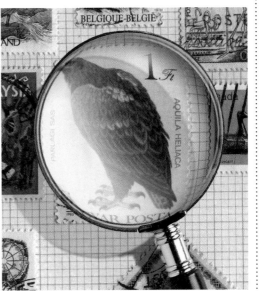

5 Press *ctrl* *T* ⌘ *T* for Free Transform. Scale, rotate and reposition the shadow layer to give the impression the magnifying glass is a distance above the background. Set the blend mode to Multiply. Finally, lower the opacity. The lighter gray fill now looks like diffusion through the glass.

6 Duplicate the background layer. Load up the glass layer's selection. Open the Spherize filter. Apply the desired amount of distortion to the copy of the background; 80% in the example. Click the shadow layer's thumbnail to make it active. Press *ctrl* *F* ⌘ *F* to reapply the filter.

HOT TIP

Using selections to constrain filters is not only used for localizing the affected area. If you also feather the selection first, the effect of the filter will be blended in or its strength lessened as it reaches the edge of the selected area.

SHORTCUTS
MAC WIN BOTH

67

Smoke without fire

PHOTOGRAPHING SMOKE CAN BE TRICKY. You need to get the lighting correct and capture the picture at just the right moment or you'll have to start again from the beginning. Even when you do have an image you're happy with, using it in a montage involves a lot of fiddly selections and masking. Creating the effect from scratch is not as difficult as you might think.

In the following tutorial we'll see how smoke can be conjured up quickly and easily using the Liquify filter. Its range of tools lets you manipulate an image as though it were oil on water; this can produce natural looking free-form effects.

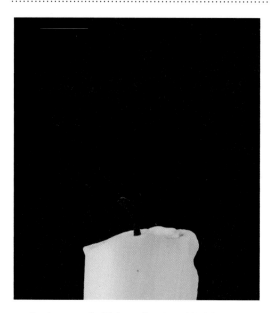

1 Here's our candle. It's been placed on a black background to make the effect easier to see whilst we're putting it together. This can always be replaced with a more fitting backdrop once it's finished. We'll begin by adding a new layer `ctrl` `alt` `Shift` `N` `⌘` `⌥` `Shift` `N`.

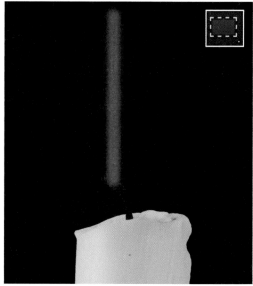

2 Select the Rectangular Marquee `M`. Draw out a long thin box from the wick to the top of the image. Fill the selection with a strong color, red in this instance; it needs to show up well in the Liquify dialog. Press `ctrl` `D` `⌘` `D` to deselect. Then add some Gaussian Blur to create a soft edge.

HOT TIP

The Liquify filter
can be a little
hit and miss.
If you make a
mistake, pressing
ctrl *alt* *Z*
⌘ *⌥* *Z*
steps backwards
progressively.
You also have
the ability to
restore areas
selectively with
the Reconstruct
tool *E*. Simply
paint over the
required area
to undo the
changes. Varying
the brush
pressure controls
the speed at
which the image
is rebuilt. If you
decide to start
afresh, click the
Revert button.
This will return
the image to
its initial state
without having
to exit from the
dialog first.

3 Now for the fun part. Open the Liquify filter from the Distort sub-menu. Experiment using a combination of the tools to spread and distort the line. Vary the brush size and pressure to create a more random effect. If you're using a pressure-sensitive tablet, check the Stylus Pressure box.

4 Add another new layer. Create a clipping group with the smoke layer *ctrl* *G* *⌘* *G*. Press *D* to restore the palette to its default. Fill the layer with the Clouds filter, which gives us a more random texture. Merge the two layers together by pressing *ctrl* *E* *⌘* *E*.

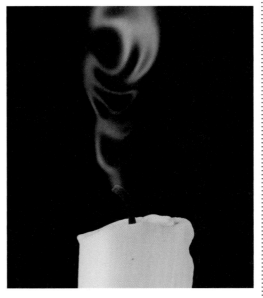

5 You can fine-tune the effect using Free Transform; hold *ctrl* *⌘* to adjust the corner points independently. Here the base of the smoke has been tapered in slightly and the top widened. The opacity has also been lowered a little to make the effect a little more subtle.

6 Create a layer above the candle itself and change its blend mode to Color Dodge. Set the foreground color to orange. Now use a soft, low opacity brush to paint in a small glow on the end of the wick. A hint of blue has been added to the smoke using a cooling Photo Filter Adjustment Layer.

SHORTCUTS
MAC **WIN** **BOTH**

Troublesome perspective

ONE OF THE PROBLEMS WE FACE when we're creating montages from different photos is the angle at which they were taken. Unless they were specifically shot for purpose, the different elements of the scene may not fit together properly because their perspective does not match.

Our example illustrates this perfectly. We have a young wizard casting a spell and a castle turret for his background. The boy's angle does not match the floor of the castle room, which was shot at a mid-level angle with a wider lens, so he looks out of place. We could try and distort his feet to match the perspective, of course, but that would be difficult and could end up looking unnatural. Instead, we'll adjust the angle of the floor. This, as we'll discover, is much easier than it sounds!

1 The image comprises two layers: the background layer and our young wizard. We won't duplicate the background this time as that will be confusing when we start distorting it. Instead, we'll convert it to a regular layer by double-clicking its thumbnail in the Layers panel.

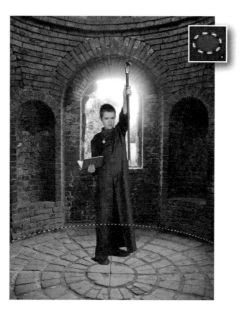

2 We don't want to distort the whole image, of course. Grab the Elliptical Marquee tool **M**. Place the cursor in the middle of the floor. Press and hold **alt** ⌥ while dragging out the selection to keep it centered. We want it to surround the whole floor area up to the edge of the walls.

3 Press **ctrl** **T** ⌘ **T** to enter Free Transform. Now drag the bottom-middle handle upwards. We can use the boy's feet to gauge the correct perspective. When it looks about right, press **Enter** to commit the changes. Lastly, deselect by pressing **ctrl** **D** ⌘ **D**.

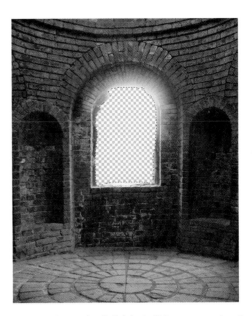

4 That's looking much better but we now have a gap at the bottom that we need to get rid of. Instead of selecting the Crop tool, hold *ctrl* ⌘ and click the castle layer's thumbnail to load its selection. Now go to Image > Crop. The image will be trimmed down. Now deselect.

5 Our castle was shot in bright daylight, not very wizardly. First, hide the boy's layer. Now, make a selection around the inside of the window. The Quick Selection tool is perfect. Soften the edge slightly with Refine Edge or Feather. Press *Backspace* to delete the area then deselect.

6 Press *ctrl* *J* ⌘ *J* to duplicate the background. Set the layer's blend mode to Multiply. This tones down the glare from the window and darkens the interior of the room, giving it a much stronger texture. Press *ctrl* *E* ⌘ *E* to merge the two layers together.

7 To finish this part of the project, go to File > Place and load the image *Moon.jpg*. Press *Enter* to set it in place. Press *Shift* *ctrl* *[* *Shift* ⌘ *[* to send it to the back of the layer stack. Use the Move tool *V* to reposition it so it matches the bright spot of the window where the sun was.

HOT TIP

This technique is not without its problems: the brickwork of the walls has been distorted where we've brought the floor up. Being an old building we can just about get away with it. If it were more prominent, however, we would need to patch it with the Clone Stamp tool or by pasting in a selection from another part of the image.

SHORTCUTS
MAC WIN BOTH

71

It's a kind of magic

CONTINUING ON WITH OUR WIZARDLY project, we're going to conjure up a magical vortex from the boy's staff. Before we do this, however, we need to make a couple of final adjustments to the scene.

Both photos were taken in daylight but our scene is now lit by the moon. This casts a blueish hue and is much cooler. We'll simulate this by adding an Adjustment Layer which affects the whole image. We also need to add a shadow of the boy to fix him into the room properly. Having done this we can go on to create our magical effect; using the ever-versatile Clouds filter to produce the power-waves emanating from his staff.

1 Select the boy's layer and make it visible again. Add a Hue/Saturation Adjustment Layer. Check the Colorize box. Drag the Hue slider into the blue range, around 220. Increase the saturation, around 50 here. Set the layer's blend mode to Multiply and lower the opacity to around 70%.

2 Next we've added a shadow cast from the moonlight coming in through the window in front of the boy. Rather than explaining it again here, the techniques for doing this, and also adding the shading on the boy's feet, can both be found in Chapter 7.

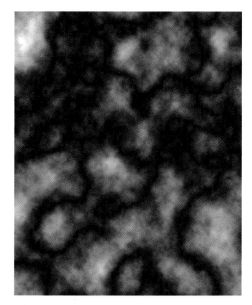

3 Create a new layer at the top of the stack. Press **D** to select the default palette. Hold *alt* ⌥ and select Filter > Render > Clouds for more contrast. Now apply Difference Clouds. We want the strong 'veiny' appearance. We can undo and reapply both filters until we get the best effect.

4 Press *ctrl* *I* ⌘ *I* to invert the colors. Open the Levels dialog *ctrl* *L* ⌘ *L*. Drag the Shadows slider across to the right; the white areas will start to disappear leaving only the brighter areas. Now use the Midtone slider to fine-tune and give us this whispy lightning effect.

5 Press *ctrl* *U* ⌘ *U* to open the Hue/Saturation dialog. Check Colorize. Drag the Hue slider into the purples and increase the saturation a little. Set the layer's blend mode to Screen. The black areas of the layer disappear leaving us with just the lightning.

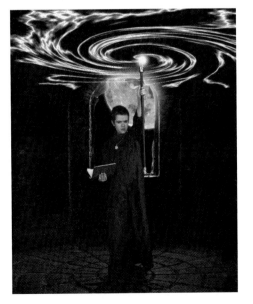

6 Open the Twirl filter (Distort). Drag the slider to around ±340°. This gives us a good effect without being overdone. Click OK to apply. Enter Free Transform *ctrl* *T* ⌘ *T*. Now hold *ctrl* ⌘ and drag the handles to distort and position the vortex over the boy's head in perspective.

7 Load the boy's selection. Now grab the Eraser tool and erase the areas that fall behind the staff to make it more three-dimensional. Deselect and erase the stray parts of the effect around the edges. Finally, grab the Brush tool and use a soft tip to dab a white glow at the top of the staff.

HOT TIP

For an extra-powerful effect, we could duplicate the lightning layer in step 5 before running the Twirl filter. The raw lightning could be edited to leave a few arcs jumping off the staff down to the floor and across the room.

SHORTCUTS
MAC WIN BOTH

Keep your composure

SOMETIMES, WE HAVE the perfect image but it's been shot at the wrong aspect. Our example would be great for a promotional flyer or magazine cover but it's a landscape image and we would need it in portrait. We'd want to keep the four people in the image too, so cropping isn't possible.

Elements now has a secret weapon: the Recompose tool. This behaves very much like Transform but with one important difference: it analyzes the image on the fly, working out what it thinks is important detail and what's not. In our case this is the grass and hills. The people remain untouched.

1 Opening our example image we can see that it's a landscape image but has a lot of space that could be reclaimed to make it narrower. If, however, we try to scale down disproportionately using Transform `ctrl` `T` `⌘` `T` the end result is

not a pretty sight. Just by scaling it down to half the orginal width the people are horribly squashed up, making the image unusable. Press the Escape key to cancel the transformation and it will snap back to its original state.

2 Select the Recompose tool `ctrl` `alt` `R` `⌘` `⌥` `R` or choose it from the toolbox; it's found as part of the Crop tool group. We immediately get a bounding box around the whole image. If we grab the middle-right handle

and start to drag across to the left we see that instead of the whole image compressing down, the wider expanse of the ground starts to disappear and the people are moved closer together but remain at their proper size.

3 Because the tool looks for less detailed areas of the image first, it took away the left edge of the photo. We can prevent this happening by using a selection to protect that part of the image. Press Escape to cancel again, or use the Undo command *ctrl* *Z* ⌘ *Z* if you committed the changes previously. Grab the Rectangular Marquee tool **M**. Now drag the boundary across the image but leave a vertical section on the left-hand side of the image clear.

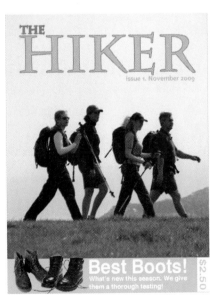

4 When we select the Recompose tool again and scale across from the right, it only affects the area within the selection, leaving us with a border which looks less cramped. Press *Enter* to apply the changes. On larger images this may take some time as the image is rendered. All that remains is to crop out the empty section of the image and we have our portrait shot ready to be used as a flyer or magazine cover. This definitely is a simple and highly effective tool!

Drawing comparisons

ONE OF THE QUESTIONS MOST FREQUENTLY ASKED by newcomers to digital imaging is which program should they choose: Photoshop Elements or the full Photoshop product. There is no definitive answer; each has its merits. The basis for the decision should be one of individual requirements.

A common misconception is that Elements is Photoshop's poor relation, only suitable for photography hobbyists who need a simple program to catalog their images and perform quick fixes such as removing red-eye from portraits or correcting color casts. Although there is a definite leaning toward the amateur market, Elements is more than capable of producing the same standard of artwork as its big brother. Elements still has around 90% of the features found in Photoshop; it merely lacks some of the more high-end functionality associated with professional pre-press. You'll find all the same filters and the majority of adjustments are present. Some are cut-down versions offering less in the way of fine-tuning, though not at the expense of their usefulness. There is also a degree of symbiosis between the two programs. Look under the hood of Elements and you'll find technologies from recent Photoshop releases packaged to perform a specific purpose. Similarly there are parts of Elements that have traversed the other way.

There is, of course, one distinct difference: the price. Presently, Photoshop will happily relieve your bank account of $600 upwards, depending on the version you choose. Elements, on the other hand, will cost you around $100 for the full product (less for an upgrade from previous versions). This makes it an ideal solution if you have a limited budget.

So, with all that said, what exactly are the differences between the two programs and can you survive without whatever it is that's missing? As we mentioned before, Elements does not feature some of the tools required for press-quality printing, such as comprehensive color management and the CMYK color space. This, however, does not mean it cannot be used professionally; the images in this book were all produced using it, after all. Most designers' applications, such as Adobe's InDesign, will convert the images and, to an extent, allow you to adjust the color. There are also many third-party utilities which perform the same function; Apple's OS X has Graphic Converter, for example.

The differences become less of an issue when you start comparing the tools and commands. Many of Elements' shortfalls can be overcome with a little lateral thinking. Here are the main 'extras' found in Photoshop, with workarounds:

Photoshop tool	What it does	Elements workaround
Pen tool	Draws Bézier paths	Use selections instead, and save as Alpha channels; save as .psd or TIFF file
Curves adjustment	Adjusts color and brightness	Use Levels instead
Vanishing Point filter	Places images in scene in perspective	Use Free Transform to distort layer
Black & White adjustment	Changes color image to monochrome	Use Gradient Map Adjustment Layer with default colors
Layer styles	More control over layer styles	Be creative with built-in styles or import styles from Photoshop
CMYK mode	Prepares artwork for commercial printing	Use third-party software to convert to CMYK mode
Smart Filters	Allows editable filters with selective masking	Duplicate target layer and lower opacity, use a mask to hide the effect
Image Warp	Allows free distortion of layers	Use Shear or Liquify filters for similar effect

There are some features in the full Photoshop that have no Elements equivalent – such as fully-featured Smart Objects, Video and 3D Layers (Photoshop Extended edition only), and support for specialist video modes. But in the main, Elements is capable of satisfying 99% of every montage artist and photographer's requirements.

■ This photograph of a man rowing has been removed from its original background and placed into a tranquil river setting. It looks far more part of the scene when it's partially hidden behind the foliage; that, and the reflection in the water, really bring the scene to life.

4

Hiding and showing

CREATING EFFECTIVE PHOTOMONTAGES is all about making layers interact with each other. And more often than not, this entails making layers partially hidden behind existing objects in the scene.

The standard way to do this is to erase the parts you don't want. But this is an irrevocable step; instead, we'll look at the tools that give Elements users some of the power of Photoshop CS5, with the ability to selectively hide and show regions of layers.

We'll also see how to blend layers together in a convincing manner, and how to arrange our montages so that they look that bit more convincing.

Exploring layer masks

ELEMENTS 9 saw the very welcome addition of layer masks; previously they have only been available when using Adjustment Layers.

If you're not familiar with the concept, a mask allows us to selectively hide areas of a layer non-destructively as, unlike the Eraser, we can restore the hidden parts whenever we want.

As we'll see here, and in the rest of the book, masks have many practical uses and are an essential part of the montage artist's repertoire.

1 This medical scientist has been experimenting with invisibility. We'll see how masks can make her disappear. To begin, we've placed her head and hands on a separate layer.

2 Make sure the head and hands layer is active by clicking its thumbnail. Now click the Add Layer Mask icon at the bottom of the Layers panel. We won't see any change yet.

3 Make sure we're working on the layer mask. Grab a large black brush. When we paint over the woman's hands and head they vanish. We can see the areas showing up on the mask.

4 If we switch the foreground color to white, we can start to paint the areas back in again. Here we've brought her hand and mouth back. The image is never affected directly.

5 Masks work on grayscale shades. Black is completely transparent, white is totally opaque. If, then, we choose a mid-gray we get something in between: a ghostly transition.

6 We can also use masks to integrate objects into the image. Here we have a goose in a doorway. It's not particularly convincing, as it appears to be both in front and behind the entrance at the same time. We can use a mask to hide the goose where it should be inside the building.

7 Switch to the background layer. Use the Magic Wand or Quick Selection tool to make a selection around the left side of the doorway. Click the goose layer's thumbnail. Now go to Layer > Layer Mask > Hide Selection. This creates a mask and fills it based on the selection we made.

8 Although we have added the mask to the goose layer, because it fills the space taken up by the doorway it gives the appearance that the goose is behind the wall. If we move the goose, however, we have a problem. As we can see, the mask moves as well leaving the poor goose tail-less.

9 We'll undo the previous step. Between the goose's thumbnail and the mask is a small chain icon. If we click it, it disappears. This means the mask is no longer linked to the image. Now we can move our goose and the mask stays in place. Here we've moved it further inside the doorway.

Smudge masking

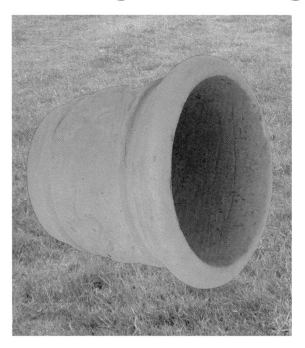

S O FAR, WE'VE LOOKED AT CREATING and editing layer masks by painting on them with the Brush tool. It works well: we can paint on a layer's mask to hide and show the object it's attached to.

But we're not restricted to painting the mask with just the Brush tool; we can use any of the painting tools. Here, we'll look at how we can use the Smudge tool to create a convincing grass effect in order to nestle the flower pot into its surroundings. As we'll see, the technique is quick and effective and far easier than painting each blade.

1 Make sure you are working on the pot layer. Hold *ctrl* ⌘ and click on the pot's thumbnail to load up its selection. Click the Add Layer Mask icon at the bottom of the Layers panel. The selection ensures that only the area around the pot is masked. We don't see any change yet, of course!

2 Select the Smudge tool *R* from the toolbox. Go to the Brush Picker in the Options bar and select one of the spatter brushes. Now set the tool's strength to somewhere around 60-70%; this controls how much of the area is affected with each stroke.

3 Pick an area at the base of the pot and start making short upward strokes with the brush. What we're doing is dragging the mask over the pot which starts to reveal the grass beneath, making it look as though it's growing up around the pot. Continue around to complete the effect.

4 Here's how the finished layer's mask looks on its own. Smudging the mask in from the edges in this way is very much easier than painting the mask, as the smudging creates a natural, fading look that matches the growth style of the grass.

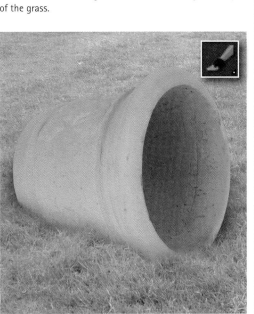

5 Now let's add some shading. Make a new layer above the pot, press *ctrl* G ⌘ G to group it with the pot; set the layer's blend mode to Multiply. Now sample a dark color from inside the pot with the Eye-dropper *I*, and use a soft-edged brush to paint shadows on the pot's lower edges.

6 Finally, make a new layer above the grass. This is where we'll paint the shadows cast by the pot. Use a soft-edged brush again, with black as the foreground color. Set the brush to a low opacity, and build up the shadow behind the pot in small stages until it looks convincing.

HOT TIP

Try changing the size of the brush to vary the density of the grass clumps. To make finer areas with only a few strands, use the outer edge of a fairly large brush, dragging up from the very edge of the mask.
If you are not happy with the way an area looks, simply reverse the stroke, using the brush to push the area back down again.

SHORTCUTS

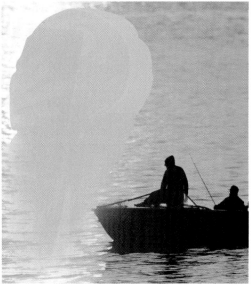

3 At the end of the previous step, our image was working well as a composition, but the color didn't match the warm orange glow of the background. Create a new Solid Color Adjustment Layer using the pop-up menu at the top of the Layers panel, and group it with the figure layer.

4 By default, a Solid Color Adjustment Layer appears as the current foreground color: black in the example. Changing this to a warm orange better suits the background. As we can see, because the Adjustment Layer is grouped with the figure, it only shows up where it overlaps the man.

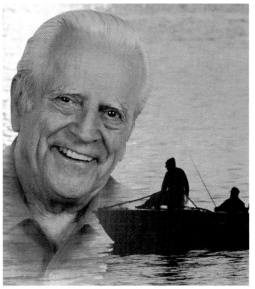

5 In order to be able to see the man through the Solid Color, we need to change the layer's mode from Normal to Multiply. Now we can see the man clearly, and the color is having its effect. But it's much too strong: we need to lower the opacity of the layer.

6 Taking the opacity of the Solid Color layer down to 50% gives us the effect we want. He now has a coloring that matches the background far more closely: the two separate images are now unified into a single montage that works as a whole.

HOT TIP

By creating a layer mask in step 2, rather than simply erasing the figure around the boat, we have the flexibility we need to move him around and adjust the mask as required. It's important that the man doesn't hide the prow of the boat, for example, but needs to wrap around it smoothly. This would be hard to achieve by simply erasing parts of the layer.

Part of the scene

B IG KIDS, LITTLE KIDS: how about giant kids? It's easy to turn a straightforward photograph into a King Kong creation by simply changing the background and adding a plane or two.

But we can go further than this. Placing a child in front of a scene may be the first step, but it's a long way from the finished montage. The trick is to bring picture elements from the background in front of any people or objects we've placed in the scene. By doing this, we're integrating our placed items in such a way as to make them appear to be genuinely part of the background, rather than merely floating on top. It makes all the difference between a straightforward montage, and a truly compelling scene.

1 We've placed the girl on the view of New York, and her feet fit neatly into the space in front of the buildings; the toy plane has been added to give her something to look at. She still appears to be pasted on top of the scene, so we'll create the illusion that she's standing within the city.

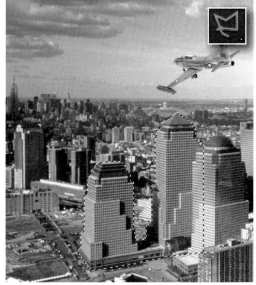

2 Hide the girl's layer by clicking its eyeball icon. Switch to the building layer. Now make a selection of the two buildings in the middle. With straight edges such as this, the Polygonal Lasso tool works best; you can also hold `alt` ⌥ with the regular Lasso to trace straight lines.

3 Now we'll create a new layer containing the buildings we selected in the previous step using *ctrl* *J* *⌘* *J*. Move this layer above the girl's layer in the Layers panel, so that she appears behind the buildings. She now looks like she's in the middle of the buildings.

4 In the last step, we left part of the girl's shoe showing beneath the new buildings layer, so we need to move her up using the Move tool **V**. Judge where she fits best within this scene, positioning her so that her feet seem to be firmly planted behind the buildings.

HOT TIP

This trick of moving background elements to the front will help in just about any kind of montage. If there aren't any suitable background objects that can be 'promoted' in this way, then create your own: an out-of-focus bush, for example, can help an outdoor montage to look that much more realistic.

5 To integrate her further, we need to add some shadows. First, create a new layer below the girl's; paint shadows beneath her foot on the ground. Then make another layer just above her, grouped with her layer; paint shadows here on her leg, as if the building is adding shading to it.

6 Finally, we can use the Move tool again to move the plane so it's right in her line of sight. Also, by positioning it slightly in front of her hand, we further help to create the illusion that she's really standing in the middle of downtown New York, batting away an attacking air force.

SHORTCUTS
MAC WIN BOTH

Polaroid-style photos

POLAROID INSTANT CAMERAS may be somewhat out of favor since digital photography became so accessible, but the familiar shape of the photos they produce remains a popular way of framing images, particularly if you're looking to create a retro theme.

The following tutorial serves not only to explain the steps to create a great Polaroid effect, but also demonstrates the use of clipping groups to crop a photo down to fit the frame; this gives us the freedom to position, scale and rotate the image within the window before commiting to any permanent changes.

1 Start by opening up the paper background file. Create a new layer by pressing *ctrl* *alt* *Shift* *N* *⌘* *⌥* *Shift* *N*. Now use the Rectangular Marquee tool *M* to mark out the shape of the frame. Fill the selection with white. Press *ctrl* *D* *⌘* *D* to deselect.

2 Draw an almost square selection inside the frame and offset it towards the top. Press *ctrl* *Shift* *J* *⌘* *Shift* *J* to create a new layer from the selection. We've filled the new layer with 50% gray here to make it visible, as it is also white, but this is not necessary for the technique.

3 Go to File > Place and select the *Girl and Dog* file. Press *Enter* to accept the default size; we'll be able to alter it later. Now press *ctrl* *G* *⌘* *G* to create a clipping group with the smaller layer beneath. Now we can only see that portion of the photo.

4 Press *ctrl* *T* *⌘* *T* to enter Free Transform. The image is quite large so you'll need to zoom out to see the whole of the bounding box. Now you can scale and rotate the photo within the frame – remember to keep the proportions constrained so it doesn't become distorted.

Best Friends!

5 Polaroid photos are thicker than normal prints so we'll add a Bevel layer style. Click the white frame layer's thumbnail to make it active, and apply the Simple Inner Bevel. The default is too large so open the Style Settings dialog and adjust the Bevel's size to suit.

6 To finish off the effect a texture has been applied to the frame using the Texturizer filter. Setting the texture to canvas with a very low relief gives us a rough but subtle effect, breaking up the solid white. A text layer has also been added; that's why the extra space is there, after all.

HOT TIP

You don't, of course, have to leave the Polaroid image square on the page once it's complete: multi-select the component layers (or link them if you have an older version of the program) and use Free Transform to make further changes. This way you still have the option to edit the text or adjust the photo a little.

SHORTCUTS
MAC WIN BOTH

Spectacular fireworks

FIREWORK DISPLAYS ARE FANTASTIC to watch but notoriously difficult to photograph, especially when there are other elements in the scene to consider; the camera has to be perfectly steady to prevent the foreground from becoming horribly blurred – not to mention the problem of timing the shot to capture the moment at its best.

With Elements, of course, we can add our own pyrotechnic delights. Although merging something as complex as fireworks into a photo might seem like an arduous task, it's surprisingly simple: using a blend mode to knock out the dark areas, allowing the background to show through, enables us to place the fireworks into the scene precisely where we want them.

1 We've placed our first firework into the scene which has, of course, hidden most of the background. There's far too much going on to be able to select it or mask it out, and lowering the opacity would cause it to become washed out.

2 The layer's background is almost black so we can use the Screen blend mode to filter it out, leaving just the bright areas of the firework visible. This gives us an almost perfect result with no harsh contrasting edges.

3 We can see the background is still visible against the original photo. Open the Levels dialog *ctrl* *L* *⌘* *L* and drag the Shadows slider in from the left a little; you'll see the light area at the bottom begin to disappear.

4 The firework is too large so press *ctrl* *T* *⌘* *T* to invoke Free Transform; now you can position and scale the firework down so it fits into the scene – remember to hold *Shift* to ensure the image remains in proportion.

5 We still have a problem: parts of the firework are in front of the tower when they should, of course, be behind. This is easily resolved by erasing, or better still, masking out the unwanted areas.

6 We've placed some additional fireworks to balance the image. Whilst we could have filled more of the sky, in this instance, we want to complement the scene, rather than totally drawing focus from it.

HOT TIP

If you're creating your firework display over a scene with an expanse of water or another shiny surface, you'll need to remember to add a suitable reflection for the fireworks as well. See Chapter 8 for more details.

SHORTCUTS
MAC WIN BOTH

Fairy gets her wings

CHILDREN LOVE DRESSING UP: either to mimic the latest movie or television characters or just to play a part in their own imagination-fuelled fantasies. With Elements at our disposal, however, we can take things a stage further and turn their fantasy into something more realistic; albeit pictorially, of course.

The following project is split into two sections: in this first part, we'll be concentrating on creating her wings. For this we'll use a layer mask to make the wings transparent. As we'll see, this gives us far more control as we are able to change the opacity selectively, rather than acting on the whole image as we would with layer opacity or blend modes.

1 Open the Butterfly Wing project file. There's already a layer mask in place. It's important to have the mask as part of the image like this, rather than using the workaround Adjustment Layer method, as that would make manipulating the image too difficult later on.

2 Select the entire image using *ctrl* A ⌘ A. Press *ctrl* C ⌘ C to copy the image to the clipboard. Now hold *alt* ⌥ and click the mask's thumbnail. We're now working on the mask itself. Press *ctrl* V ⌘ V to paste the image in. Now deselect *ctrl* D ⌘ D.

3 We can't see any change, of course, because we're looking at the mask. Click the image thumbnail again; we can see that most of the image is hidden. Click the mask thumbnail again and press *ctrl* **I** **⌘ I** to invert it. Now most of the mask is lighter and we can see the wing again.

4 Keeping the mask active, open the Levels dialog *ctrl* **L** **⌘ L**. We'll begin by dragging the Highlights slider in from the right. This increases the brighter areas of the mask which makes the black of the wings more solid but leaves the colored areas almost unaltered.

5 To change the opacity of the colored areas, we use the Midtone slider. Dragging to the left makes them more solid, to the right more transparent. We could also affect the whole image using the Output Levels slider: dragging from left to right to make it more solid and vice versa.

6 Now we can add the wings to our fairy. We've cut her away from the background and added some space so we can fit the wings in. The wing layer has been duplicated then distorted to fit with Free Transform. One layer is in front of the girl with a small part erased to fit her body.

HOT TIP

A really good way of seeing how changes to the mask affects the image is to open a new viewing window. From the View menu, select New Window for filename. When you set one of the windows to edit the mask, you can keep the second window as a standard image view. As you adjust the levels of the mask you can see the transparency changing dynamically.

SHORTCUTS
MAC WIN BOTH

Extending the scene

FINDING THE PERFECT IMAGE for a montage isn't always easy and you can waste many hours trying. Unless you go out to take your own, specifically with the idea in mind, there will doubtless be something that means it doesn't fit exactly as you intended.

Our project image is a case in point: it's a wonderful image of some toadstools, ideal for our fairy image. The trouble is there isn't enough space to comfortably fit the fairy on the main toadstool. We need to increase the height of the photo – for this we'll use the much overlooked ability of the Crop tool to expand the area of a photo. We will, of course, need to fill in the additional space we have created; we could use the Clone Stamp tool but there is not much to work with in the background and the result would look messy. Instead, we'll bring another photo into the image and blend it in with a layer mask.

1 Grab the Crop tool **C**. Zoom the image out so we have some space around the photo. Click and drag the crop boundary around the entire image. Now drag the top-center handle up to mark out the additional space. Once applied, the area is filled with the background color.

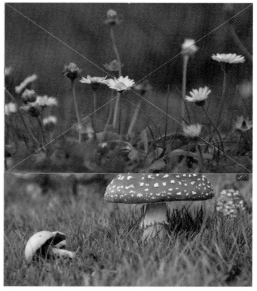

2 From the File menu, select Place and select the file *Daisies.jpg*. The image is automatically scaled to fit. Click and drag the new image to the top of the document. Press *Enter* to set it down, then select Simplify Layer from the Layers menu to convert it to a regular layer.

94

HOT TIP

It's a good idea to turn off the option of resizing windows when you zoom in and out, as it saves you having to manually drag the window in order to see the space around the image. Press *ctrl* K ⌘ K to enter the General Preferences then uncheck Zoom Resizes Windows.

3 We obviously need to blend in that harsh edge. Add a layer mask to the new layer by clicking the mask icon. Once it's in place we can start to paint away the area of the mask where the two images overlap. Paint in black using a large soft brush so we get a good, seamless blend.

4 We need to match the focus of the original image. Make sure we're working on the image by clicking its layer thumbnail. Open the Gaussian Blur filter, check that Preview is enabled. Now start to move the slider to the right, visually comparing the two photos until it looks realistic.

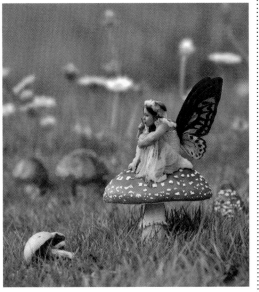

5 The color of the two images doesn't quite match. This was fixed simply by using the Auto Smart Fix command *ctrl* *alt* M ⌘ ⌥ M. Although these 'magic' options don't always give the best results, it's certainly worth trying them first as they can save a lot of time.

6 All that remains now is to add our fairy. We've imported the saved file from the previous project and scaled it to fit. We've used Levels to adjust her color and contrast slightly, and added a shadow to fix her into the scene. All the techniques for doing this are here in the book, of course.

SHORTCUTS
MAC WIN BOTH

Panorama power

SO MANY OF OUR GADGETS now either come with, or can be fitted with, a digital camera. No matter where we are, we will almost always have a way of taking photos. This is great, of course, but there is a downside. Devices such as cell phones have limited space in which to place the camera lens, so they are generally fairly small and rarely have a zoom facility – some have digital zoom but the less said about that the better. This makes taking pictures of buildings or other large landmarks difficult because you have to be at a fair distance to capture the whole thing. This is often impractical or, if it is possible, the results lack clarity and the resulting prints may not be as detailed as they could have been, even with today's high megapixel camera phones.

There is a solution, of course. Elements has an incredible panoramic stitching feature. All we need do is move closer to our subject and take several photos in overlapping sections. Here we took shots across the top half of the building first, then moved back along the bottom. This way we were able to keep the images fairly level. We feed these into Elements which then goes off and does its magic, producing one complete image at the other end. Fantastic!

The final image has a length of just over 11 inches at 300dpi. This could probably be blown up two or three times without loss of quality. That's nearly 3 feet long from a 2 megapixel camera phone. Imagine the size you could achieve if you did the same with a high-resolution DSLR!

1 We'll begin by opening the Panorama dialog: File > New > Photomerge Panorama. Click Browse to locate and open the Panorama Power folder. Select all the images by clicking the first file, holding **Shift** while clicking the last file. They'll appear in the dialog window.

2 We'll leave the Layout option set to Auto and make sure that Blend Images Together is checked. Click OK and it will begin to perform its magic. The initial result is a little ragged but Elements has a trick up its sleeve: the Clean Edges dialog will appear. Click yes and wait a while.

3 Elements has used its new Content Aware Fill technology to analyze the areas around the edge of the image and fill them to blend in. It's made a great job of it, with only a couple of small problems on the left by the tree and at the bottom of the grass.

4 We need to fix the photo's crookedness: select Filter > Correct Camera Distortion. Alter the angle using the central spire as a guide; 2.9 degrees is about right. This does leave gaps, however, so we can increase the Edge Extension a little to compensate.

5 Here's our finished image. The minor problem areas from before were removed when we scaled the image up to adjust out the edges. Overall, it's an astonishingly good result with very little effort required and no need for cloning or additional cropping, thanks to the incredibly clever Clean Edges feature introduced in Elements 9.

SHORTCUTS
MAC WIN BOTH

Digital cameras

BEING AN ELEMENTS USER, it's likely that you'll already have a camera of some type, even if it's not digital. You may, however, be looking to buy your first, or upgrade from your current model, and with so many different cameras on the market, choosing the right one can be a difficult decision. There are many factors to take into consideration and they are largely based on how much you intend to use it and for what purpose; you don't really want to be carrying huge amounts of equipment around with you if you're only interested in taking the occasional snapshot and similarly, if you're a keen photographer, you might be disappointed with the lack of features on a smaller model.

There are three main types of digital camera: let's begin with the compact models. Firstly, small is not necessarily a sacrifice in quality or features. Even at entry level, 3 megapixels (Mp) will give you a perfect quality 7" x 5" print and a reasonable one at Letter or A4 size. Some have a fixed lens whilst others offer a moderate amount of optical zoom – don't fall for the digital zoom gimmick, though; the results are often lower quality because the image is enlarged by the software in the camera, and not by the lens. The features vary from set point-and-shoot modes to a reasonable amount of manual control, depending on the model.

Next in line are the mid-range cameras, sometimes referred to as prosumer (from professional-consumer). These are bulkier than the compacts but are generally higher quality having larger image sensors and more manual control of the settings. The lenses are larger with a good zoom factor; again, many still include the digital zoom feature in an attempt to make the package more attractive to the buyer.

Finally, we have the DSLR (Digital Single Lens Reflex) cameras. These are the most expensive, and largest, but do give the best image definition: most producing photos that can be printed at A3 with no degradation. They have the same control features as their film-based brethren and their lenses are interchangeable. Many share the same mounts as their analog predecessors, giving you the option of using your existing ones, if you choose the same manufacturer.

It's worth noting that when it comes to the resolution of a camera, bigger isn't necessarily better, especially on the compact cameras which use a smaller sensor; the receptors need to be more tightly packed and the definition of the image can suffer as a result. For most purposes anything between 5 and 12 megapixels is sufficient. Professional DSLRs tend to start at 6Mp and can go as high as 20Mp or more, but you'll be paying out serious money at that level.

Once you've decided on the type of camera, you then need to choose the specific make and model: this can be another minefield, of course, and it's certainly a good idea to read reviews, both in magazines and online. There are two websites well worth visiting: **www.dpreview.com** and **www.stevesdigicams.com**; both offer highly in-depth information about almost every camera currently available — and sometimes advanced previews of the latest technology, as well as archives of the older models too.

From a photo-montage perspective, having a good camera certainly helps when it comes to sourcing images for your artwork. We'll talk about stock libraries elsewhere in the book and whilst you're almost certain to find the image you need on at least one of the sites, there's still no substitute for taking your own; you are in full control of the pictures and can get just the right angle and distance to suit your needs. You can create your own library of images, especially if you have a camera that you can carry with you easily at all times; that way you'll always be ready to capture those interesting scenes and textures. You can also set up a small home-studio for photographing smaller objects, either by buying a dedicated light box and lamps or, if you're feeling particularly adventurous, you could build your own – there are numerous websites with instructions on how to do this.

You might even consider uploading your own images to one of the many free stock libraries and add to the constantly growing resources. You may think that your contributions will be just a drop in a very large ocean, but you may just provide someone with a picture of something nobody else has. If your pictures are of high enough quality you could subscribe to one of the micro-stock websites such as **www.istockphoto.com** or **www.shutterstock.com**. You never know, you may start earning some extra money from it, especially if you sign up with a lot of different ones. There's always the excitement of seeing one or more of your pictures in use on someone's website or in a book such as this, perhaps.

■ The Palace of Westminster is one of London's best-loved and most-photographed attractions. But the dull, gray sky that's almost as much a London landmark makes the whole image look dull. How much better when we substitute a blue sky with fluffy clouds. It isn't hard to do, even though that tree may look fiddly.

Elements 10

5

Image adjustments

DIGITAL CAMERAS are the best gadget the Elements user can own. But even the best camera can't produce sunny skies on an overcast day, or make snow from thin air, or change the color of a car. Fortunately, we have a solution.

Elements allows us to make any changes we like to an image: literally anything we can imagine can be changed within a single image. We can turn silver into gold, alter the time of day, and give the impression of speed.

But we can also enhance our images without adding anything new. Got a dull, lifeless photograph? We'll see how to liven it up in just a few steps – and how to recover apparently lost information from shadows and burnt-out highlights.

Adjusting images with Levels

1 When we open the Levels dialog using *ctrl* **L** ⌘ **L**, all the sliders are in their starting position: the black and white triangles to the extreme left and right, and the gray triangle sits in the middle.

ELEMENTS INCLUDES SEVERAL METHODS for adjusting the brightness, contrast and tonal range in images. By far the most powerful – and the most versatile – is Levels, which gives a large degree of control over your pictures. Getting to grips with Levels will mean you're able to fine-tune your images to get perfect results.

The Levels dialog is in three parts: the histogram, the graph which shows the spread of tones in the image; the Input Levels, which allows you to adjust highlights, shadows and midtones; and the Output Levels, which controls the final brightness and contrast of the finished image.

2 Dragging the small white triangle in the Input section to the left will brighten the image overall. Similarly, dragging the black triangle to the right will darken it.

3 A good way to balance an image is to drag the black and white triangles so they touch the extreme edges of the histogram. This gives the image the full tonal range and makes it much crisper.

4 Dragging the center gray slider will affect the midtone values. Here, dragging the slider to the left brightens the image, without changing the brightest and darkest areas.

5 Dragging the black Output triangle to the right makes the image brighter; dragging the white triangle to the left would make the whole thing darker. Moving either will reduce image contrast.

6 Pressing the Auto button will examine the histogram and produce what Elements thinks is the best result. Often, pressing this button can produce a marked improvement at a stroke.

7 Levels also gives access to the individual red, green and blue channels, using the pop-up menu. Here, dragging the midtone on the green channel to the right reduces the total amount of green.

8 When we drag either the black or the white Input triangles, the middle gray triangle moves with it to remain spaced halfway between light and dark.

9 By dragging this midtone gray marker towards the light end, we can produce a strong, graphic effect.

HOT TIP

If you make a mistake and feel everything has gone horribly wrong, don't panic: press the Reset button to return the dialog to its original state.

You can use the three Eye-dropper tools to adjust the image automatically. With the black (left) dropper, click in the darkest part of the image; click the brightest with the white (right) dropper. Use the gray (center) dropper to click on a neutral gray in your image (if there is one), to color balance the image.

SHORTCUTS
MAC WIN BOTH

103

Shadows and highlights

EXPOSURE IS THE ONE factor that photographers worry about more than any other. Professional photographers will always 'bracket' their exposures – that is, they'll take a range of exposures of the same image to make sure they've got the right one.

The real difficulty comes when we're faced with an image like this: a view through a window. In the image captured by the camera, above, we can see that the room itself is too dark (we can barely make out the blind texture among those deep shadows), while the view is so bleached out as to be wholly indistinct.

We can fix both of these problems in one go, with the Shadows/Highlights adjustment. It's a hugely powerful tool, which can rescue even the most poorly exposed photographs.

1 After opening the image, go to Enhance > Lighting > Shadows/ Highlights, and the dialog above will appear. As long as the Preview button is checked, any changes you make here will be visible immediately in the image. The default setting for this adjustment is to Lighten Shadows by a value of 25% and, as we can see here, this setting manages to rescue some of the darker areas of the image. We can already see that there's a yellow pattern in the blind, for example.

2 That's not enough for our purposes. Let's increase the value significantly – here, we've dragged the slider to raise it to 80%. Now, the pattern and texture in the blind can be clearly seen. In addition, we can see that the dark field outside the window has now acquired some definition: the trees on the hill are now distinct from the plowed field in front of them.

3 Now let's turn our attention to the highlights. As the image stands, the sky is greatly over-exposed. Dragging the Darken Highlights slider addresses this problem: the further to the right we drag it, the more detail we're able to see in the sky. We've dragged it here to a value of 70%, and this means that the clouds now stand out from the sky behind them.

4 Although we could stop there, it's worth looking at the final slider – Midtone Contrast. Generally, we'd welcome contrast, as it provides definition within the image. Here, though, the result of tweaking both the shadows and the highlights has resulted in a window frame that's so well defined that it overpowers the view through it. By lowering the midtone contrast we take out a little of that over-defined molding, drawing the eye through the window to the view instead.

HOT TIP

Not all cases are as extreme as this one. The adjustment is also useful when a person has been photographed with side lighting: by lightening the shadows and darkening the highlights, we're able to give the impression that the lighting came directly from the front.

105

Bee flat to bee sharp

WE ALWAYS STRIVE to get the best possible images but sometimes, even with the best equipment, we can end up with an image that is slightly soft.

In our example the combination of the extreme close-up and the bee's movement has resulted in a less defined photo. There is, of course, no way to get a clearer image once it's been taken but we can enhance it to give the impression of it being a lot sharper. We'll have a look at two different sharpening methods here, each providing a slightly different effect.

Rather than working directly on the image, however, we'll use a grayscale copy and blend it with the original; this way we have far greater control over the final effect.

1 Here's our slightly soft photo in need of a little attention. We're not going to work on the image directly so the first step is to duplicate the background layer. Both techniques require a grayscale layer so we need to desaturate the layer by pressing *ctrl* *Shift* *U* *⌘* *Shift* *U*.

2 For the first technique we'll use the Unsharp Mask adjustment. This can be found at the bottom of the Enhance menu – in previous versions it can be found in the Filter menu under Sharpen. The dialog may look a little daunting but it's surprisingly straightforward.

3 The default settings are fairly tame and have little effect on our image. Drag the Amount slider to the right. Don't be afraid to increase it higher than you would normally, it won't look as severe when we blend it with the original. In this case we raised it to 350%.

4 Without the adjustment applied we can overlay it onto our original image. Set the blend mode to Soft Light. The image is looking a lot sharper whilst retaining much of its tonal qualities and color balance, something that might have been affected if we'd applied the effect directly.

5 The second technique makes use of a little-known filter called High Pass; this resides in the Filter menu under Other. There is only one slider and, unlike Unsharp Mask, we only need to make a small adjustment to achieve good results – we've used a setting of 3 pixels here.

6 As before, we need to change the blend mode; this time, set it to Hard Light. This is a more subtle effect than the Unsharp Mask version, concentrating more on the edges than the entire image, but still gives superb results and leaves the original color almost unchanged.

SHORTCUTS
MAC WIN BOTH

RAW adjustment

YOU WOULD BE FORGIVEN for thinking that RAW is something that should be left in the realm of the professional photographer. This is not the case, however, as more and more compact and so-called 'prosumer' (the not-quite-DSLR type) cameras are now able to record their images in RAW.

So what is so special about this format? When you take a photo the camera records the data its sensor sees into memory. Normally this would then be converted to a JPEG by the camera and stored on its memory card. Various enhancements are carried out during this process, making sometimes irreversible changes, and being compressed, there is already a slight degradation in quality. RAW images are not processed by the camera. The recorded image is saved unaltered (more or less) to the memory card. The data is instead decoded by the software on the computer. This gives us far more editing power as we can work on the separate color channels to make more precise corrections. The main benefit, however, is RAW's non-destructive editing. Whenever a change is made, the original image remains untouched. The alterations are written to a control file which in turn tells the software how to display it. These changes can be output to a separate version of the image, either by opening it in Elements or saving it as a .dng (Digital Negative) file directly from the Camera Raw dialog.

1 Go to the File menu and open the example photo *RAW adjustment.crw*. Before we start working on the image, make sure we are working in full screen mode. This can be done by pressing **F** or by clicking the button just to the left of the histogram window.

2 One of the first things we notice is that the image is crooked. Select the Straighten tool from the toolbar (or by pressing **A**). Find a suitable guideline – the opposite ends of the bridge work well. A boundary appears showing the change in angle. Pressing **Enter** sets the changes.

3 We can also crop the image down a little. Select the Crop tool **C**. The skew-adjusted boundary appears again. We want to keep the same image aspect: hold **Shift** and drag the bottom-right corner in – enough to remove the cut-off ship and its mooring. Press **Enter** again to set it.

4 Now we can start color correcting and enhancing the image. Firstly we'll set the white balance; this generally defaults to As Shot. The image was taken in sunny conditions so set it to Daylight. This gives us a slight blue hue and brings out the color of the sky and water.

5 It's always worth trying the Auto correction option. Even if it's not perfect, it serves as a good baseline. It's done a pretty good job here. If we weren't happy with the changes, we could select Reset Camera Raw Defaults from the fly-out menu on the tab bar to return it to its initial state.

6 We'll concentrate on the lighting adjustments first. Recovery deals with blown highlights. There are very few in this image. Press **O** to turn on the highlight clipping warning. A small red area appears on the boat on the right. Drag the slider to the right until most of the red area is gone.

7 Blacks is the opposite to Recovery, dealing with the heavy shadow areas. Again, there aren't too many in this image. Press **U** to display them; they show up in blue. There's a very small area on the hull of the boat. This time drag to the left to tone them down.

8 The previous adjustments have left the image slightly washed out. Grab the Clarity slider and drag it to the right. This acts as a subtle form of sharpening by boosting the midtones of the image. A value of 60% works well here and takes away the haziness.

9 The last adjustment we'll use is Vibrance. This boosts the less saturated color whilst leaving more saturated ones untouched. It really deepens the sky and the softer colors of the buildings. Finally, we can save all our changes by clicking Done. They will be there next time we open this image.

HOT TIP

The standard tool cursors can get in the way, particularly if you are zoomed right out of the image. You can temporarily switch to precise crosshairs by pressing the Caps Lock key. This is especially useful for the Straighten tool, where you often need to pinpoint a particular area of the picture. To return to normal cursors, simply press Caps Lock again. This shortcut also works for most tools within Elements' Editor workspace.

SHORTCUTS
MAC **WIN** **BOTH**

Photomerge: exposure

ONE OF THE DIFFICULTIES with photography is the inability to capture both bright and dark areas of the scene at the same time. Unlike our eyes, which can create a happy medium between the two extremes, the camera falters, leaving us with horribly blown out highlights when we try to capture shaded areas and disappointingly dreary shadows if we expose for the bright areas.

Fortunately, we have a solution. The Photomerge Exposure command basically compares the differences between two or more photographs at different exposure levels to blend and output one composite image comprising the best of the batch. The photos can either be shot separately at the time, exposing for light, shadow and midtone – the filter will also realign the images if necessary – or, as we will see here, create them using the Camera Raw dialog where we can save different exposures of the exact same image, so they will be perfectly aligned from the outset.

There are two modes: automatic and manual. The former is the default and will often do the job without any need for alteration. It's not perfect, however, so we can also get our hands dirty and define the regions of the image ourselves to perfect the result.

1 Open the project photo *Photomerge exposure.dng.* The image will appear in the Camera Raw dialog. The image has already been straightened and auto-adjusted. We can see that the image has been exposed for the sea; the foreground is dark and the sun and sky are a little too bright.

2 We'll use the starting image as our base. Click the Open Image button to open the photo in Elements. We have to save the file as we cannot open more than one version of the same file. We'll add the word 'Mid' to the end of the original filename as it's a midtone equivalent.

3 Open the original .dng file again. Drag the Exposure slider to the left. We want to tone down the blown highlights. We can also add a little Vibrance to bring out the blue sky. Open the image in Elements. Save it as before but this time append the filename with Dark.

4 Open the original image one last time. Increase the Exposure to brighten up the rocks in the foreground. Save the file, appending the filename with Light. Now make sure the Project Bin is visible; if it's not, you can make it visible by clicking its entry in the Window menu.

5 Select all three images in the Project Bin. Go to File > New > Photomerge Exposure. When it's finished processing we have our merged photo. It's done a reasonable job but the colors are a little strange. We have a limited adjustment control but not enough to make a difference.

6 Click the Manual tab. Click and drag the *Mid* file from the Project Bin to the right-hand (background) window. Now click the Dark file's thumbnail to make it the active foreground. Make sure the Selection tool is enabled. Paint a zig-zag line over the sky to replicate it to the background.

7 Now click the *Light i*mage and paint over the rocks in the same way. We now have a much more evenly balanced image. If we click the Show Regions box, we can see where the image has been blended. It's an even split but more complex images would have many blending areas.

8 The sky is a little too intense. Click the Dark thumbnail to make it active. Now drag the Transparency slider to the right. This works like opacity, allowing the background image to become more visible. It's always best to make the middle exposure image the background for this reason.

9 When we're happy with the effect, we click Done to return to the Editor window. A new document will be created containing both the original mid-exposure image and the merged image as a layer. We can now save it as a Photoshop file to keep the layers or as a single JPEG image.

HOT TIP

On complex images with finer detail, you may find yourself accidentally spilling over into the wrong area of the image when working with the Selection tool in manual mode. We can still undo the last few actions but, if we've gone too far to do this, there is the Eraser tool. We can erase the section definitions which remove that area from the background image. Remember to make the relevant photo active first by clicking its thumbnail in the Project Bin.

111

All that glitters...

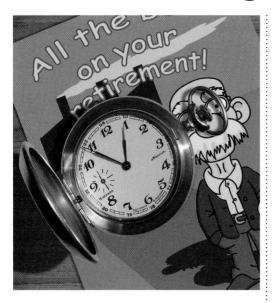

CHANGING A SILVER OBJECT to gold is not a difficult task. The two metals are very similar. They both have the same specular properties: the way light is reflected back from their surfaces (once polished, of course). Silver has a high content of blue, giving it its colder appearance. Gold, on the other hand, is predominantly red and green. It's simply a matter of adjusting the hues to give us the familiar warm color. Although you might be tempted to use a Hue/Saturation adjustment, we'll use the Levels dialog. By working with the color channels individually, we have far greater control.

1 Here's our silver watch. The face has been cut away from the rest of the image and placed on a separate layer. We only want to color the body, after all. Because of its slight angle, we used the shape selection technique from Chapter 3.

2 Make sure the body layer is active by clicking its thumbnail in the Layers panel. Open the Levels dialog by pressing *ctrl* *L* *⌘* *L*. Select the Blue Channel from the menu. Move the midtone slider over to the right. This removes some of the blue and the color becomes noticeably greener and closer to gold.

3 Now switch to the Red channel. This time increase the amount by moving the Midtone slider across to the left; not too much, subtlety is key here. As we can see, our watch is now beginning to look much more valuable. It still seems a little dull though, so in the next step we'll finish off with a little bit of digital polishing.

HOT TIP

You can also select the individual channel views from the keyboard. Holding *ctrl* ⌘ and **1** **2** or **3** will switch between the red, green and blue channels respectively. Press *ctrl* ⌘ and the ~ (tilde) key to return to the composite RGB view – not the more logical 0, as you might think. This, of course, is the reserved shortcut for the Fit on Screen view mode.

4 Switch back to the composite RGB view. Start to slowly drag the Highlight and Shadow sliders toward the middle of the histogram window. As we do this we can see the darker areas begin to deepen and the brightness in the lighter areas increases. This gives us a much richer range of tones to the color as well as giving us the impression that the metal is much shinier.

SHORTCUTS
MAC **WIN** **BOTH**

The perfect respray

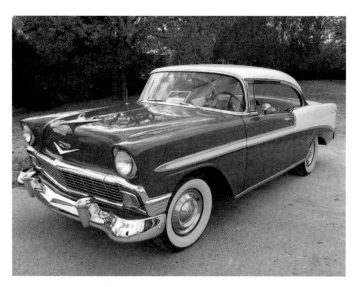

THERE ARE NUMEROUS WAYS to change the color of an object. Most, however, are designed to affect the entire image. We could, of course, use the selection tools to isolate the parts we need to work on. This is a time-consuming practice and often more trouble than it's worth.

For tricky jobs, such as this car with all that complex trim, by far the best method is to use the Replace Color tool. With this we can selectively alter the hue, saturation and lightness of an area without the need to separate it from the rest of the image.

IMAGE: PEGGY S. SIMONI/MORGUEFILE.COM

1 Press *ctrl* *J* *⌘* *J* to duplicate the background layer. Open the dialog by going to Enhance > Adjust Color > Replace Color. The white area in the preview shows the selected area after clicking a section of the car's body. We've set the Fuzziness to its maximum, and we'll adjust it later.

2 Instead of applying the new color straight away, we've lowered the Saturation completely; this shows up the more subtle shades of red not included initially. We can add these areas to the selection by holding *Shift* and clicking them with the Eye-dropper.

3 We've isolated all of the car's color but we now have a problem: looking at the preview, a large amount of unwanted areas have been included from the rest of the image. This is where we'll use the Fuzziness setting to fine-tune the result.

4 By gradually lowering the Fuzziness value we can see the selection start to tighten up in the preview. Some of the previously selected color will begin to reappear. Zoom in a little and start to add these back in. If necessary, adjust Fuzziness a little more until you have a good balance.

5 Now we can add the new color by raising the Saturation and altering the Hue to the desired shade. As we began by duplicating the image, we can simply erase the unwanted areas, such as the 'for sale' sign in the window and the trees in the background, to let the original show through.

6 You may notice that there are still places where the original hue remains. Often this will be noticeable in the highlights and reflections. As a final touch, grab a soft brush. Set its blend mode to Color. Now you can carefully paint over these areas with the target color.

HOT TIP

The Fuzziness setting of the dialog works in a similar way to the Tolerance feature of tools such as the Magic Wand. By increasing the value, Elements will select a greater tonal range of the chosen color. This can be used to avoid harsh lines where two hues meet. It's rarely possible to achieve a perfect result with no excess areas affected. If we keep refining the balance by adjusting the fuzziness and adding in small amounts to the selection, we can keep problems to a minimum.

SHORTCUTS
MAC WIN BOTH

Shifting the seasons

W E CAN'T ALWAYS BE in the right place at the right time to capture a scene. Our example image was taken during the summer and whilst it's already a very picturesque scene, wouldn't it look more beautiful in the fall, with the reds and browns of the leaves framing the chapel nestled within.

In the previous project we changed the color of the car with Replace Color; this works well when the subject has a uniform color. If the image has more varied hues, as with the leaves in our example, we might not get the best results as there would be too much to change in one go. Instead, we'll break the task down into several smaller steps and build up the effect gradually for a much better effect.

1 Duplicate the background layer *ctrl* *J* ⌘ *J*. Now use the Quick Selection tool to make a selection around the chapel. Soften the selection slightly with Refine Edge or Feather. Press *ctrl* *Shift* *I* ⌘ *Shift* *I* to inverse it. Now only the trees will be affected.

2 Open the Replace Color dialog from the Enhance menu. Click the Selection button so we can see the area of the effect. Choose a suitable starting point such as the large leaves on the left. Click the eye-drop cursor on one of the leaves. The area shows up as white in the preview.

3 Rather than trying to get the right color using the Hue slider, we're going to be a bit bolder. Click the color chip in the Replacement area. Select a fairly deep red/brown hue. We've picked up a little of the green here. Click OK to accept the color change.

4 We need to add a few more tones in. Click the Add to Sample (middle) icon in the Selection area. Click a few of the areas next to the reds to add them in – not too much as we don't want to include too many shades. Now use the Fuzziness slider to fine-tune the selection. Click OK to apply.

5 Open the Replace Color dialog again. Select a different range of greens and adjust them as before. This time, use a slightly more orange tint in the Color Picker. Try not to make the colors too bold as they can end up looking unrealistic. Repeat the technique for the rest of the image.

6 With our new colors, the chapel looks a little stark. Inverse the selection again. Now create a Photo Filter Adjustment Layer. The chapel will be masked from the selection. Select the Warming (85) preset and increase the Density to give the impression of a warm fall glow.

SHORTCUTS
MAC WIN BOTH

Photomerge Style Match

MOST DIGITAL CAMERAS have built-in settings that adjust the image automatically when we take the shot. Some can convert to black and white, or sepia, or add other creative effects. Wouldn't it be great, though, if we could tell our camera to take our pictures in any number of specific styles; an Ansel Adams high-contrast landscape image, for instance, or maybe the popular gritty HDR style of Dave Hill?

Well, we may not be able to do this in-camera just yet, but in the meantime we have a really superb alternative: Style Match. This is another addition to the Photomerge series in Elements.

We can open one of our own images and tell the program to apply the tones and colors from any photo we choose, either from the supplied presets or one we have sourced ourselves. As we'll see here the results can be stunning!

1 The first thing we need to do is open an image. We've chosen a view along the coast with some prominent wooden posts. Now select File > New > Photomerge Style Match. The dialog will open with the photo already placed in the destination slot. We can see the Style Bin at the bottom.

2 Now we'll choose an image from the presets to apply to our photo. This will look great as a heavily contrasted black and white image. We've dragged the Pier Rope image onto the style slot. Initially this only affects the tone of the colors. Not a bad effect in itself but not the effect we want.

3 Go over to the control panel on the right and check the Transfer Tones box. This forces the colors of the style image to be mapped onto the destination photo. We've switched to the After only view here and, as we can see, it's done a superb job without any need for further adjustments.

4 We'll try out a different effect now. Using another seascape image, we'll try changing from a sunny daytime scene to a fiery sunset. Here we've placed the Sunset preset in the style box. Without transferring the color tones its effect is not very good at all.

5 Clicking the Transfer Tones box has a much better result but it still has some problems. The definition of the clouds and sky is not great, and there are some harsh areas causing ugly bright spots of orange on the otherwise dark beach in the foreground.

6 We'll go back to the control panel. The Style intensity slider reduces the amount of the overall effect. We'll leave this as it is. We'll increase the Clarity slider to 3. Although it seems we are making the image worse here, it's just the initial step in the process.

7 We'll use the Enhance Details control to reduce the harsh areas of the image. Lowering it to -3 removes the bright specks from the foreground but because we boosted the Clarity, we still retain much of the definition in the clouds. It's not perfect but it's still a really great image.

8 So far we've used photos that are similar to the styles we are applying. Let's see what happens if we try something a little unusual. Here we have a picture of President Obama. We'll apply the Silver Hotel preset. Curiously, it's produced an effect not unlike a pastel drawing.

9 If we go one step further and apply the color tones we now have a sketched effect. The initial result is a bit dark. We'll click Done to go back to the Editor. Now we can open the Levels dialog and brighten him up a little. A surprising and rather interesting effect!

HOT TIP

Like many of the automated adjustment filters and tools, the results we get with Style Match are not going to be perfect every time. The effects may not work at all on some photos but on the whole it can produce great images.
Often, as is the case with our second image, we can only adjust the problems up to a point. Once we've saved the image, however, we can sort out any major issues – such as the smudge on the tip of the sculpture – in the Editor with one of the retouching tools.

119

A splash of color

LEAVING LARGE AREAS of prominent color in an otherwise monotone image to make it leap out at you is by no means a new idea; although it was used to great effect in the movie *Sin City*, which we'll be paying homage to in this project. It has always been possible to create this effect in Elements, of course, but with version 7 came a new tool which makes the whole thing much easier.

The Smart Brush is a combination of the Quick Selection tool and Adjustment Layers: as you click or paint, the selected area dynamically builds a mask, so only that part of the layer's effect is visible. The great thing is that because they are Adjustment Layers, we can change the look of the image in an instant by simply choosing another preset or by altering the opacity or blend mode.

1 Here's our starting image. It's fairly striking to begin with but we can make it really stand out with just a few simple steps. Begin by grabbing the Smart Brush tool **F**; go to the Preset Picker, select Photographic from the drop-down list and choose Natural Tone BW.

2 It makes more sense to work on the areas we want left intact, and switch them later, than to spend time on the background. We'll start with the lower part of the dress. Using a fairly large brush, but making sure it stays within the confines of the dress, click once to begin the selection.

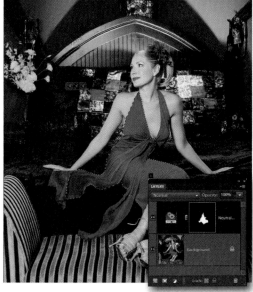

3 The small square that appears marks the starting point of the selection and is color coded for when there is more than one effect layer applied. Add some more areas in by clicking once each time. If we look at the Layers panel we can see how the effect is starting to build up.

4 Continue clicking around the dress, varying the brush size accordingly. The tool is good but not infallible and some areas have spilled onto the bed and parts of the skin. We can remove these by holding *alt* ⌥ to temporarily switch to subtract mode and click/paint over them.

5 We've added as much as is possible with the Smart Brush. Pressing *F* again gives us the Detail Smart Brush. Using this, only the immediate area is affected so we can resize the brush and paint the rest of the areas in. We can also use it to touch up any other areas around the dress.

6 Here's our image with all the areas painted in. We're almost ready to reveal the final effect but as a last piece of tidying we can use Refine Edge (see Chapter 1 for more detail) to clean up the fringing that's been left around some of the dress.

7 Clicking Inverse in the Options bar swaps the areas around and gives us a stunning result. We found the black and white to be a little too bright so we've changed the Adjustment Layer's blend mode to Color, as this gives us a slightly even contrast.

HOT TIP

By default, whenever we select the Smart Brush or Detail Smart Brush, the Preset Picker appears. This can be very off-putting, especially when switching between the two as we have done in this project. Fortunately, we can turn this off: open the picker window and open its fly-out menu. Click Show on Tool Select to uncheck and disable it.

SHORTCUTS
MAC WIN BOTH

121

Smart bling

THE PREVIOUS PROJECT introduced us to the power and ease of use of the new Smart Brush. We only used a single layer for the effect but, as we'll see, you can apply as many as you need. Each can be a stand-alone effect or one that enhances the rest of the artwork.

There is a whole host of preset styles available by default and they can also be installed. Because they are standard Adjustment Layers, we have hundreds of possible effects at our disposal: we can even import Photoshop-only layers, which gives us extra scope.

The custom presets used here, along with installation instructions, can be found in the Goodies folder on the website. Details on how to access this are at the back of the book.

1 Our starting image is just a simple embossed image created using a similar technique to the wax seal in Chapter 9. It's a bit dull and looks like pressed plastic at present – not very exciting at all. This is all about to change, of course: select the Smart Brush 🅕 and choose the Gold preset from the Style Picker window.

2 Using a large brush, paint across the whole of the artwork; we can quickly select it in just one or two strokes. We're not simply changing the color, however, we're also altering the tones of the image – in essence we're dynamically applying the technique we used in the silver to gold project at the beginning of this chapter.

3 Now to create the impression that the surface is polished. Firstly, deselect *ctrl* D ⌘ D, to force the tool to add a new effect layer. Go back to the Style Picker and select Metallic. As we can see in the inset, painting over the object again applies a new texture on top of the gold layer which, in turn, interacts to create the shiny surface.

4 Let's really add some value with some diamond encrusting. Deselect again and choose the Diamond preset. Decrease the brush size so it fits comfortably within the dollar emblem and start to paint. We have a bit of a problem, though: because some of its edges are low contrast, the texture has spilled out. We'll deal with this next.

5 We'll use the Detail Smart Brush *F* to clean up the problem areas, as we can work much more accurately. Remember to switch to subtract mode, either by holding *alt* ⌥ or by clicking the icon in the toolbar. As the texture has covered up the shape, we can lower the opacity of the Adjustment Layer to enable us to see more clearly.

6 Here's our completed artwork: not bad for only a few minutes' work. Once we have our effects in place we can easily alter them too: we could, for example, swap the gold for silver and the diamonds for gold. This is done simply by selecting the relevant layer and choosing another style from the Style Picker.

HOT TIP

The colored icons that appear on the document are visual links to the individual effect layers. Left-clicking on one takes us straight to the corresponding layer – very useful when we have many different effects. Right-clicking gives the option of editing the settings (unless it's not a native function of Elements). We can also opt to delete the current effect or select another layer by name.

SHORTCUTS

123

Changing skies

THE BACKGROUND ERASER is a fantastic tool for removing areas of similar color. It works by sampling the color beneath the crosshair and deleting all the pixels of that color within the radius of the brush. Here, we're going to use it to replace the dull sky in this photograph of London's Houses of Parliament.

Although we could select and delete much of the background using the Magic Wand tool, that won't select inside fiddly areas such as the tree: this is where the Discontiguous setting of the Background Eraser comes in handy, as we'll see in this example.

Before we start with this tool, it's important to duplicate the layer you're going to work on, hiding the original so there's always a copy we can return to later.

1 Select the Background Eraser tool **E** and change its limits from Contiguous to Discontiguous. A Tolerance setting of around 40% works well for this plain sky. Click and drag around the tower to delete the background, but be sure not to let the crosshair stray onto the building.

2 When we move into the tree area, we get a problem. Once the crosshair touches the branches, that's the color that's sampled – and so that's the area that is deleted. We need to find another way to remove the sky in there. Undo that step and we'll try again.

3 Make the Eraser brush size much larger – we've used a 175 pixel brush here. Click on a clear area of blue sky within the tree branches and all the sky within the radius of the brush will be deleted. Make sure you don't click on the branches by accident.

4 Continue erasing all the sky within the image, varying the size of the brush as you need to. Don't worry if some areas of the picture are erased that shouldn't be; we can get those back later. For now, concentrate on getting rid of all that sky.

5 When we now bring in a new sky layer behind the buildings, we can see a few mistakes: the clock face has been erased and we can see the new sky through it, and the same applies to one or two parts of the buildings. Just as well we were working on a copy of the layer!

6 Make selections around the missing building parts using the Lasso tool. Now return to the original (hidden) layer and press *ctrl* *J* ⌘ *J* to make a new layer from the selection. Move this layer above the clouds layer and the image is complete.

HOT TIP

There are several settings for this tool. The first is choosing between Contiguous and Discontiguous: the former will find edges and the latter will look inside bounded regions such as the branches of the tree.

The Tolerance setting depends on how uniform the background is. The higher the Tolerance, the wider the range of deleted colors will be. It's a matter of judgment for each image individually; start with a setting of around 50% and increase or decrease it as needed.

SHORTCUTS
MAC WIN BOTH

Miracle healing

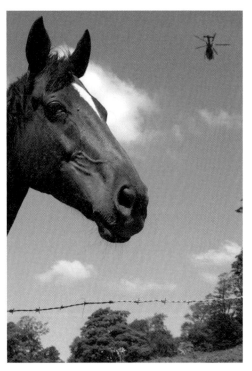

W E'RE NOT ALWAYS IN CONTROL of what appears in our photos when we take the shot; something could move into the frame just as we press the shutter or there could be something that we just can't avoid.

We're going to look at fixing problems using the Spot Healing Brush. A new feature that was added in Elements 9 is Content-aware fill. Previously, the tool only had the Proximity Match option, which samples the area immediately around the brush cursor. This works well but has its failings. Content-aware fill differs greatly as it analyzes the entire image looking for possible areas that match the affected spot. As we'll see here, the results can be quite remarkable; the tool is now capable of removing complicated items from an image, often in a single stroke.

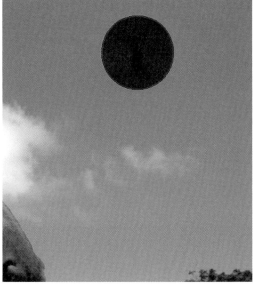

1 We'll start by removing the flies from the horse's head. Grab the Spot Healing Brush tool **J**. Set its type to Proximity Match. Choose a fairly small brush. Now we can simply click once on each fly to remove them. The tool does a great job; we'd never know they had been there.

2 We'll set our sights a bit higher now: increase the brush size to just larger than the helicopter. Click once and release the mouse and it disappears without a trace. Although it seems like a simple fix, being on a plain sky, there are still a lot of varying tones to match and blend.

3 Although we were able to remove the flies and helicopter easily with a single dab of the brush, this isn't always the case. If we want to remove the barbed wire we can't use single clicks, as the tool uses the surrounding area to repair the point where you have the brush. The result, as we can see here, is no good at all; it sees the trees and clouds as different to the pixels directly beneath the brush and assumes it's OK to use those to repair the area. To remove objects like this we need to paint over the whole thing in one go.

4 Undo the last attempt by pressing *ctrl* Z ⌘ Z. Make the brush size around that of the barbed wire, including the barbs. Go to the Options bar and change the Type to Content-aware. Now trace along the entire length of the wire from one edge of the image to the other. When we release the mouse the result is very different. Aside from some slight blemishes, it's almost impossible to see where the wire was. The problem areas are fairly isolated so we will not have much trouble removing them. We can switch between Proximity Match and Content-aware in order to tidy up the places that were missed – the strands of hair caught on the barb, for example – or where the tool didn't do such a good job. Overall, what might have taken hours to fix in the past can now be done in a matter of minutes.

HOT TIP

Whilst the Content-aware option of the brush can remove and repair parts of an image with astonishing results, it's not infallible. It works best when there are large areas of a repeating pattern, such as trees or bricks.

Sometimes, however, it's not the tool that's at fault, it's us. We know how the image looked originally and we see problems that other people may not notice. It's often worth walking away for a couple of minutes and looking at the image again.

SHORTCUTS

MAC WIN BOTH

Cleaning up the scene

THE HEALING TOOLS work well for smaller, less detailed areas of an image, but what if we need to work with a much more complex image? Well, thanks to an impressive feature in Elements, what would have been a laborious and highly time-consuming task has been made as simple as making a few strokes of the pen.

The aptly named Scene Cleaner is one of the Photomerge set of commands in the Guided Edit section; its function is to remove unwanted people or objects from around the subject of the photograph. This might be a popular scenic view with a steady flow of visitors or, as with our example, a particularly popular attraction at a show. In situations like this, it's not always possible to stop people moving into the frame, but what we can do is take several shots in roughly the same position but with enough time in between for different areas to be populated. When we open the images in the cleaner, they are automatically aligned so we can blend different areas from each together and hopefully finish up with a largely uninterrupted scene.

All the project images can be downloaded from the website. See the end of the book for details.

1 Opening all four images, we can see the people are in different positions in each one but none of the images is good enough individually. Select the New > Photomerge > Scene Cleaner. A dialog will appear asking you to choose the images. Click Open All.

2 Once we're in the Scene Cleaner's dialog, we need to select our base photo: we've chosen Car 2 by dragging its thumbnail from the Project Bin over to the final image frame. We can see the images have been cropped slightly; this is due to the automatic alignment process.

3 Now we can start work on the image: the first task is to remove the three men standing behind the car. To do this we need to choose a suitable source image from our set. Clicking through each of the photos, Car 3 has the least obtrusive background, so we'll use that.

4 Grab the Pencil tool and set its size; it doesn't need to be large, around 20 pixels is sufficient. Now paint over the man in white; start from his head and loop around his body – the color reflects the source photo you are currently working on. When we release the mouse, he disappears!

5 Painting over the man in blue results in both being removed, well almost. There is still a part of a red shirt visible through the window of the car. If we try to remove it, however, we bring in the man in blue from the source image. Fortunately, we can undo this: ctrl Z ⌘ Z.

6 We'll switch to a different source photo now. Car 4 seems the best choice. We only need to click once to remove the remnant of the red shirt; this is replaced by the man's head in the distance, which is much less distracting. That's all we need this image for at present.

7 Now we can focus on the area at the rear of the car. Looking at our image set, Car 1 looks like the ideal candidate. We'll concentrate on the man in the suit: draw across him so all areas are marked. When we release, we see that the man behind the car is also removed; clever stuff!

8 Although the man in the suit has been removed, his reflection in the body of the car remains. We can remove that just as easily, of course. We could replace it with the man in the white shirt, as it should be, but that's too noticeable; instead, we'll use the reflection area from Car 4.

9 Our scene is just about complete now. It's worth pointing out some of the additional options: if we check Show Regions, we get a color overlay showing where areas have been replaced and blended. We can also fine-tune by using the Eraser to remove sections we don't want.

SHORTCUTS
MAC WIN BOTH

Making rainbows

WHETHER IT'S THE PROSPECT of finding the fabled pot of gold or simply its beautiful colors, a rainbow can really lift your spirits on an otherwise dreary gray day. The problem is that the conditions have to be just right for us to see one. The sun has to be low and behind us, and it has to be raining, of course. This is not a common combination.

We don't have to rely on science and nature to call the shots, however. We can make our own rainbows in dry comfort. In just a few steps we can not only paint a spectrum across the sky but conjure our own rain as well.

As well as using the technique for photographic effects, we could just as easily use it to create bolder graphic objects to highlight stationery or brighten up collages and album pages.

1 Start by creating a new layer. Grab the Rectangular Marquee tool **M** and draw out a selection from the bottom-left corner to around halfway across the document. The height determines the rainbow's width; we don't want it too wide to begin with as we'll be scaling it up later.

2 Select the Gradient tool **G** and pick the Transparent Rainbow preset from the Options bar. Make sure Linear Gradient is selected and, holding **Shift**, click and drag inside the boundaries of the selection from the bottom to the top. Release the mouse and deselect **ctrl D** **⌘ D**.

3 Grab the Rectangular Marquee again, hold **Shift** to keep it square and click and drag from the bottom-left corner of the image to the far right of the gradient. Select the Polar Co-ordinates filter (under Distort) and choose Rectangular to Polar; click OK and deselect.

4 Enter Free Transform *ctrl* *T* *⌘* *T* and scale the rainbow up proportionally; it will help to zoom out *ctrl* *–* *⌘* *–* so we can see outside of the image bounds. We can also stretch it horizontally to gain more of an arc. Press *Enter* to commit the changes.

5 We don't want the bottom part of the arc so use a soft-edged Eraser *E* to remove the excess. Now apply some Gaussian Blur to make it more hazy; the exact amount will vary, depending on the image size. Finally, we'll lower the layer's opacity to fade it out a little.

6 We couldn't have our rainbow without rain, of course. Create a new layer above the rainbow, then fill it with 50% gray using the Fill Layer dialog *Shift* *Backspace*. Now add some Noise: check the Gaussian and Monochromatic boxes and push the Amount up to around 100%.

7 Now open the Motion Blur filter. There are no definite settings for this, it's just a case of experimenting with the angle and distance until we get a reasonable rain effect. Click OK to apply the filter. Use Free Transform to scale the layer up slightly to lose the harsh edges the filter left.

8 Holding *alt* *⌥*, create a Levels Adjustment Layer. Check the Group With Previous Layer and click OK. Now we can adjust the strength of the effect: bring the Shadows up to the edge of the histogram then adjust the Midtones and Highlights to produce a lighter amount of rain.

9 Click the rain layer's thumbnail to make it active again and set its blend mode to Screen. This hides the black, leaving us with just the rain. Using an Adjustment Layer means we can go back at any time and edit the settings to increase or decrease the amount as we see fit.

0–60 in ten minutes

APTURING THE ESSENCE OF MOVEMENT in a photograph can be really tricky. The motion is often frozen and the shot can look static and lifeless.

Fortunately it's not difficult to put the drama back, or, as we'll be doing here, creating movement from a stationary image. We'll explore two different ways of doing this: the first mimics the use of a slow shutter speed by blurring the object in front of a static background. The second creates the opposite effect: the car remains still whilst the background is blurred. This would be the result of panning, i.e. following the subject movement with the camera whilst taking the shot.

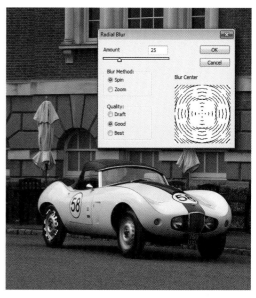

1 The first task is to isolate the car from its background. A combination of the the Quick Selection tool and the Selection Brush is best for doing this, the latter being used to tidy up the tricky areas of low contrast. Copy the car to its own layer by pressing `ctrl J` `⌘ J`.

2 One common trait of speed is the wheels. Use the Elliptical Marquee to select one of the wheels (not the tire). Open the Radial Blur filter and set the Method to Spin. The Amount depends on the required effect; we've used 25 here. Deselect `ctrl D` `⌘ D` and repeat for the other wheel.

3 First we'll create the effect of the car zooming past. Open the Motion Blur filter – make sure Preview is enabled. Start by setting the distance. Keep this subtle to avoid it looking too much like a cartoon. Now adjust the angle to suit the direction of the car's movement.

4 You'll notice there's some blurring in front of the car as well as behind, most prominently around the tires and far right of the bodywork. This, of course, wouldn't happen unless it was being vigorously shaken. Select a large, soft Eraser. Use the edge to carefully remove the unwanted areas.

5 Here's a different approach. After completing step 2 above, make the background layer active. Apply the Motion Blur filter; as before, set the Distance and Angle. You can add a slightly heavier effect this time. Once again there are some unwanted areas. We'll deal with those next.

6 Select the Clone Stamp **S**. Using a small soft tip, go around the car painting over the sections where the overspill is most pronounced. Finally, switch back to the car layer. Use a small Eraser to remove the windows to reveal the blurred background of the original image.

HOT TIP

When you're cloning in parts of a blurred image you can often afford to be a little less precise than you would be where the detail is visible. As long as there are no obvious areas where there's a repeating pattern or misalignment, a little artistic license will most likely go unnoticed.

SHORTCUTS
MAC WIN BOTH

Real world modeling

THIS TECHNIQUE IS STYLED AROUND an effect known as Tilt-Shift, which is derived from a specialist camera lens of the same name. Its main purpose is to prevent perspective convergence when photographing subjects such as tall buildings. When using this equipment to capture normal scenes, however, it was discovered that the results could end up looking like scale models, due to the extremely shallow depth of field it produces. We are used to seeing larger areas in full focus and small objects with heavily blurred backgrounds; when this is swapped around our brains can be confused.

The best images to use with this technique are ones that are taken from above the scene – although it can work with different views, such as that shown in our example. It's also good to keep the subject area fairly tight in the frame as we are less likely to be fooled by an image that extends for miles into the distance, as models generally don't have that degree of detail and would take too long to construct.

Gaussian Blur

OK

Cancel

☑ Preview

100%

Radius: 6.0 pixels

1 Here we have our starting image: a picturesque fishing village. It almost looks like a model to begin with so our technique is going to work really well. The first thing we need to do is duplicate the background layer *ctrl J* *⌘ J* as we'll be working exclusively with the copy.

2 Now we'll apply some Gaussian Blur. We don't want to completely obliterate the scene, just knock out the detail. A radius of around 6 pixels works well in the example; the amount will vary for different images, of course, depending on their size.

3 The next stage is to add a mask to the layer. This will allow us to selectively hide parts of the blurred image so the sharp layer below can show through. Click the Add Layer Mask icon at the base of the Layers panel. Nothing happens yet, of course.

4 Pick the Gradient tool **G**, choose the Black, White preset and set the Type to Reflected. Holding *Shift*, click and drag up from the middle of the image to where the trees meet the sky. We now have a narrow area in sharp focus which softly fades to a blur.

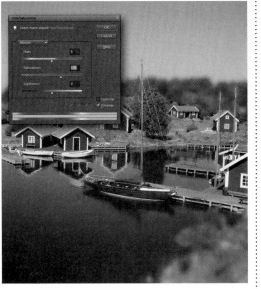

5 It's beginning to look good but there are still a few adjustments to be made. Because we're looking straight at the scene, the masts of the boats should still be in focus. Still working on the mask, use the Polygonal Lasso to outline them and then fill the selection with black to hide the blur.

6 We can use a fairly soft black brush to paint out any additional areas, such as the top of the trees behind the mast, or blur more of the background by painting in white. Finally, we'll add a Hue/Saturation adjustment above the blur layer and raise the saturation to enhance the illusion.

135

Sunset silhouette

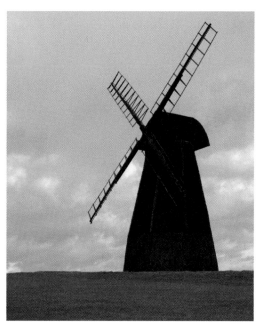

EARLIER IN THIS CHAPTER we looked at replacing a washed out sky with a more impressive one. Simply changing the existing sky isn't always enough, however: depending on the type of scene we want to produce, we will often need to adjust the foreground to match. We'll demonstrate this by transforming our uninspiring photo of a windmill into a lovely evening silhouette.

As the sun sets its light changes, becoming a richer, more orange tone which, in turn, affects the scene's colors. We can mimic this by adjusting the levels of the image; it's important not to darken the subject too far as we still want to be able to see some detail.

1 Here we've duplicated the background layer and removed the sky: the Magic Wand in discontiguous mode made easy work of the fiddly areas of the sail frames. Our sunset image is then placed on a layer behind. It's not looking particularly convincing at this stage, though.

2 Make the windmill layer active and load its selection by holding *ctrl* ⌘ and clicking its thumbnail in the Layers panel. Create a Levels Adjustment Layer; the selected area becomes a mask so the changes we make will only affect the foreground image.

3 Drag the midtone slider across to the right to make the tones richer and darker. Increase the Shadows slightly and bring the Highlights up a little by dragging the slider to the left. Select the Red channel *ctrl* **1** *⌘* **1**. Drag the midtones a little to the left to deepen the red hue.

4 We'll add a shadow to complete the scene: load the windmill layer's selection. Only the outline is needed so grab the Polygonal Lasso tool, hold *Shift* *alt* *Shift* ⌥ to switch to intersect mode, and draw across the windmill's base. Follow on with a loose selection around the rest.

HOT TIP

It's often not possible to remove all traces of the background, particularly in small, intricate areas of the photo. When placed against a darker image these lighter areas can show up as a halo around the isolated object. We could zoom in with a smaller Eraser to tidy it up but this is fiddly and we could end up removing parts of the image we meant to keep. Instead, use the Burn tool to darken and blend in the offending areas; this can also be used to paint over any brighter elements in the scene that the Levels adjustment doesn't affect.

5 Create a new layer above the Adjustment Layer and fill the selection with black. Deselect and enter Free Transform mode *ctrl* **T** *⌘* **T**. Distort the shadow into position by holding *ctrl* *⌘* and dragging the corner handles – you'll need to zoom out to stretch it past the bottom edge.

6 The shadow is too harsh so we'll use a small amount of Gaussian Blur to soften the edges and lower the opacity a little so it's not completely black against the background. As a final step, we've used the Ripple filter to add the effect of the shadow falling across the uneven grass.

SHORTCUTS

That's snow business

WE DON'T SEEM TO GET THE SAME amount of snow as we did in years gone by; whilst some people would say this is a good thing, it is a shame not to see the stunning white backdrop blanketing the streets and countryside – it does make a particularly great photo opportunity, after all.

This is not a problem for the montage artist, however. With a little effort we can take almost any scene and add a little wintry magic; a layer of snow on the pyramids, perhaps?

1 First we'll make a selection of the girl using the Quick Selection tool **A**. We don't need to worry too much about the fine detail. Once you've made the selection press *ctrl* *J* *⌘* *J* to create a copy on a new layer. This will allow us to add snow both in front of and behind her.

2 Now to start creating the snow. Make a new layer *ctrl* *alt* *Shift* *N* *⌘* *⌥* *Shift* *N* above the girl's layer. Fill this with 50% gray. Now go to Filter > Noise > Add Noise and set the Amount to around 100%. Check the Monochromatic box and click OK.

3 Now open the Gaussian Blur filter. We're looking to achieve a soft, mottled effect here. Somewhere around a 6 pixel radius gives us the best result on our example image; any more would not contain enough contrast for the technique to work correctly.

4 Open the Levels adjustment *ctrl* *L* *⌘* *L*. Start by dragging the Highlights arrow over to the left so it meets the right edge of the histogram. Now pull the black Shadows control over towards the Highlights arrow. As we do this the image tightens up, creating snow-like flecks.

138

5 Setting the layer's blend mode to Screen removes the black, leaving us just with the snow. This works well as it is but we can take it a step further. Duplicate the snow layer and hide the original for the time being by clicking the eyeball icon next to its thumbnail in the Layers panel.

6 Press *ctrl* **T** ⌘ **T** to enter Free Transform. Make sure Constrain Proportions is checked. Now type 50% into the Width field. The layer will shrink to a quarter of its size. Drag it over to the top left of the image and press *Enter* to set the transformation.

7 Press *ctrl* **J** ⌘ **J** to duplicate the layer. Use the Move tool **V** to slide it over next to the original. Now go to Image > Rotate and flip the layer both horizontally and vertically. This gives us a better pattern without obvious repeats. Press *ctrl* **E** ⌘ **E** to merge the two layers.

8 Create a duplicate of the merged layers. Move it beneath the copy and flip it both ways as before. Finally, merge the two layers. We have a problem though: there are ugly joins across the image. Grab a soft-edged Eraser and paint them out, being careful not to leave large holes.

HOT TIP

Remember when using the Move tool or Free Transform, you can hold *Shift* while you drag the layer to keep it constrained to horizontal or vertical movement. This is very useful for techniques such as this, where keeping layers aligned is essential.

9 Drag the layer down between the girl and the background in the Layers panel. It now looks like the snow is in the distance. Make the original snow layer visible again. The combination of the large foreground flakes and the smaller ones in the background makes it more realistic.

10 Snow tends to mute the colors of a scene, especially in the distance. As a final step add a Hue/Saturation Adjustment Layer between the girl and the background. Lower the saturation slightly to tone down the colors in the background. This also gives more focus to our subject.

SHORTCUTS
MAC WIN BOTH

139

But is it art?

THE ART WORLD CAN BE A FICKLE and sometimes intimidating place. Whilst the majority of its denizens are more than happy to welcome new concepts such as digital art with open arms, there will doubtless be the old-school stalwarts who balk at the very notion of something as utilitarian as a computer being the medium for any kind of creative expression. This is nothing new, of course: photography also received the same amount of steely renunciation when people started using it as anything other than a functional method of preserving images of people and places. It took the work of the late, great photographer Ansel Adams and others like him to prove that the photograph could have just as much visual impact and provide the same aesthetic pleasure as paintings by the old masters.

Unfortunately, as with many things, there can also be a degree of fighting within the ranks as well. There are those who frown upon certain aspects of digital art, such as photo-montage and 3D imagery, seeing it as compensation for lack of talent because it's not created from scratch and often uses other people's work as a constituent. This is, of course, a ludicrous way of thinking. Nobody thinks to question the validity of art forms such as decorative floristry, which quite obviously doesn't necessarily require the flowers to be grown by the artist beforehand; it is, after all, the end result that matters and not how it was achieved.

Squabbling aside, one of the main accomplishments of the digital age is its ability to unlock and uncover artistic flair. We may shy away from trying out our ideas, often because we lack confidence in our abilities, believing that we'll make irreversible or costly mistakes. Another reason might be one of space and time, or the lack thereof. A studio requires a fair amount of working space and it's not always practical to set one up permanently; it can take a while to ready the materials and pack them away after a session, all of which does nothing to aid the creative process.

This is where computers come into their own. In general they're fairly self-contained, taking up only a small proportion of space and they can be ready for action in just a few minutes. What really sets them apart, however, is their forgiving nature: make a mistake on canvas and you've got a fair amount of tidying up ahead of you – at worst you'll have to paint over it and start afresh, which is demoralizing to say the least.

Working digitally is a different matter entirely. With technologies such as layers, non-destructive adjustments and styles, and not forgetting the trusty Undo function, you can afford to think more freely in the knowledge that you have these safety nets to catch you, should you falter and lose your artistic balance.

It's not all plain sailing, of course. The standard equipment that comes with a PC, usually a mouse, is great for moving the cursor around the screen to point at links in web pages, menus and highlight passages of text in a word processor, but not so good for creating a masterpiece. Imagine trying to draw with a pencil shaped like a soap bar: it's not impossible, but it can be awkward and become uncomfortable after a while. If you're considering any kind of digital art as a serious hobby or even as a profession then a graphics tablet is an essential purchase. They can take a while to get used to, however; there's often a period where hand-eye coordination causes problems — we are usually more accustomed to looking directly at what we're drawing, rather than away to a screen. Once you have overcome this, it's unlikely you'll want to stop using it: outlining and selections can be achieved in half the time and you can really see the difference with the painting tools. Using a pressure-sensitive device makes shading an absolute delight, rather than the constant size and opacity changing nightmare it once was. Many tablets have configurable buttons on the stylus which can be set to emulate key-presses; for example, you could set one up as the Spacebar, allowing you to pan around the image whilst zoomed in for close-up work. Some also have an Eraser function when the stylus is flipped over, which also saves time.

There are, of course, some things that even the most powerful computer technology can't provide you with: imagination and determination. You're on your own there, but without the constraints that may have been holding you back before, you're free to express yourself in whatever way you see fit. There is no rule book to abide by here, just do what seems good at the time.

Who knows, those images you had locked away in your head might be just what the art editor of a magazine is looking for, so get creating!

The text above fits neatly enough onto its plaque, but it looks rather painted on. How much more impressive if the wording appears to have been carved into the wood. The words 'First Class' in this example use a metal style not detailed in this chapter, but it's available to download and install from the website to import into Elements and use in your own work.

6

Working with text

WE USE TEXT FREQUENTLY IN ELEMENTS. Although you may not think of it as being an essential component of most images, there are often times when adding a caption can lift an image.

But there's more to text than mere captions. Think how good it would look if you could engrave an invitation on stone, or carve it into a piece of wood. How good your holiday slideshow could appear if the first frame showed the title written in a sandy beach. Or imagine customizing a photo of a classic car so that its owner's name was written in gleaming chrome along the side.

We'll look at all these techniques and more in this chapter.

Carving in stone

STONEMASONS TAKE YEARS to learn their craft: after all, the one thing that's certain about carving lettering into stone is that there's no Undo key. Make a mistake and it will cost you dearly.

Fortunately, Elements is rather more forgiving when it comes to carving. All we have to concern ourselves with is arranging the text to its best advantage; we can leave it to Elements to add the bevel effect automatically.

As we'll see here, we don't even need to choose a color for the text. This, too, is added directly by Elements, building on the texture already in the stone for added effect.

We'll demonstrate this technique by adding an inscription to this blank gravestone, in memory of the unfortunate captain of the mutinous ship *Bounty*.

1 Begin by typing your text – centered – for a gravestone. Choose a serif font, such as Caslon Bold, for authenticity. No need to worry about the text color at this stage as we're only using it as visual aid; in fact, making it as contrasting as possible helps with the technique.

2 Now lay out the text for emphasis, adding spaces in between the individual blocks of text using the `Enter` key. Hold `ctrl` `Shift` `⌘` `Shift` and press the `>` and `<` keys to make selected text bigger and smaller — notice how the different sized lettering still remains in proportion.

3 In order to distort the text, we first need to make it into a regular layer: choose Layer > Simplify Layer. Now enter Free Transform and distort the text in perspective by holding *ctrl* ⌘ and clicking and dragging the corner handles. We can use the lines of the stone as our guide.

4 Hold *ctrl* ⌘ and click on the text layer's thumbnail to load up the selection. Then hide the text layer, switch to the background layer, and press *ctrl* *J* ⌘ *J* to make a new layer from it. Choose Simple Sharp Inner from the Layer Styles panel to make the basic bevel.

Although we created the text on a new layer, we later discarded that layer, instead loading its selection from the original background. This allows us to keep the stone texture, making the carved lettering look that much more convincing.

When choosing a font for stone carving, be sure not to pick one that's too light or the bevel effect will make it unreadable. Always choose the bold version of a font, where possible.

5 We now need to modify that bevel, so open Layer > Layer Style > Style Settings. Change the bevel type from Up to Down to make it carved rather than raised. Adding an Inner Glow, using the default settings, brightens the carved lettering as well.

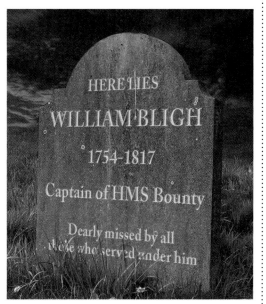

6 To make the carving more realistic, carefully erase the layer with a small Eraser where the grass goes over it. Here, we've also darkened the background layer using the Levels adjustment, and added a new somber sky to complete the spooky graveyard effect.

SHORTCUTS
MAC WIN BOTH

145

Neon signs with layer styles

ELEMENTS COMES WITH A BUILT-IN selection of neon styles – called Wow Neon. But they're brash, too bright, and look unconvincing on the screen; they're also set to colors that will look dull and muddy when printed out.

For this reason, we've created a set of custom neon layer styles. They can be found on the book's website in the Goodies section, along with installation instructions; refer to the end of the book for details on how to access the downloads. Be sure to load them in before you start the project!

As a first step, though, we'll look at how to round off our basic sign design to give it the sort of smooth corners required for the neon to work properly.

1 We'll begin with a standard piece of black and white artwork. We've created a simple text-based sign here. The design could be more complex, of course, incorporating graphic objects. This has been flattened to a single layer.

2 We need to soften the edges as they are far too angular for a neon sign. We'll begin by applying a Gaussian Blur. We've used a 6 pixel radius blur, which applies quite a high degree of smoothing.

3 Now for the clever part. Open the Levels adjustment and drag the white and black sliders together so that they almost touch the gray slider. This tightens up the blur, producing a round-cornered version of the artwork.

4 Grab the Magic Wand tool **W**. Uncheck the Contiguous option. Click one of the letters. Go to Select > Modify > Contract. Set a value of around 6 pixels and click OK. Now press *Backspace* to delete the selected areas.

5 Now click the Magic Wand in the area outside of the letters to select the background. Go to Select> Modify > Expand. Set a value of 1 pixel. Hit *Backspace* to delete the pixels and we're left with just the outline of the lettering.

6 Press *ctrl* *D* ⌘ *D* to deselect as we no longer need the selection active. The lettering is currently a little difficult to see. Press *ctrl* *I* ⌘ *I* to invert the image. The artwork is now white instead of black.

7 Now we can add our neon layer style. Go to the Effects palette, click the Layer Styles icon and select the Cheat Styles (which you remembered to install beforehand, of course!). Here we've applied the Neon Pink preset.

8 We can change the colors of the different parts of the sign. Here we've made a rough selection around the word 'cafe'. We've cut it to its own layer by pressing *ctrl* *Shift* *J* ⌘ *Shift* *J* and applied the Neon Green style.

9 The components of neon signs are not made from one continuous tube. We can simulate the breaks by selecting a hard-edged Eraser and erasing a small section on each of the parts. The layer style fills around the gaps.

HOT TIP

The Gaussian Blur/Levels technique used in steps 2 and 3 can be used to smooth out any artwork, adding rounded corners to just about anything. The more you blur, the more rounded the corners will be. Drag the white, gray and black sliders to the left or right to change the thickness of the lettering after blurring it: experiment to see what works best for your design.

Note: you can't change the color of the inner glow in layer styles in Elements before version 5.

SHORTCUTS
MAC WIN BOTH

147

Instant chrome

ELEMENTS OFFERS A WIDE VARIETY of ready-made layer styles you can apply to your artwork – among them is a selection of good-looking chrome effects.

As with most layer styles, though, some adjustment is needed before they fit the artwork perfectly. You'll almost always need to adjust the bevel size and the rather over-enthusiastic drop shadow in order to make the style work with your image.

Here, we'll go a step further and make the chrome reflect its background to match the chrome detail already present on this car.

1 Here's our initial lettering: it's set in the freeware font Deftone Stylus, which is easy to find online. After typing the text, turn it into a regular layer using Layer > Simplify Layer, so we can distort it more easily.

2 Use Free Transform to shear the text so that it fits the side of the car. Hold *ctrl* ⌘ as you drag a corner handle to add a little perspective to it: the lettering gets slightly smaller towards the right-hand side.

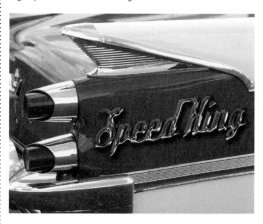

3 Now open the Layer Styles panel and go to the Wow Chrome section. Drag the first style, named Wow Chrome Beveled Edge, onto the layer to apply the effect to the text.

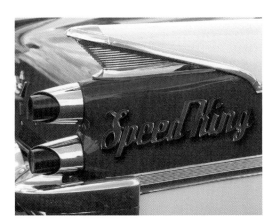

4 That's far too big a bevel for our purposes. Double-click the Layer Styles icon in the Layers panel and change the Bevel size to around 8 pixels. Make a note of this number, as we'll need to use it later.

5 We need to reduce the drop shadow amount, too: a far smaller shadow with a smaller offset is needed. By dragging the Lighting slider clockwise, we can also get a better chrome effect.

6 Now for the inner part of the lettering. Hold *ctrl* ⌘ as you click on the layer's thumbnail in the Layers panel to load it up; then choose Select > Modify > Contract and reduce the size of the selection by 8 pixels.

7 Make a new layer and fill with any color. This is a red sampled from the car body. It looks fairly convincing as it stands, as the inner color matches the car well, but we can make it better still.

8 Go to the background layer and select a portion of the reflection in the fender with the Lasso tool. Make a new layer from the selection and drag it above the inner color text layer as shown here.

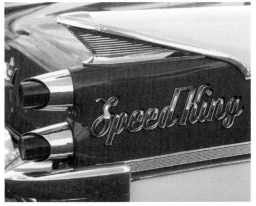

9 Now press *ctrl* G ⌘ G to group the reflection with the inner color layer. Enter Free Transform and scale the reflection so that it fills the whole of the lettering. The chrome's now a perfect match to the original car.

HOT TIP

In step 9, you may have some difficulty making the reflection fit the full extent of the inner part of the text. Don't worry if it doesn't quite reach the edges: you can always use the Clone tool to copy any of the texture out to the sides, and any missing portions of the top can easily be painted in by sampling and then painting with a soft-edged brush.

SHORTCUTS
MAC | WIN | BOTH

149

No mess pumpkin carving

A TRADITIONAL PART OF HALLOWEEN is the scooping out of pumpkins to make Jack-o'-lanterns. This is all very messy and time-consuming, of course.

We can achieve a similar image effect to use in our design, without going near the pumpkin's innards. We'll be using a dingbat style font which, instead of having the standard individual letter characters, has entire words or images. This allows our artwork to be completely re-editable; we can change the motif at any time without having to redo the whole image.

This is an impossible image, of course; there are areas where the text is floating, which couldn't really be achieved, but we can afford ourselves a little artistic license here as it makes a great party invitation or poster.

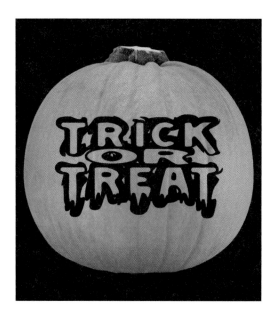

1 Here's our pumpkin with the text layer. We've used a dingbat font: the aptly named Trick or Treat, which gives us the whole artwork in one go by typing one character, in this case the letter A. At present it's looking somewhat flat and not at all like it's been carved.

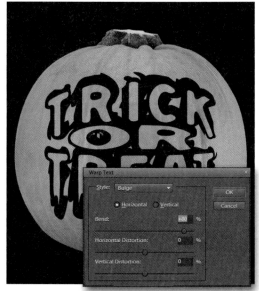

2 Make sure the text layer is active and the Type tool **T** is selected. Go to the Options bar and click the Warped Text button; select Bulge from the menu and choose horizontal as the direction. Now drag the Bend value to the right to try and match the curve of the pumpkin.

3 Choose the Bevels presets from the Layer styles; choose Simple Sharp Outer and apply it to the text layer. The effect needs adjusting so double-click the style indicator to the right of the layer's label. Adjust the Bevel size, around 10 pixels for this image, and change the direction to Down.

4 Create a new layer above the text layer and load the pumpkin's selection. Go to Select > Modify > Contract. Enter a value of around 15 pixels and fill it with 50% gray. This creates a smaller copy that we can use for the texture inside the pumpkin.

5 Select the Texturizer filter; set the texture to sandstone and the scaling to 200%. Apply a small amount of Gaussian Blur to soften the effect. Now use Hue/Saturation *ctrl* **U** ⌘ **U** set to Colorize and change the color to a warm yellow hue. Press *ctrl* **D** ⌘ **D** to deselect.

6 Grab the Dodge tool **O**, set the mode to Highlights and use a large, soft brush to create the impression of a glow radiating from the center. Create a clipping group *ctrl* **G** ⌘ **G** with the text layer to hide the excess. Finally, we've added a candle and shading to complete the effect.

SHORTCUTS
MAC **WIN** **BOTH**

151

Creating text on a path

ONE OF THE THINGS that Elements has been lacking is the ability to create text that follows the outline of a shape. This is an essential part of design work so it's great to see it's finally been added in the latest release.

There are three different options available to us: we can create a shape using one of seven presets (some more practical than others!), we can create the path based on a selection, or we can draw a freehand path. In this project we'll cover the basics by adding text to the label of a vinyl record using the Shape preset – the technique for creating the record itself can be found in Chapter 9.

1 Here's our record with its blank label ready to have some text added. Begin by selecting the Text on Shape tool **T**. Go to the Options Bar and choose Ellipse from the Presets menu. Holding **Shift** to constrain the dimensions, draw out a circle to match the whole area of the label.

2 If we hover over the path outline, the cursor changes to the one shown in the inset. When we click on the path we get the standard text cursor. The typeface and size can be set in the Options bar; we've used Elephant 10pt. When we start typing the text follows the contour of the curve.

3 This is good but the angle of the text is not right. Switch to the Shape Selection tool **U**. If we hover the cursor over the text, it changes to the one shown in the inset. If we click and drag to the right, our text shifts clockwise. It will snap into place when it hits the center point.

4 We now need our text on the label. Press `ctrl` `T` `⌘` `T` to enter Free Transform. Now hold `alt` `⌥` to constrain the proportions and drag a corner handle in to scale the path down. Unfortunately, the text doesn't update dynamically, so there's some guesswork involved.

5 We'll add some text at the bottom of the label. Grab the Text on Shape tool again. Position the cursor at the bottom of the path so the text path cursor appears again. As before, click and start typing. Although we haven't created a new path, our new text is created on a separate layer.

6 The problem here is the text is upside down. Switch to the Shape Selection tool again. Center the text as before. Now, click and drag the cursor inside the circle. The text will flip over to display the correct way up. Now we just need to use Free Transform to scale the text up to match.

HOT TIP

It's also possible to move the text around without using the Shape Selection tool. Whilst you are still working with the Text on Shape tool selected, holding `ctrl` `⌘` and clicking on the text will also give you the positioning cursor, although this only appears when you hold the mouse down. You must first select all the text, however; this makes it difficult to see what you are doing. The Shape Selection tool will always work straight away.

SHORTCUTS
MAC WIN BOTH

153

Three-dimensional text

WHEN WE WANT TEXT TO STAND OUT
we tend to use a bold font, often in a
different typeface to the rest of the document.
To really draw attention to it we can take it a
little further and give it a three-dimensional
effect so it jumps off the page at the viewer.

Three-dimensional text is usually generated
by dedicated programs or by using plug-ins;
but, as we'll see in the following tutorial, we
can create the effect in a few simple steps using
the standard Type tool and a crafty trick with
selections, layers and the Move tool.

The technique can, of course, be used to add
emphasis to your artwork as a heading; you
could also use it as part of a montage, creating
a sign to place over a store, for example,
or, as the image above shows, adding some
personalized jewelry to a photo.

1 We'll begin by creating a new text layer: grab the Type
tool **T**, set the Alignment to center and click in the
middle of the document to place the cursor. Select a suitable
font: larger, rounded styles work especially well. Type out
your text, remembering to leave some space around it.

2 Create a new layer and load up the text's selection. Grab
the Gradient tool, choose the copper gradient from the
Presets panel and set the mode to Reflected. Holding **Shift**,
click and drag from the top of the text to the bottom to give
a varied range in tones. Press **ctrl D** **⌘ D** to deselect.

3 Unsurprisingly, our text does not look very golden at all.
We chose the copper gradient because it gives us a good
contrast with strong highlights. A Levels adjustment can be
used to alter the hues. The technique for this can be found
in Chapter 5.

4 Turn the original text layer off to avoid confusion. Enter Free Transform *ctrl* *T* *⌘* *T*, hold *ctrl* *alt* *Shift* *⌘* *⌥* *Shift* and drag the top-left corner handle up a little to add some perspective. Keeping the keys held, drag the top-middle handle to the left to tilt the text back.

5 Press *ctrl* *A* *⌘* *A* to select the canvas. Grab the Move tool *V*, hold down *alt* *⌥* and, using the cursor keys, nudge once to the right and once upward to copy the pixels. We'll repeat this rhythmic sequence until the letters have the desired thickness.

6 Press *ctrl* *J* *⌘* *J* to create a new layer from the current selection. This will become the face of our text; we can alter this separately from the rest of the effect. This also serves as a mask so we can add shading to the edges of the lettering without affecting the front.

7 Make the rear text layer active again. Grab the Burn tool *O*, set a fairly low exposure and choose a large, soft tip. Using a combination of Midtone and Highlight modes, darken the areas that would be in shadow. Hold *alt* *⌥* to switch to the Dodge tool to add in some extra highlights.

8 Switch back to the top layer and add some additional highlights across the face of the text; being shiny metal, it would pick up random reflections and lighting. We can also add a layer style to add a slight ridge to the front; being a separate layer it doesn't apply to the solid backing.

9 To finish off we've filled the background with black to set the gold off. A new layer has been created above the text and we've added some small sparkles on the brighter points: these are made with the Crosshatch brush under the Assorted tip presets in the Brush Picker.

The addition of shading really helps to bring an image to life. A traditional artist might use different shades of the same color to produce highlight and shadow in their picture; we can brighten or darken the exisiting color using Dodge and Burn – in effect, painting with light. By switching between the Midtone and Highlight modes, areas can be put into shadow, the color made richer and hotspots added; this is especially good for metal effects. It is, however, worth noting that the results can be fierce if overdone so it's good practice to use a low exposure and build the effect up gradually.

Writing in the sand

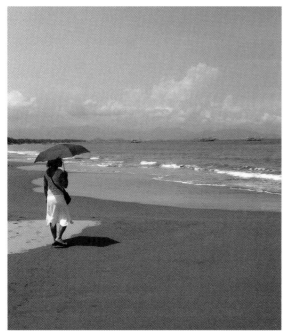

THERE'S SOMETHING ABOUT AN EXPANSE of smooth, untouched sand that begs us to carve something into it; this could be a message of adoration to a loved one or simply a declaration to prove you were there.

We're going to recreate the effect here using distortion and layer styles in a similar way to the stone carving we made earlier in the chapter, except that we'll create the excess sand around the letters where it would have been scraped out.

This quick but effective technique lets us write whatever we want, all without getting a single grain of sand between our toes; it won't get washed away, either.

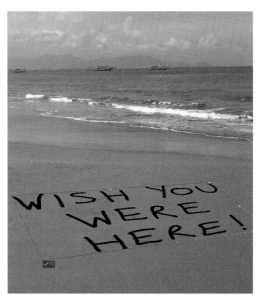

1 Make sure you're working on the text layer by clicking its entry in the Layers panel. Press `ctrl` `T` `⌘` `T` to enter Free Transform; hold `ctrl` `⌘` and drag the corner points to position the text in perspective on the sand. Press `Enter` to accept the changes.

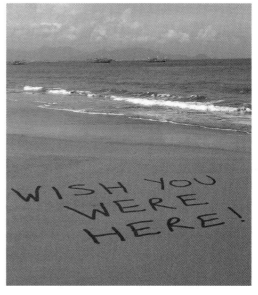

2 Load up the layer's selection. We can hide the layer now by clicking its eyeball icon. Make the background layer active. Press `ctrl` `J` `⌘` `J` to copy the selection to a new layer. Change the layer's blend mode to Multiply to make it darker against the background whilst retaining its texture.

3 Apply the Simple Sharp Inner bevel preset from the Effects panel. Double-click the layer's Style icon in the Layers panel to open the Style Settings dialog. Lower the Bevel value, adjust the Lighting Angle and set the Direction to Down to create a carved appearance.

4 Add a new layer and reload the text's selection. Select Stroke from the Edit menu and set a suitable value for the width; use the Color Picker to select a suitable color from the sand, set the Location to Outside and apply to create an outline around the text. Press *ctrl* D ⌘ D to deselect.

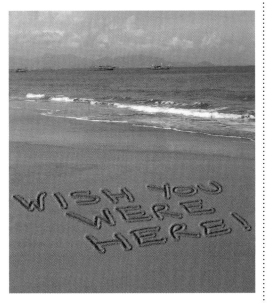

5 Apply a small amount of Noise to add some texture; we used the Uniform, Monochromatic setting with an amount of around 12% here. Add a Simple Inner bevel and decrease its width a little; this time keep the Direction set to Up to give it a raised appearance.

6 Set the blend mode to Dissolve and lower the opacity to give the outline a broken-up, grainy effect. We've also lowered the base text's opacity and darkened the two layers a little using Levels, giving the impression of the wet underlying sand showing through.

HOT TIP

The Dissolve blend mode is great for creating grainy effects or for eroding parts of the image. Unfortunately, because it uses the opacity of the layer to determine the intensity, you cannot soften the pixels by applying a blur. To get around the problem, first create a new layer beneath the target layer then merge them together. The resulting layer preserves the effect which will no longer be affected by blurring or further changes to the opacity.

SHORTCUTS
MAC WIN BOTH

Chop and change

1 We'll start by creating the cut-away effect to show the background beneath the fabric. Grab the Type tool **T** and place some text above the background layer. We've used Poplar Std here as it's a nice clear font; the color is not important as we'll only be using it as a template.

IT'S FAIRLY SAFE TO ASSUME that you wouldn't consider mercilessly plunging a scalpel into a priceless painting solely to advertise your upcoming art exhibition; unless, of course, it was one of those avant-garde affairs, in which case it would be positively frowned upon if you didn't. That aside, it's surprising how often we start hacking into our images without a moment's thought and, whilst we do have the safety of the Undo command, there are far better ways to take chunks out of our artwork.

By using a combination of text layers, clipping masks and layer styles, we can create the effect of words being cut out of a piece of material (or almost any other substance) to reveal a surface beneath. What's more, this technique is completely editable as we never actually cut into the image; we simply create the illusion of doing so.

2 Click the planks layer in the Layers panel and make it visible by clicking its eyeball icon. This will be the texture that shows through the fabric. Press `ctrl` `G` `⌘` `G` to group it with the text. This hides everything apart from the area taken up by the text.

3 It's not looking too convincing at the moment; there's no sense of depth. Make the text layer active and go to the Effects panel; select Layer Styles and from there choose Inner Shadows from the menu. Select the Low preset by pressing Apply or by double-clicking its icon.

4 That's looking a lot better. Before we add the cut-out text itself we'll make some space for it on the artwork. Grab the Move tool **V** and drag the text down towards the bottom. Because the style is applied to the text layer the effect also moves, so we can position it wherever we want.

5 Holding *alt* ⌥, click and drag the text layer's thumbnail to the top of the layer stack. This creates a copy without having to relink the original's clipping mask. Duplicate the background layer and drag it above the new text. Finally, create a clipping group with the two new layers.

At the time of writing, the current version of Elements does not have the option to adjust the inner shadow layer style. Although the default settings work well in our example, they may not look as good on different image sizes. To compensate for this we've included a collection of presets to download from the book's website. Go to the Goodies section where you will also find instructions on how to install them.

6 We still have the previous style set from the copy. Right-click the style indicator icon and select Clear Layer Style. Now go back to the Effects panel and select Drop Shadows from the drop-down list. The Low preset works well here.

7 We need to reposition the new text but this time we want the pattern to move with it. Click the text layer's label (not the thumbnail), hold *ctrl* ⌘ and click the texture layer's label to form a group. Click the chain icon at the bottom of the Layers panel to make the group permanent.

8 Press *ctrl T* ⌘ *T* to enter Free Transform; we can now move and rotate the text and its overlay into position in unison. The bounding box seems far too large compared with the text but remember, we are transforming the entire texture layer. Press *Enter* to apply the changes.

9 With everything in place we can change the text without having to reapply the effects and textures. Double-click the type layer to edit it. This works both ways, of course: you could just as easily change the styles or replace the backgrounds, leaving the text intact.

Elements of design

Y OU MAY NOT REALIZE THIS but with Elements we have at our disposal a highly competent layout tool for both text and graphic-based design such as newsletters, posters and flyers. Many functions are already built-in and others can easily be emulated. With rulers, grids, paragraphs, layers and much more to work with, we can produce professional-looking documents with relative ease.

In the following project we'll be looking at some of these features and building a simple, column-based layout as we might find in a newspaper or magazine article. The principles for creating a full page are the same, we'd just need to add more columns and arrange them across the page.

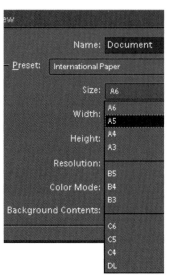

1 When we start a new document we have a host of different presets to choose from or we can create our own custom size, of course. We need to take care when doing this as it may cause problems when we go to print it.

2 One of the most important parts of the design process is the grid. This can be found under the View menu and can be toggled on and off. We can also adjust its size and color from the program Preferences `ctrl` `K` `⌘` `K`.

3 We have rulers `ctrl` `Shift` `R` `⌘` `Shift` `R` for creating designs to a specific size. We can set the measurement units in Preferences. We can also change their origin by clicking and dragging from the top-left.

4 We can add horizontal and vertical guides by clicking on the ruler and dragging down or across onto the document. We can reposition them using the Move tool. Drag them back to the ruler to remove them.

This is a paragraph text box. We can move it around, resize it, and even skew it. The text inside will automatically resize to fit the new size and shape.

If there is not enough space to contain the whole paragraph, a small cross will appear in the bottom-right corner handle. We can choose to resize the box, or alter the size of the font.

5 Normally, when we add text, we click the cursor at the point we want it to start and type. If we click and drag, however, we create a text box which can hold individual paragraphs.

6 Let's put this into practice: we've set up a blank document on which we've created a typical layout comprising a border and three columns spaced with gutters (separation areas for the text and graphics). We can

enable the Snap to Grid and Snap to Guides options from the View menu. This makes positioning the design elements much quicker.

Sweet success!

Congratulations go to Margaret Jones for winning the Horticultural Society's home-produced jelly contest for the second year running. There seems to be no stopping her when it comes to preserves; and we're not about to try, they're delicious!

She attributes her success to the home-grown fruit and a secret extra ingredient

which goes into each and every jar.

"And my patience and dedication, of course." She adds, smiling broadly.

We look forward to seeing (and tasting) more of her produce; long may she reign as the queen of the fruity spreads. **A.J.**

7 Here's the completed article demonstrating how the paragraphs are laid out around the image. Unfortunately, Elements doesn't automatically hyphenate or flow text

from one column to another, but it's not too much effort to do this manually. To the right we have the Layers panel showing the structure of the document.

HOT TIP

HOT TIP

A useful trick when adding images to the document is to duplicate the layer and create a clipping group. This way you can use Free Transform to scale the only base layer, which gives us the ability to hide areas of the photo without the need to resize or crop it permanently.

SHORTCUTS
MAC WIN BOTH

161

Image size

UNDERSTANDING IMAGE SIZE is a conundrum that puzzles many Elements users. Just what is 'dots per inch' and how do they relate to the megapixel sizes quoted by the manufacturers of digital cameras? What resolution is required for printing, or saving files for the web?

Image size is traditionally measured in dots per inch (dpi), even if you're accustomed to working in centimeters. You can, of course, work in centimeters per inch, but we'll stick to dpi here to be in tune with the convention.

Computer monitors typically display images at 72 dpi. This means 72 pixels across and 72 down, which amounts to 5,184 physical pixels in each square inch of screen space. This is the resolution you should work at when designing for the web. In Elements, when you view an image at '100%', you're seeing it at 72 dpi: in other words, each pixel in the image precisely matches one pixel on the screen. Viewing images at a smaller size – say, 50% – means that each pixel on the screen displays an average of the colour of four pixels in the original document. If you zoom in further, to say 800%, you can see each pixel with much greater clarity; they'll clearly appear as squares.

Commercial printing uses only four basic colors: cyan, magenta, yellow and black. All other colours are simulated by overprinting these four. The bigger the printed dot, the more of that colour is seen, so if in one region there are equally sized cyan and yellow dots, you'll see green. If the cyan dots are twice the size of the yellow, the result will be turquoise. Clearly, these dots need to be tiny if we're not going to notice them, and the smoother the paper, the smaller the dots can be. Newspapers print at around 100 dpi and glossy magazines at around 250 dpi, occasionally more.

When printing on an inkjet printer, however, the color is made up from arrays of tiny dots of equal size. The more dots that are clustered together, the stronger the density of that color. Inkjet printers typically print at 1200 dpi, which produces a smooth tonal range with a dot that's barely perceptible. That doesn't mean you need to work at 1200 dpi in Elements: a size of 150 dpi is more than adequate for getting excellent color prints from most inkjet printers.

Digital cameras capture pixels on a CCD chip: the better the camera, the more pixels on the chip, and so the higher the resolution at which the image can be

| Original image, composed of smooth colors | Image converted to square pixels on computer monitor | Image printed using dot clusters on inkjet printer | Image printed using different sized dots in magazine |

recorded. If a camera is quoted as having an image size of 3.2 megapixels, it will produce images that measure 2048 pixels wide by 1536 pixels high. Multiplying these values together – the total number of pixels in the image – produces 3,145,728 pixels overall, or rather over three million pixels, and that's what the 3.2 megapixel name refers to.

If its images were printed in a newspaper, a 3.2 megapixel camera could produce a high quality image at up to about 10 x 8 inches. The same image in a glossy magazine could be used at up to around half an A4 page; if printed any larger than this, the pixels in the image would be larger than the printed dot size, and we'd start to see ungainly pixelation in the finished result. When shown on a web page, however, the same image would easily fill the entire area of a huge 30 inch monitor.

The software that comes with most flatbed scanners tends, confusingly, to offer the ability to adjust both the size and the resolution of scans. In fact, these both amount to the same thing; it's the number of pixels captured in total that counts, not the relative dimensions. The easy solution is to scan an image at the size you're going to want to use it, at a resolution appropriate for the medium on which it's going to end up – printed out or on the screen. Err on the high side: you can always reduce an image's size in Elements, but you can't easily increase it without loss of quality. Bear in mind, though, that the larger the file, the slower it will be to work on in Elements.

The Image Size dialog in Elements has the ability to resample images to any size and resolution you choose. But if you uncheck the Resample Image button, it will adjust the size and resolution together. This is a useful method for turning, say, digital camera captures – which typically have a resolution of 180 dpi – into screen-ready files with a resolution of 72 dpi.

It's not difficult to create a simple montage like this one – a boy sitting on the White House lawn. But while he may be in the correct place, the image above looks unconvincing. By adding shadows, both on the boy and beneath him, we greatly increase the sense of realism, making it appear as if he was really photographed in this location.

7

Light and shade

WHEN WE COMBINE IMAGES from several different
sources, we can scale them, rotate them and distort them
to fit the space – but they still won't look quite right. In
order to achieve a true, realistic appearance, we need to
add shadows. Whether they're cast on the ground, the
wall or on other objects, it's shadows that will help your
montages to work as complete images and to look less
like obvious compositions.

Of course, there's a lot more to light and shade than just
adding shadows. In this chapter we'll also look at how to
make fire from scratch, how to add a spotlight effect to a
stage curtain, and how to turn day into night.

Light and shade
Shadows on ground and wall

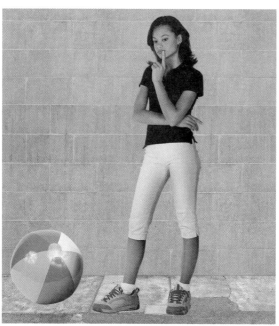

SHADOWS CAN MAKE THE DIFFERENCE between a convincing montage and one that looks like several images placed together. And yet, shadows are often overlooked in the rush to get things done.

It's easy to make shadows on the wall and on the ground – easier still if the base of the wall is at right angles to the viewer, as it is here. The ball, the girl and the background are three separate layers, which makes it easy for us to place shadows between them.

We'll look at two different methods for creating shadows: the girl and the ball require different treatments to produce their effects.

1 Begin by loading up the girl as a selection by holding *ctrl* ⌘ and clicking on her thumbnail in the Layers panel. Make a new layer, feather the selection using *ctrl* *alt* D ⌘ ⌥ F, and fill with black. Deselect, move this layer behind the girl, and drag it out to the side.

2 Now make a rectangular selection of the shadow at about knee height. Enter Free Transform with *ctrl* T ⌘ T, and drag the top-center handle down to meet the bottom of the wall. Then hold *ctrl* ⌘ as you drag the bottom-center handle to meet her feet.

3 With the floor section of the shadow complete, we can move on to the wall part. Select the remaining piece of shadow with the Marquee tool and simply drag it down until it meets the ground. Stretch it vertically slightly if you need to.

4 All we need to do now is to reduce the strength of this layer so we can see through it. We can change the opacity by dragging the slider at the top of the Layers panel; a simpler way is to use the number keys – **3** for 30%, **5** for 50% and so on. We've used a 50% opacity.

5 The ball's shadow requires a different treatment. As it's a spherical object, it will cast an elliptical shadow, so use the Elliptical Marquee tool, on a new layer, to make a selection. Feather it as before, and fill with black. Make sure it's behind the ball layer.

6 Lower the opacity of the ball shadow to match that of the girl, and then move it so that its position corresponds with the angle set by the girl's shadow. As it's a separate layer, it's easy to move and transform it until it looks exactly right.

HOT TIP

The distance of the shadow from the girl is determined by her distance from the wall: the closer she is to the wall, the closer her shadow will be.

Not all objects on the ground are as obliging as this ball: for more complex shapes, paint the shadow on a new layer with a soft-edged brush, working at a low opacity to build it up.

If you're working with a wall that isn't parallel to the bottom of the picture, you'll need a slightly different technique. In step 2, cut the bottom half of the shadow to a new layer; distort both parts, and erase any overlap.

SHORTCUTS
MAC WIN BOTH

167

Painting soft shadows

ON THE PREVIOUS PAGES we looked at how to create shadows cast on a wall and on the ground, by duplicating the figure and filling with black. But some kinds of shadow can't be created this easily: seated figures, such as this one, need shadows to be painted by hand.

As well as adding shadows beneath the figure, we need to add some shading to the figure itself in order for the effect to work properly. The technique we'll use here is more efficient than painting directly onto the figure and gives us greater flexibility and accuracy.

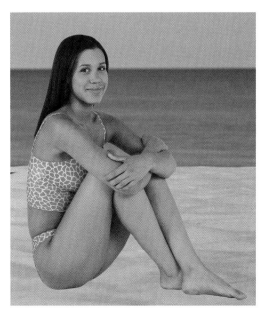

1 When we place our figure of a seated girl onto this beach background, she looks as if she's hovering above the surface: we need to add shadows to place her more firmly on the ground.

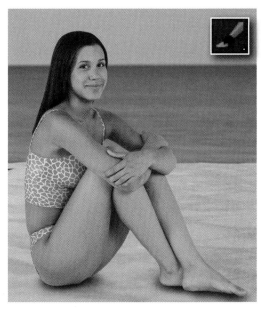

2 Begin by making a new layer between the girl and the background. Using a soft-edged brush set to an opacity of around 40%, paint the shadows beneath the places where she's touching the surface. By working at a low opacity, we can build the shadow up in stages.

3 Now switch to a larger, soft-edged brush and reduce the opacity of the brush still further. We can now paint the shadows cast by her body and her legs: they're fainter than those directly beneath the points of contact and the lower opacity will help us achieve this effect.

4 We also need shadows on the girl herself, to make sense of those cast beneath her. Although we could paint directly onto her layer, here's a better method. First, hold *ctrl* ⌘ and click on the thumbnail of the girl's layer in the Layers panel to load this area up as a selection.

HOT TIP

The best way to paint shadows is to use a pressure-sensitive graphics tablet. If you don't have one, then use a low opacity and build the shadow up in small stages. If the finished shadow looks too dark, then remember you can always lower the opacity of the shadow layer to reduce the effect.

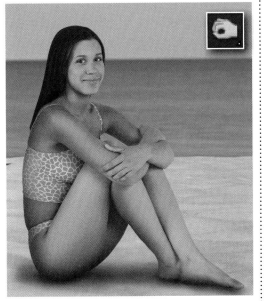

5 Make a new layer and, in the dialog that appears, set the mode to Hard Light and set it to fill with a Hard Light neutral color (mid-gray). Then inverse the selection using *ctrl Shift I* ⌘ *Shift I* and delete the area outside her: here's how the layer would look if it were set to Normal.

6 When set to Hard Light, the gray is invisible. But when we use the Burn tool, set to a soft-edged brush, to paint on this layer, we can darken it up. Add shading to her undersides, beneath her legs and bottom, to link her shadow into the shadows we've already painted beneath her.

SHORTCUTS

169

Light and shade

Turning day into night

TAKING PHOTOS AT NIGHT generally requires the use of a tripod to avoid shaky or fuzzy images. You won't always have one with you, especially if you're just out for the day and happen to spot a scenic view such as the quaint English pub in the above photo. Whilst it's a great picture in its own right, it probably looks equally as good after dark.

In the following tutorial we'll fast-forward to a night view almost exclusively using Adjustment Layers to create the effect. This way we can have total control over the look and feel of the final image or take it back to daylight whenever we wish.

1 Use the Magic Wand `W` to select the sky; hold `Shift` to add the different sections together. Any stray areas can be tidied with the Selection Brush or Lasso tools. Inverse the selection `ctrl` `Shift` `I` `⌘` `Shift` `I`. Now press `ctrl` `J` `⌘` `J` to create a copy of the foreground.

2 The next stage is to isolate the glass of the street lamp and the windows that will be lit. The Polygonal Lasso is best for this job: hold `alt` `⌥` to switch to the Freehand Lasso to select the tricky areas around the leaves. Add a light feather to the selection and copy to a new layer.

3 Create a Levels Adjustment Layer between the building and the layer you just created; accept the defaults for now. Add a Solid Color layer above that. Select a midnight blue color; this will create the night effect. Set its blend mode to Multiply and drop the opacity to around 80%.

4 Now we'll create the lit areas. Click the color layer's mask thumbnail. Now select a soft brush set to a low opacity and begin to paint in black over the areas where light would fall: around the lamp and windows. This hides the color layer to reveal the original daylight image beneath.

5 We need to adjust the lighting a little. It's too harsh for our image. Double-click the Levels Adjustment Layer to bring up its settings. Darken the shadows by dragging the left slider toward the middle. Add some warmth by raising the red channel's midtones and lowering the blue.

6 Create a new Solid Color layer above the windows. Choose a fairly deep orange hue, set the blend mode to Linear Dodge and drop the opacity to tone the effect down a little. Now press *ctrl* G ⌘ G to create a clipping group and restrict the color to the light sources.

Making fire

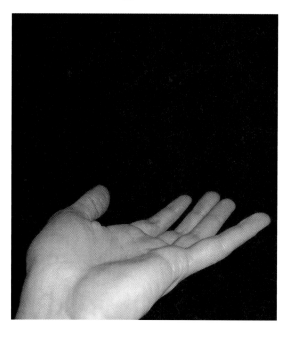

HERE'S A METHOD of creating fire from scratch, the only photograph being the hand we choose to place it on. Of course, you could set fire to anything – a house, a car, a landscape; whatever you choose, bear in mind that the effect will work very much better if you start with a black or very dark background. Flames rarely have the same impact on a bright summer's day.

This is the kind of image you can keep working at until the result looks exactly as you want it: there's a lot of fun to be had from continuously tweaking those flames.

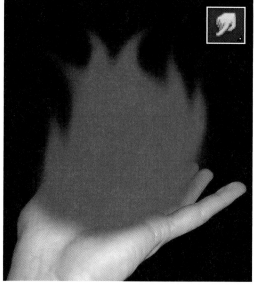

1 Begin by painting a blob, using a soft-edged brush, on a new layer. The shape and size don't matter that much at this stage, as we'll transform both later in the process; this is just the starting point.

2 Use the Smudge tool, set to a strength of around 70–80%, to smudge that red blob into the beginnings of flame-like structures. Make sure the tool is not set to Sample All Layers, or you'll end up smudging the hand as well.

3 To make the basic texture, first lock the layer's transparency by clicking the Padlock icon at the bottom of the Layers panel (or press ◢). Set the foreground and background colors to red and yellow, and apply Filter > Render > Clouds.

4 We need a bright heart at the center of this flame. Using a soft-edged brush, paint a yellow glow covering about a third of the flame area; then switch to white and paint a much smaller blob of color right at the bottom. It's already starting to look quite flame-like.

HOT TIP

Locking the transparency in step 3 allows us to apply the Clouds filter just to the flame area – otherwise it would fill the whole canvas. We need to unlock it again in step 6, so that we can distort the flame layer. Getting from step 5 to step 6 took longer than the whole of the rest of the process: it's a slow and painstaking procedure to get this to look right. Don't rush it and you'll be rewarded for your efforts.

5 Using the Smudge tool once more, tweak up that yellow and white into fire-like shapes, reaching up into the body of the flame. This is also a good time to darken the hand: open the Levels dialog and drag the middle gray triangle to the right, about 80% of the way along.

6 Now unlock the transparency on the layer and work on the flames with the Smudge tool once more. Switch between large and small brush sizes to work on large areas and details; remember, you can smudge down from outside the flame area as well as up from the middle of it.

SHORTCUTS
MAC WIN BOTH

173

Instant candlelight

EVEN THOUGH CANDLES have long been obsolete as a source of lighting, we still rely on them for the warm atmosphere they bring and for the sense of occasion they lend to any event.

On the previous pages, we looked at how to create a fireball. Making a single candle flame is a slightly different process, in that it's painted entirely 'by hand', using no filters.

This isn't a difficult procedure, but it can result in a spectacular image: the trick is to paint each stage slowly, building up the effect as we go along.

If you want to take it a step further and add smoke to your flame, you can see how it's done in 'Smoke without fire', in Chapter 3.

1 Start by placing your candle on a dark background so the flames show up well. We've used a deep red curtain.

2 On a new layer, paint a rough shape in pale orange, using a soft-edged brush. Don't worry too much about the exact shape yet.

3 Use the Burn tool **O** set to Midtones, and darken the bottom of the flame around the wick to give the flame depth.

4 Switch to the Dodge tool, set to Highlights, and use it to brighten the center of the flame, turning it from orange to yellow.

5 Continue painting the flame in with the Dodge tool until the center is a brilliant, glowing white (but don't overdo it).

6 Now use the Smudge tool **R**, with a large brush size, to twist the candle flame into a more appropriate shape.

7 Continue smudging the top of the flame, perhaps switching to a smaller brush, until you're happy with the overall shape.

8 Changing the mode of the flame layer from Normal to Hard Light gives it added impact by increasing the strength of the tones.

9 It's possible to create a huge variety of flame shapes by distorting the original painting with the Smudge tool – particularly handy when you want to make a row of candles. No need to paint each flame, just duplicate and smudge it.

10 For a stronger result, try painting a soft glow on a new layer behind the flame, using the same orange we started with (but at a low opacity). Darkening the background also draws attention to the flame itself.

HOT TIP

When we started to brighten the flame in step 4, we brought the yellow down into the orange a little way. Continuing with the Dodge tool in step 5 hardens the edge between the yellow and the orange, automatically producing the subtle glow effect we see at the base.

SHORTCUTS
MAC WIN BOTH

Stage lighting

WE ALL WANT TO BE ON THE STAGE. Now, thanks to Elements, we can easily achieve this ambition.

The trick to creating stage lighting is to think in reverse. You might imagine that the way to add a spotlight effect would be to place a bright disk over the affected area, but you'd be wrong. Rather than adding light to the spotlit region, we'll subtract it elsewhere – in the form of a shadow with a circular hole in it.

And just for good measure, let's add a glow from the spotlight just out of shot and a shadow cast on the curtain behind.

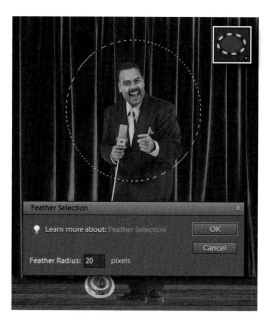

1 Begin by making a circular selection: hold *Shift* as you trace with the Elliptical Marquee tool to make a perfect circle. Now use *ctrl* *alt* *D* *⌘* *⌥* *F* to bring up the Feather dialog and add a large feather radius – about 20 pixels is sufficient for this task.

2 Make a new layer and inverse the selection by pressing *ctrl* *Shift* *I* *⌘* *Shift* *I*. Now, everything except the feathered circle is selected. Press *D* to make the foreground color black, then *alt* *Backspace* *⌘* *Backspace* to fill the selection with the foreground color.

3 At the end of the previous step, the shadow was so strong that we were unable to see anything through it. Lower the opacity of the shadow layer, either by dragging the slider at the top of the Layers panel or by pressing a number key: pressing **7** gives an opacity of 70%.

4 Now for the visible light. Make a rectangular selection and feather it as before, with a feather radius of 20 pixels. Choose a very pale yellow color and, on a new layer, use the Gradient tool set to Foreground to Transparent to drag from left to right, making a faded glow.

5 Use Free Transform (*ctrl* *T* *⌘* *T*) to rotate and distort the glow so that it comes in from the top left of the picture. Holding *ctrl* *alt* *Shift* *⌘* *⌥* *Shift* while you drag one of the corner points produces a perspective distortion, giving the impression of the beam getting larger.

6 Finally, add the shadow behind the man. Load his selection by holding *ctrl* *⌘* as you click on his thumbnail in the Layers panel. Use the technique described earlier in this chapter to make a shadow that sits on the curtain behind him and runs along the ground to his feet.

SHORTCUTS
MAC WIN BOTH

Divine light

SOMETIMES IT'S NECESSARY to exaggerate an effect (for the purpose of illustration, for instance) and as long as we don't overdo it, a little hyper-reality can really make an image stand out.

We'll demonstrate this by creating the impression of light beaming through a stained-glass window and projecting its image on to the floor of the church. Whilst this is not an unnatural occurrence, it's unusual to see it in such bold effect.

We don't have to use stained glass, of course; we could apply the technique to a normal window, for instance, projecting the shadows of the frame instead of the colors of the glass.

1 Begin by making a selection of the window. The Magnetic Lasso or Quick Selection tool work well here. Now press `ctrl` `J` `⌘` `J` three times to make as many copies. Turn the last two layers off by clicking their visibility icons in the Layers panel.

2 We'll start off the effect by brightening up the window as though the sun is behind it. Make the first copy's layer active by clicking its thumbnail in the Layers panel. Add a Simple Outer Glow layer style; we can leave it at its default settings. Now set its blend mode to Color Dodge.

Radial Blur

Amount 100 | OK | Cancel

Blur Method:
○ Spin
● Zoom

Blur Center

Quality:
○ Draft
○ Good
● Best

3 Now for the light rays: make the second copy active and visible again. Open the Radial Blur filter, set the Method to Zoom, raise the Amount to maximum and select Best for the Quality. Now click and drag the Blur Center so the majority of the lines are pointing down. Click OK to apply.

4 Enter Free Transform *ctrl* *T* *⌘* *T*. Now, holding *ctrl* *⌘*, click and drag the bottom corner points out to distort and elongate the rays down the aisle and extend them a little more at the top. Press *Enter* to commit the changes. Finally, set the layer's blend mode to Screen.

5 Switch to the top layer and make it visible. Open the Gaussian Blur filter and set a moderate amount of blur: enough to soften the window's detail. Flip the layer vertically via Image > Rotate and now use Free Transform as before to move and distort the layer so it lays along the floor.

6 Change the blend mode to Hard Light – or Vivid Light for a more intense effect – and lower the opacity to fade the colors slightly. Finally, use a small, soft Eraser *E* to tidy up where it overlaps unwanted areas such as the ornament in the foreground and the front edges of the steps.

HOT TIP

The Radial Blur filter works really well here as we are viewing the window head-on. If, however, the picture was taken at an angle, it would be a slightly different technique: we would need to duplicate the blurred layers and flip one horizontally so we could have the rays emanating in different directions.

SHORTCUTS
MAC WIN BOTH

179

Shading using Hard Light

1 When we place the girl on the nightclub background, she looks quite artificially placed in the scene: her coloring in no way matches the tones of the background image. To begin, hold `ctrl` `⌘` and click on the girl's thumbnail in the Layers panel to load it up as a selection. Make a new layer and, in the dialog, set the mode to Hard Light, filled with Hard Light neutral color.

W HEN WE LOOKED AT SHADOWS earlier in this chapter, we were always painting with dark colors. But in this scene, set in a nightclub, we want to add the impression of the singer being lit by multicolored stage lighting from different angles.

Rather than painting directly onto the girl's layer, we'll create a new layer in Hard Light mode. By painting on this, we can add the effects we want without damaging the original layer; we can also edit the effects later, to produce exactly the effect we want.

2 Group this new Hard Light layer with the girl's layer, so it only shows up where the two overlap. Using a soft-edged brush, sample some of the pink color from the background and paint it on the girl's shoulder to look like light reflecting off her.

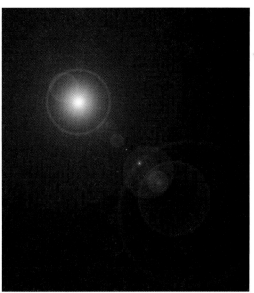

3 Continue sampling colors from the background, painting them on the Hard Light layer as appropriate. You'll need to choose fairly dark colors to paint with: too bright and the effect will look artificial. As it's a separate layer, if we make a mistake we can easily paint over it.

4 Let's add some Lens Flare to make the scene more impressive. First make a new layer in front of the girl. Fill this with black. Then choose Fliter > Render > Lens Flare and position the flare in the preview window so that it's pointing down from the left.

5 When we change the mode of this Lens Flare layer from Normal to Screen, all the black disappears so we can see through it to the scene beneath and move it into place.

6 In the previous step, the Lens Flare layer appeared where we created it – right at the top of the layer stack. But if we move it beneath the Hard Light layer, then it appears to originate from behind the girl's head. We can still see an outline of the ring it created in front of the girl, but the dazzling white center is hidden by the Hard Light layer.

HOT TIP

By creating the lens flare on a separate layer, we have far more control over its positioning and effect than if we'd applied it directly to the background or to the girl's layer. Here we have the option to move it around the scene and to place it in front of the girl or behind.

SHORTCUTS
MAC WIN BOTH

181

Deceiving the eye

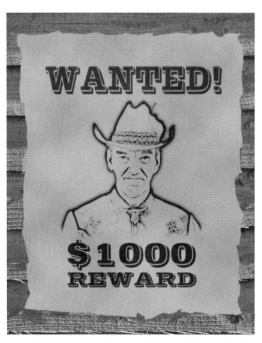

HOW WE PERCEIVE THE SURFACE of an object visually is largely due to how light falls across it. Everything from the waves of the ocean to the contours of someone's face are defined by the variance in the tones.

In this project we have a wild-west style Wanted poster. In its current state, it looks two-dimensional and lifeless, especially when set against a real background.

We can enhance the image immensely simply by adding a shadow but we can take it further still. Folding over a corner instantly portrays depth and by painting in areas of highlight and shadow using the Dodge and Burn tools we can create the impression that the poster has been wrinkled, as though dried in the high-noon sun.

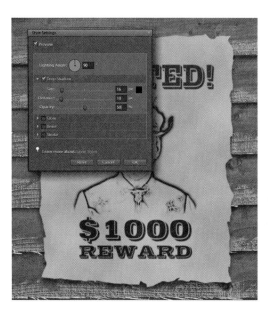

1 First we'll add a Drop Shadow Layer Style to the poster layer using the Low preset. It needs adjusting slightly so select Layer > Layer Style > Style Settings. Set the Lighting Angle to 90° to match the background's shadows. Drop the Opacity to 50% and lower the Size and Distance a little.

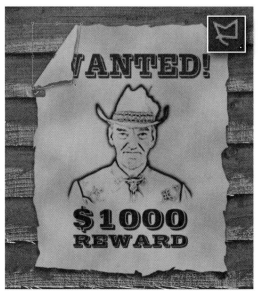

2 Grab the Polygonal Lasso **L**. Mark out one of the corners of the poster. Press *ctrl* *Shift* *J* ⌘ *Shift* *J* to cut the area to a new layer. The shadow style will be applied to the new layer. Now use Free Transform *ctrl* *T* ⌘ *T* to rotate and distort the folded corner into position.

3 Press *ctrl E* *⌘ E* to merge the fold and the poster layers. Create another new layer above the poster layer. Load the poster's selection again. Now press *Shift Backspace* to open the Fill dialog and set the Contents to 50% Gray. This will be our shading layer.

4 Set the shading layer's blend mode to Hard Light. Grab the Burn tool *O*. Choose a medium-sized soft brush. Set the Range to Highlights in the Options toolbar. Set the Exposure to around 40–50%. We'll begin by following one of the edges of the fence to make a crease.

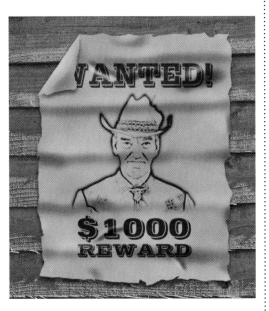

5 Hold *alt* *⌥* to temporarily switch to the Dodge tool. Now add a highlight just above the shadow you just painted. Continue to add horizontal creases – remembering not to go over the top of the corner fold, of course. Try to vary the tones to give a more uneven effect.

6 Add some random wrinkles at different angles and sizes across the poster to break up the linearity. If we swap the highlights and shadows, we get a dent, rather than a bulge. We can also add some shading to the folded corner to give the impression it's silghtly rounded.

HOT TIP

Drawing the creases is made much easier if you're using a pressure-sensitive tablet, as you can control the amount of effect as you paint. If you don't have one, you may want to lower the Exposure setting a little more and make several sweeps for each crease to build up the effect. If the final result seems too strong, we can always lower the opacity of the shading layer.

SHORTCUTS
MAC WIN BOTH

Flashlight illumination

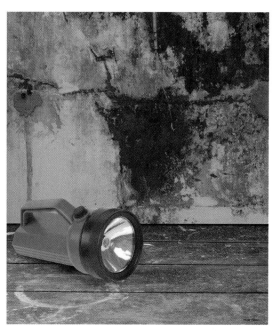

DARKNESS CAN PROVIDE AN IMAGE with a much needed change in mood; a technique frequently used in horror or thriller movies – the lurking terror is very rarely in a well lit, designer basement, after all.

Our starting image is a bit dull and lacks any sense of purpose: it's just a flashlight in a lit room that may just be in the process of being renovated. Its owner's probably gone off to find his sandwich. By turning out the lights and switching on the flashlight, however, we instantly add an air of mystery to the scene: where is this place, and why has the flashlight been left lying on the ground in what appears to be a derelict house?

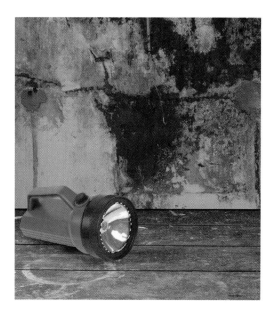

1 Make sure the flashlight layer is active by clicking its thumbnail. Now make a selection around the lens. This is quite tricky because of the angle; see the sidebar for a tip on how best to achieve this. Once done press *ctrl* *J* ⌘ *J* twice to create two new copies.

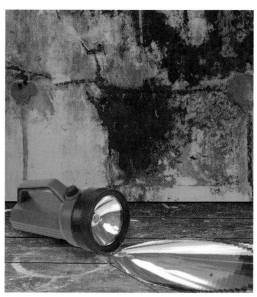

2 Press *ctrl* *T* ⌘ *T* to enter Free Transform. Now stretch out one of the lens copies to create the shape of the beam area on the floor in front of the flashlight. You'll need to zoom out to see the handles as they will be outside of the canvas area. Press *Enter* to apply the transformation.

3 Press *ctrl I* *⌘ I* to invert the colors of the layer. Now apply some Gaussian Blur; we can use a large amount as we don't want too much of the original detail showing. Finally, set the blend mode to Linear Dodge. Most of it will disappear, creating the effect of the beam pattern.

4 It's beginning to shape up but something's not right: the flashlight needs to be switched on to cast its light, of course. Make the second lens copy active and set its blend mode to Linear Dodge. This has the effect of making the already light areas much brighter.

5 Load up both the light beam and lens layers' selections by holding *ctrl Shift* *⌘ Shift* and clicking their thumbnails in turn. Now create a Levels Adjustment Layer at the top of the stack. We need to invert the mask *ctrl I* *⌘ I* so all but the light areas will be affected.

6 Drag the right-hand Output levels slider across to the left to lower the overall brightness. Now push the Shadows value to the right to give a richer effect. Finally, load up the flashlight's selection and use a soft black brush to paint out the mask inside the bezel to lighten it up.

SHORTCUTS
MAC WIN BOTH

Cooking up a storm

LIGHTNING IS NOT THE EASIEST OF phenomena to photograph. Firstly, electrical storms are not as common in some parts of the world as they are in others and secondly, there's the problem of braving the weather – not the best of environments for a camera. There's the issue of getting a good image as well; the best we can hope for is one or two lucky shots, let alone getting a picture of lightning striking just where we need it! Even if it does, the chance of being ready to capture it is not very likely, and lightning never strikes the same place twice, of course.

In this project we'll find out that it's not at all difficult to create a stormy scene and place a realistic lightning strike just where we want it.

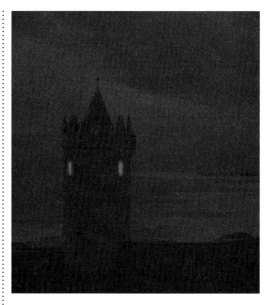

1 This picture of an isolated castle on the coast will make an ideal starting image. We have everything here: it's dark, mysterious and we already have some menacing-looking clouds as a backdrop. All we need now is to add some raging, untamed weather.

2 Create a new layer *ctrl Shift N* ⌘ *Shift N* and fill it with white. Now take a soft black brush and paint a slightly jagged line down from the top of the document to the bottom. This will become our bolt of lightning. Finally, use a larger brush to fill one side of the canvas with black.

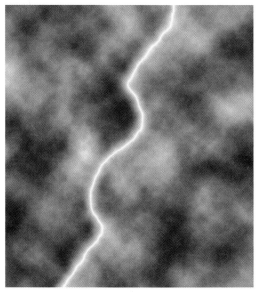

3 Make sure the default colors are set by pressing **D**. Now apply the Difference Clouds filter. This gives us a narrow and more defined line. Press *ctrl I* ⌘ *I* to inverse the image and we can see our lightning bolt beginning to take shape.

4 Change the layer's blend mode to Screen to filter out the black areas. Now open the Levels dialog and drag the shadows and midtones sliders to the right until most of the cloud texture has disappeared. The rest can be removed with the Eraser tool **E**.

5 Instead of scaling the lightning, we can just choose a suitable portion and erase the rest, then move it into position. Open Hue/Saturation *ctrl* *U* *⌘* *U*, check the Colorize box and drag the Hue slider to the right to add a tinge of blue; we can also increase the Saturation if needed.

6 Create a new layer above the lightning. Use a soft, low-opacity brush to build up a small glow where the lightning hits the tower. Now add a Simple Outer Glow layer style; double-click the style icon in the Layers panel to change its color to the same kind of hue as the bolt.

7 Finally, our image wouldn't be complete without a heavy downpour. We've taken the technique from the rainbow project in Chapter 5 and used much stronger settings to give the impression that our tower is in the midst of a truly ferocious storm.

HOT TIP

We've created a simple example of the effect here but we could just as easily add more layers to build up a really tropical or magical storm. We could also use a very low opacity brush to paint in brighter areas on the clouds to give the effect of them being lit up by the lightning as they extend off into the distance.

SHORTCUTS

MAC WIN BOTH

187

Can I get a job doing this?

THE SHORT ANSWER IS: YES. The longer answer is: Well, yes – if you have the skill, determination and free time available, and if you happen to bump into the right people.

The question of whether it's possible to make a career out of doing photomontage work occurs, at some stage, to just about everyone who's ever dabbled in Photoshop or Elements. It's an appealing proposition: the idea of spending one's days tinkering with images for profit sounds like a great way of occupying oneself.

The trouble is, the world just isn't crying out for more photomontage artists. It's not like studying to become a dentist or a plumber. There's no standard course, no regular qualification, and absolutely no guarantee of a career of any sort at the end of the line. This, coupled with the fact that you're not alone in wanting to pursue this path, means that there are far more people out there capable of manipulating images than there is demand for such services.

But if you're really determined, then there are several steps you could take to make the dream a possibility. It all depends on whether you have the free time to develop your skills without being paid to do so.

The first, and most important step, is to get your work published. Art editors are notoriously busy and preoccupied people, who are driven by deadlines and the need to fill the space between the text and the advertisements in their publications. What matters to them are four main factors: Can you interpret a brief? Do you have the skill needed to turn in a good job? Do you have an interesting or unique style? And, above all: Can you be sure to meet a deadline? For ultimately, it doesn't matter how good or inspired your work is if you're unable to turn it in on time. If you don't meet the deadline, you'll never hear from them again.

Art editors are far more likely to take a chance on commissioning work from an unknown artist (yourself) if you can demonstrate that others have already placed their faith in you. Of course, it's something of a catch-22 situation: you can't get the work unless you've already had work published, and you can't get work published unless someone gives you the work.

One solution is to begin by offering your services, for free, to publications or websites who couldn't afford to pay for them. This might include local newspapers, community and sports magazines, charity websites, church and workplace newsletters, and so on. Get as much work in print or on websites as you can, to show that you're capable of sustained effort.

Only when you have a fair body of work to show should you then approach magazine and newspaper art directors. But start small: writing to *The New Yorker* offering to draw their covers is unlikely to produce a positive response, at least in the early days.

Self-promotion is a key part of bringing your skills to the attention of those who matter. These days, it's easy to set up and maintain your own website, and you should take the opportunity to show off as much published work as you can in this way. Feel free, as well, to show 'personal' work done for your own entertainment – but be aware that this won't carry as much weight with potential employers as work you've been commissioned to do.

Another way of getting started is to get a job in a publishing office, doing menial tasks such as scanning and filing photographs. Before long you'll come across an image that needs tweaking; show what you can do, and if you're any good your skills will be recognized.

You can, of course, set up a website offering your services directly to the public. Many people offer photo restoration, custom greetings cards, and photo caricature services; a few make a reasonable living out of it.

Decide where your strengths lie. You may be proficient at restoring photographs, removing ex-spouses from family shots, or caricaturing politicians. Develop your area of expertise and find new ways of performing the task. People are far more likely to use you if you can offer a service that no one else can.

A simple still life, above: the fruit bowl, candlestick, and bottle are all on separate layers, as are the table and the curtain behind. Adding the shadows was straightforward enough, but the scene is dull and looks unrealistic. Adding reflections to that wood surface really brings this picture to life, giving it an extra dimension.

Shiny surfaces

GLASS, METAL AND WATER all have one thing in common: they're shiny. Which means that any objects placed on these surfaces will have reflections.

Making reflections can be as easy as simply flipping an object vertically and lowering the opacity. But it can also be much more complex, if the object in question is photographed from an angle. We'll show how to split an object into its constituent planes in order to reflect each one individually.

We'll also look at making rippled reflections in water, show how to place people and things inside bottles, and look at that most easy and powerful tool for making instant liquid – Plastic Wrap.

Shiny surfaces

Upon reflection

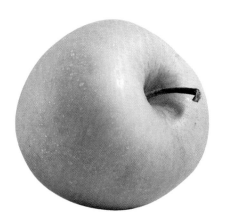

ADDING A REFLECTION TO A SURFACE converts it from being flat and matt to bright and glossy. The more vivid the reflection is, the shinier the surface appears. Different materials produce varying levels of reflectivity depending on how much light they absorb or let through. A piece of glass on its own will let most of the light through. This results in a sharp but faint reflection. Add a backing to it, such as silver, and you have a mirror. This bounces most of the light back, giving a perfect copy of the person or object.

In the following tutorial we'll create a soft reflection by fading it out as it extends further away from the original object. This gives us a similar appearance to the acrylic surfaces used in product photography.

1 Here's our subject. It's already on its own layer. We'll need to duplicate this to use as our reflection. Press *ctrl J* ⌘ *J*. We'll be using the lower layer for the reflection. This will allow us to place it behind the original, giving the impression of depth and substance.

2 Select the reflection layer. Flip it vertically via Image > Rotate > Flip layer vertical. Use the Move tool *V* to drag the layer down. Hold *Shift* to constrain the movement vertically. This ensures the two images remain aligned. Leave an overlap so the reflection layer remains slightly behind.

3 We have a mirror image of the apple but it's too perfect, we want the effect of a shiny plastic surface where the reflection would gradually fade out. We'll begin by adding a mask. Make sure the reflection layer is active. Now click the Add Layer Mask icon at the bottom of the Layers panel.

4 Grab the Gradient tool **G**. Select a Linear Black, White gradient. Click the layer mask's thumbnail to make it active. Position the cursor at the bottom of the document. Holding **Shift**, click and drag the cursor up. I took it to around a third of the way up the original apple here.

HOT TIP

You can adjust how the mask affects the reflection without having to recreate the gradient each time. Click the mask's thumbnail to make it active. Open the Brightness/ Contrast dialog. Increasing and decreasing the Brightness changes the opacity. Altering the contrast determines how smooth the blend becomes. A higher value produces a much harsher transition whilst lowering it gives a much more gradual fading effect.

5 We'll add some blur to the reflection to give it slightly more softness. Click the reflection layer's thumbnail to make it active again. Open the Gaussian Blur filter. You won't need to use a lot for this effect; just enough to knock it out of focus a little.

6 To finish off we'll add a shadow. This is created with another copy of the apple filled with black. See Chapter 7 for more on the technique. For reflective surfaces such as this the shadow needs to be much lighter than if it were cast on a matt surface.

SHORTCUTS
MAC WIN BOTH

Complex reflections

O N THE PREVIOUS PAGE we created a reflection for an object that had been photographed head-on; a simple task of flipping the image vertically and placing it beneath the original. Problems start, however, when the photo is taken from an angle, as we can see from the example image. Elements can only work in two dimensions so inverting the image gives undesirable results.

For tricky jobs such as this we first need to break the object down into separate layers; we can then distort them individually to produce the correct effect.

1 The first step is to divide the object into separate layers: grab the Polygonal Lasso and make an outline around one side of the box. Press *ctrl* *J* *⌘* *J* to copy it to a new layer. Now repeat this for the other side remembering to make the original box layer active again, of course.

2 Go back to the front panel layer and flip it vertically, then press *ctrl* *T* *⌘* *T*. Drag it down and match one of the corresponding corners on the base of the original box. Hold *ctrl* *Shift* *⌘* *Shift* and drag the opposite center handle up to skew the panel into position.

3 Repeat the last step to add the side panel. At present we have two boxes on top of each other; a good effect in itself but we need to make it more like a reflection. The first thing to do is drop the opacity; around 30% works well here – do this for both layers.

4 We need to fade the reflections out but we cannot do this in one hit because the angles on the front and side are different. Add a layer mask to both the front and side layers by clicking the Add Layer Mask icon at the base of the Layers panel.

5 Select the Gradient tool **G** and choose a Linear Black, White gradient. Click one of the mask's thumbnails to make it active. Now click halfway along the bottom edge of the panel, then drag straight up to the top of the reflection. Repeat this for the other panel.

6 Finally, we'll add a shadow to place the crate firmly on the ground. Create a new layer above the background; use the Polygonal Lasso to draw a selection around the bottom of the crate. Fill this with black, blur it slightly and lower the opacity a little.

Shiny surfaces

Window reflections

THE VIEW THROUGH THIS WINDOW is far from inspiring: the side of the house next door adds little life to the scene. We'll replace this view with a new one to improve our outlook.

The complications arise when we begin to place figures in the scene. A person in the room will look convincing enough just standing in front of the window, as long as he appears at the right scale for the room; but, if we leave it at that, we're ignoring the fact that there should be glass in the window, which should create a reflection.

Adding a reflection certainly makes the glass itself exist as a medium. But how do we make the glass cope with multiple reflections? The answer is to subtract one reflection from the other, to create a wholly convincing effect.

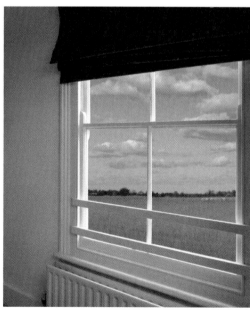

1 We can easily select the window area using the Lasso tool. By making a new layer, filled with a solid color, we create a mask for the window; any view placed on top of this layer, and grouped with it, will be seen 'through' the window.

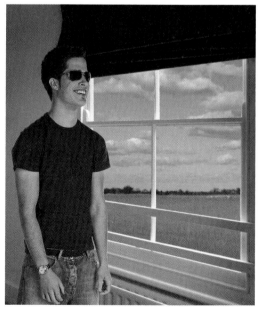

2 Placing our figure in the scene, looking obliquely down the field, adds that human element that brings the image to life. But the window itself looks distinctly empty and we need to add glass to it.

3 Because of the angle of view – and the symmetry – of our figure, we can simply duplicate him and position a slightly reduced copy (to allow for perspective), grouped with the view, at a low opacity – here, around 50%.

4 The man is reflecting in the window, and we should be able to see a reflection of the rest of the room as well. Almost any suitable interior will do, as long as its horizontals match that of the window perspective: it doesn't need to be a view of the same room.

HOT TIP

Our man happened to be at exactly the right angle to allow us to 'translate' him through the window. In most cases, you'd need to flip your figure horizontally in order for the reflection to work properly. It's a lot easier if the window isn't at an angle as extreme as the one in our example.

5 The trouble with the previous step was that we could see through the man to the room behind. Of course, his reflection should obscure the room. So hold *ctrl* ⌘ and click on his thumbnail to load his selection; then switch to the room reflection layer and delete from there.

6 We made the reflection of both the room and the man strong enough to see what we were doing in the previous few steps. In reality, we'd expect a much less visible reflection. Here, we've reduced the opacity of both layers to just 20% for a more convincing result.

SHORTCUTS
MAC WIN BOTH

From railway to waterway

CREATING REFLECTIONS IN WATER requires a slightly different approach to those of solid surfaces such as metal or wood. Being a liquid, it has different properties to take into account such as turbulence and refraction. We need to distort the reflection to match the state of the water. This could be anything from the subtle ripples on a pond to the hazy elongated lights of cars on a rain-soaked road.

In the following example we'll convert this railway platform into a canal. By using a combination of layers, filters, and distortion techniques, we can quickly create a realistic water effect which can be tailored to suit many different images, for example: beautiful lakeside scenes, rock pools for a sea life project, or simply puddles on the ground.

1 First we'll create the reflection: draw a selection using the Polygonal Lasso following the perspective of the platform; I've used the yellow letters as a guide. Create the rest of the selection around the top of the image. Now save the selection via the Select menu.

2 Copy the selected area to a new layer *ctrl* **J** ⌘ **J**. Flip the layer vertically to make a mirror image. Select Image > Transform > Skew. Hold **Shift** and drag the layer down to line the layers up, then pull the right-middle handle up to correct the perspective.

3 Hide the reflection layer for now and click the background layer's thumbnail to make it active. Select the line at the edge of the platform with the Magic Wand; hold **Shift** to add any missing areas. Add a small amount of feathering; 1 pixel will be fine here.

4 Inverse the selection `ctrl` `Shift` `I` `⌘` `Shift` `J`. Go to the Select menu and load the selection we saved earlier. Make sure Subtract from Selection is checked and click OK. Now grab the Polygonal Lasso, hold `alt` `⌥` and remove the area of the platform from the foreground.

5 Create a new layer between the platform and the reflection. Fill the selection with 50% gray and deselect. Paint in a slight unevenness to the back edge using a hard brush; remember to make it less pronounced as it moves further into the distance.

6 Add another layer above the last. Press `D` to select the default palette, now fill the layer with the Clouds filter to generate a random pattern. Choose the Glass filter from the Distort menu. Set the Texture to Frosted, now use the sliders to create a fine-rippled effect.

7 Use Free Transform to distort the water into place. This doesn't need to be a perfect fit; the texture can become too pixelated if it's stretched too much. We need to adjust enough to stop it looking too flat. Once you've done this, press `ctrl` `G` `⌘` `G` to group it with the base layer.

8 Make the reflection layer visible again. Set its blend mode to Soft Light and group it with the water layer. We need to add some ripple to the reflection itself as it would be distorted by the water's surface. This is easily done with the Ocean Ripple filter.

9 Select a large, soft Eraser; using the edge, erase some of the lower area of the reflection to fade it out. We'll also add a little tint to the water. We've used a Photo Filter Adjustment Layer set to Cooling at a very low density. You could use a Hue/Saturation adjustment set to Colorize.

HOT TIP

Although it's generally good practice to avoid using the Eraser, there are times when it's quicker and more practical to do so. If you're worried about making a mistake, duplicate the layer as a precaution.

SHORTCUTS
MAC WIN BOTH

199

Goo, slime... and molasses

ELEMENTS IS AWASH WITH FILTERS for performing special effects – everything from knocking up a quick pointillist Seurat painting to making an image look like it's reflected in rippling glass.

Sometimes, though, filters can have surprising results. One of our favorites is Plastic Wrap, which – surprise, surprise – makes objects look as if they're wrapped in plastic. This isn't a job it does very well, but what it can do is to make glistening, slimy liquids from the most basic of ingredients.

Here, we'll show how to use the Plastic Wrap filter to add a few spoons of molasses to the top of this man's head. Why? Well, why not?

1 Begin by making a new layer. Select a mid-gray and, using a hard-edged brush, paint in the area to be taken up by the goo. If you're having trouble painting convincing drips down the face, try using the Smudge tool **R** to smear the color where you want it to go.

2 Now add some shading to it using the Dodge and Burn tools, set to Highlights. Remember, if you hold *alt* ⬝ when using either tool, you'll get the other one temporarily. All we're aiming for here is a random lumpy texture, to give Plastic Wrap something to work on.

Plastic Wrap can be used to create all kinds of liquid effects – spilt wine, dripping water, vinegar, coffee, and oil – just by changing the hue and the brightness. It's also good for creating icicles and all kinds of shiny, lumpy surfaces.

The real effectiveness of this filter depends on getting the shading right in step 2: keep applying the filter, using Undo if it isn't right, then adding more shading and reapplying the filter until it works. Subtlety is the key here: don't go for deep shading, but paint in the shadows and highlights with a very light touch.

3 Choose Filter > Artistic > Plastic Wrap. (Why is it in the Artistic section? No idea.) Push the Highlight Strength and Detail settings up to their maximum – no half measures here – but leave the Smoothness round about the mid point to add some texture to the stuff.

4 Here's the result of that Plastic Wrap filter: a glistening dollop of – well, something gray. We can fix that in the next step. If you find you don't get the effect you want, undo the filter, add a little more shading, and use *ctrl* F ⌘ F to apply it again without having to open the dialog.

5 When we change the mode of this layer from Normal to Hard Light, using the pop-up menu at the top of the Layers panel, all the gray disappears, leaving us with just the highlights and shadows. As it stands, this looks more like water than molasses.

6 We can add color using the Hue/Saturation dialog, checking the Colorize button and dragging the Hue slider until we get the color we want. If we left this slider at the far right, we'd get a convincing impression of a bottle of red wine poured over his head. Your choice!

201

Preserving your memories

WOULDN'T IT BE WONDERFUL if we could bottle our memories of events and occasions and open them every once in a while to relive the experience? Sadly, the technology to do this is a little way off yet but in the meantime, we can still have a little fun with Elements!

In this project we'll be looking at placing objects behind glass – a jar in this instance. The trick to making this look realistic is retaining the original reflections and textures of the jar, whilst still allowing the picture within to be seen. We'll do this using layer masks and a technique similar to that used to make the fairy's wings translucent in Chapter 4.

1 We'll begin by making the beach photo layer active by clicking its thumbnail in the Layers panel. Press *ctrl* *G* ⌘ *G* to create a Clipping Mask with the jar layer. Now only pixels that fall inside the area of the jar can be seen. We can now use the Move tool *V* to reposiiton the scene.

2 Create a duplicate of the jar layer. Drag the *original* jar layer above the photo layer so as not to break the clipping mask. Before we continue, we'll use the Spot Healing Brush *J* to remove the rear part of the jar's base. We shouldn't be able to see that when the jar is full.

3 Load the top jar's selection by holding *ctrl* ⌘ and clicking its thumbnail. Press *ctrl* V ⌘ V to copy the selection. Next, click the New Layer Mask icon. Now, holding *alt* ⌥, click the layer mask's thumbnail. Press *ctrl* V ⌘ V to paste the copied pixels of the jar into the mask.

4 Hold *alt* ⌥ and click the mask thumbnail again to exit edit mode. Open the Levels dialog *ctrl* L ⌘ L. Hold *alt* ⌥ and click the mask thumbnail again. Now drag the Shadows slider across to the right. We can see the photo start to emerge through the glass.

HOT TIP

If you want to photograph your own container, make sure it's against a plain white background: a white sheet of paper behind it will work well. And try not to use the flash on your camera or you'll get an ugly glare off the glass surface.

5 The glass has thickness so our image shouldn't go right to the edges. Switch to the photo layer. Go to Select > Modify > Contract. A value of 10 pixels works well here. Click OK. Now create a layer mask. This clips away a small amount of the photo's edge, giving the jar more substance.

6 Finally, we'll mask out some of the larger areas. Set the foreground color to black. Select a fairly soft brush *B*. Now paint over the mask to remove the sky from the lid. We can also paint out some of the sand around the the base of the jar, particularly the corners where the glass is thicker.

SHORTCUTS
MAC WIN BOTH

Keeping it real

POSSIBLY THE GREATEST COMPLIMENT you can receive for one of your montages is when the viewer does not realize it is one in the first place. This need not be as time-consuming and laborious as you may think: a large part of producing a convincing image, after all, is creating an illusion to fool the viewer. It may not survive close scrutiny, but unless we're trying to conclusively prove to NASA that we had reached the moon long before Neil Armstrong, we can afford a little artistic license.

Creating a realistic image depends on a number of factors: most importantly the individual components of the artwork need to fit together as seamlessly as possible. The direction at which the people and objects are lit needs to be the same – there's no point having someone caught in a spotlight, for instance, if their face still appears to be in shadow. We also need to make sure the shadows themselves are correct and, more importantly, present to begin with; everything casts a shadow of some sort, even if they are too faint to notice initially — they help to define depth, placing their associated object within its surroundings. Getting the color right also plays an essential role: be careful not to use garish hues as this could result in an unnatural-looking image.

So, with all that said, how do we go about translating it into our artwork? The answer is often staring right back at us: a lot of the time we'll be adding to an existing photo so we can take our cues from there, adjusting the new elements accordingly and sampling the colors and tones, comparing them as we go. Things become trickier when it comes to building a picture from the ground up where our clues aren't there to guide us — we're far from helpless though.

Just as a traditional artist studies their subject and surroundings to set it to canvas, we can do the same. It's by no means a crime to use reference material to make sure we achieve the correct effect and it's certainly preferential to trying to use guesswork alone. A good starting point is, of course, the internet and image search engines such as Google or Yahoo are superb resources. It's highly probable that we'll find what we're looking for and, because we're not actually including the image within our artwork, copyright is not an issue; also, we need not be too concerned with the image's dimensions as long as it's possible to see the detail. We can, of course, take our own reference shots as well: again, these don't need to be award-winning photographs, they just need to be of a good enough quality to see the effect, so even quick snaps from a cell phone should be sufficient.

There will be occasions when we need to see different versions of the same effect and also have the ability to view it from different angles; something that a still image cannot offer. In these situations improvising with props is often a great solution as they don't necessarily need to be the exact objects and only need to be crudely put together; as long as the outcome is a good representation, we can transpose it to our design. It's surprising how many things we can find within immediate reach with which we can improvise. We might, for example, want to see how a shadow falls across an uneven surface such as a staircase; so instead of grabbing the nearest family member and have them stand in different positions, we can quickly put together an impromptu mock-up by folding a sheet of paper and positioning a suitably illustrative object, then use a flashlight or similar maneuverable light source to create the desired effect.

We're not always going to be producing images depicting plain old reality, of course. We'll often be creating montages that are highly stylized or in a fantasy theme: there will always be a demand for fairy princesses and other such magical pictures, after all. This often demands more attention to detail than with their more sublime counterparts; people tend to scrutinize them far more closely, even though they know they cannot be real. It's highly unlikely we'll stumble across a real photo in a search but we can still apply the same principles from the real world to our artwork: reflections, shadows, and color still play their part in creating a convincing scene. We do have the advantage that nobody can really say how a picture of this ilk really should look, so we can be a little more lenient with the rules.

Finally, remember that there will always be flaws and unexpected elements in a real scene: try not to make your images too clinical. Try adding some random areas of light and shadow — it's often the smallest details that have the most impact.

■ Textures can make all the difference to a piece of artwork. Here are two versions of a wedding album layout. The first is flat and uninspiring; everything is clean and squared off. The second, with its satin background and gold-framed images, sets the mood and adds that all-important interest factor.

Materials and textures

OUR SURROUNDINGS ARE DEFINED BY TEXTURES. We can, for example, see at a glance that something is made of wood simply because of its familiar grainy appearance. We recognize certain materials such as silk by the way the light catches its folds and creases.

In this chapter, we'll look at ways of creating textures such as wood and cloth from scratch. This gives you more freedom as you are not constrained to the size of your source images.

We'll also see how existing images can be manipulated to match your theme: torn edges for newspaper clippings or ticket stubs, or ageing an object by covering it in dust.

Conjuring curtains

ALL THE WORLD'S A STAGE, as William Shakespeare would have us believe, and what stage would be complete without the familiar heavy red and gold drape curtains?

The following tutorial demonstrates a quick and easy way of creating an undulating texture resembling the folds of heavy hanging material. This has many potential uses: you may want to mock up some decor for a room in the house. You could also use the effect to create a template or intro for a home movie DVD. Why not create a montage and give a family member the stardom they deserve?

1 We'll begin by creating a new document `ctrl` `N` `⌘` `N`. Make a new layer and fill it with 50% gray. Press `D` to set the default palette colors of black and white. Go to Filter > Render > Fibers. We want a nice mix of lights and darks for this technique. Click OK to apply the filter.

2 Although this gives us a rough material-style texture it's not quite right for this purpose. Go to Filter > Blur > Motion Blur. Set the Angle to 90° so the effect is vertical. Now drag the Distance up until we have a smooth set of lines but still with a slight variance here and there.

3 Apply a small amount of Gaussian blur to smooth out the texture; we used a 3 pixel radius here. Open the Levels dialog `ctrl` `L` `⌘` `L`. Add some more contrast by increasing the shadows and midtones. This gives the impression of the folds being deeper in some places.

4 We'll be using the Displace filter later on so this is a good place to stop and create the displacement map. Go to Layer > Duplicate Layer. Set the Destination to New. Give it a name and click OK. This will create a new document. Save this to disk and close the document's window.

5 Make sure the curtain layer is active. Open the Hue/Saturation dialog *ctrl* *U* *⌘* *U*. We're going to make the curtains a rich red. Check the Colorize box. Drag the Hue slider over to the far left. Now bring the Saturation slider up to around 60. We don't want it to be too overpowering.

6 We need to sort out the harsh cut-off at the bottom; the pleats should follow on to give an uneven edge. Grab the Move tool *V*. Hold *Shift* and tap *↑* on the keyboard twice to nudge the layer up. This will give us enough space to work with.

7 We'll apply the distortion to a separate layer. Grab the Rectangular Marquee tool *M*. Set the Feather radius to 1 pixel – this ensures we won't have a hard edge. Now make a fairly wide selection along the bottom of the curtain. Press *ctrl* *J* *⌘* *J* to copy it to a new layer.

8 Go to Filter > Distort > Displace. We only want the effect to be vertical, so set the Horizontal Scale to 0. We also want the effect to go down, so set the Vertical Scale to -10. Click OK. Choose the displacement map you saved earlier from the file selection dialog and click Open.

9 Nudge the layer down a little with the Move tool so it's visible below the curtain. Open Hue/Saturation again. Click Colorize. This time set the Hue to a rich yellow color and increase the saturation. Finally, merge the two layers together by pressing *ctrl* *E* *⌘* *E*.

HOT TIP

The Displace filter has many uses but it is difficult to get to grips with. Unlike most filters, it does not have a live preview, which makes it impossible to know what the outcome will be. Getting the correct effect is really a question of trial and error. It's an idea to spend some time fiddling with the options and values to see how they behave.

SHORTCUTS

209

Quick and easy wood grain

PHOTOS OF WOOD TEXTURES can be found in almost any stock library. You can, of course, take your own. As abundant as they may be, sometimes you may not be able to find just the right style to use in your artwork. Here's where filters come to the rescue.

On the previous pages, we saw how the Fibers filter can be used to create the effect of plush material. Here, we'll use it to generate the effect of wood grain – it's very versatile. To further the realism, various inconsistencies such as knots and twists are added. Just like the real thing, once made you can use it to apply to all sorts of objects: an ornate picture frame (as the inset shows), some polished flooring, or simply as a backdrop for your images.

1 Create a new document ⌃ *ctrl* **N** ⌘ **N** to the desired size; we've used the same dimensions as the example image. Duplicate the background layer ⌃ *ctrl* **J** ⌘ **J**. Fill the layer with 50% gray; the Fibers filter won't work on an unfilled layer. Finally, duplicate the layer again.

2 Make sure the foreground and background colors are set to the default black and white by pressing **D**. Go to Filters > Render > Fibers. Adjust the settings until you have a fairly reasonable-looking grain. Variance gives more randomness; Strength gives more contrast to the effect.

3 We'll add some bends and knot holes. Open the Liquify filter. Grab the Turbulence tool. Choose a medium brush size. Set a fairly low Turbulence: we don't want the effect to be too wild. Now click and drag the cursor down in short strokes randomly around the document.

4 Add a few more knots and distortions; experiment with the different tools like Bloat and Twirl. When you're happy with the effect, click OK. Set the layer's blend mode to Overlay. Although you won't notice any difference just yet, we're setting the layer up to allow color to be added.

5 Click the plain gray layer's thumbnail to make it active. Open up the Hue/Saturation dialog *ctrl* U ⌘ U. Check the Colorize box. You'll see the effect immediately. Use the Hue, Saturation and Lightness sliders to create the shade you want your wood to be.

6 You may decide the grain layer is too dark or coarse. Try experimenting with different blend modes. You could also use the Levels dialog to change the contrast, making it lighter or darker. Here, we've changed the blend mode to Soft Light and lowered the opacity a little.

HOT TIP

Just like many of the other tools in Elements, holding down the *alt* ⌥ key (referred to as the modifier key) when you're using a tool in Liquify temporarily changes its behaviour. For example, if you have the Twirl Clockwise tool selected, holding the modifier key will switch it to the Counter-clockwise tool.

SHORTCUTS
MAC WIN BOTH

211

Lying on a bed of satin

CREATING COMPLEX TEXTURES from scratch is not necessarily as difficult as it may at first seem. Here we are going to combine gradients and blend modes to create a random and fluid effect resembling the intricate folds and wrinkles of finer fabrics such as silk or satin.

The major advantage of generating your own materials in this way is you are never tied to the size of a stock image. You can create the pattern to suit the dimensions of your artwork, without the fear of repeating areas of the texture letting the effect down.

1 Hide the rose layer. Click the backgound layer's thumbnail to make it active. Select the Gradient tool **G**. Choose a Linear Black, White gradient. Set the mode to Difference, then click and drag the guide from corner to corner. This creates a good base for the effect.

2 Pick a random starting point. Click and drag out another gradient. Make it shorter than before and repeat this several times. Change the position, length and angle on each. Try to create a good balance of small, intricate areas and larger smooth sections.

3 The initial result is a little harsh, so we'll soften it with a little Gaussian Blur. Set a fairly low value: enough to remove the sharpness from the lines and produce a smooth transition between the tones. The amount will, of course, vary depending on the size of the document.

4 Go to the Stylize filters sub-menu and select Find Edges. This produces a smoother version of our pattern and leaves the ridges well defined. It's looking good so far but we need to bring back some of the contrast. This is easily done by applying Auto Levels `ctrl` `Shift` `L` `⌘` `Shift` `L`.

5 Open up the Diffuse Glow filter from the Distort sub-menu. We'll use this to add some texture and spread out the highlights. Push the Graininess up: around half way is sufficient. Add a small amount of Glow; be careful not to wash the image out. Set the Clear Amount to its maximum.

6 As a final step we'll add some color. The Hue/Saturation adjustment is perfect for this. Remember to check the Colorize box. Some shading has been added to the rose along with a shadow to gel the scene together. More on this can be found in Chapter 7.

SHORTCUTS
MAC **WIN** **BOTH**

The jean genie part 1

FOLLOWING ON WITH THE THEME of materials, we'll now have a look at creating another type of cloth: this time it's denim. Once again we'll be making it from scratch using just filters and layers.

This quick, simple and very effective technique could be used in your designs as a styled backdrop for scrapbooking or your website.

This also forms the first of a three-part project. In the next part we'll add a pocket to the image and then finally, in the last part, we'll use the new text on a path feature of Elements 10 to create the stitching around it.

1 Create a new blank file ctrl N ⌘ N. The size we use here is 800 x 885 pixels, if you want to follow along exactly. The settings used will work at almost any size, however. Make sure the background is set to white. Click OK to create the new document.

2 Now we can begin creating the effect. Make sure the default black and white palette is set by pressing D. Now go to Filter > Sketch > Halftone Pattern. Set the Pattern Type to Line. Reduce the size to 1, its lowest setting. Set the Contrast to 0. Now click OK to apply the filter.

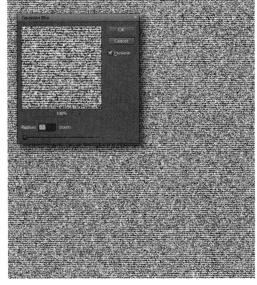

3 We'll apply another filter directly on top of the pattern. Go to back to the Filter menu. This time select Pixelate > Mezzotint. Select the Fine Dots preset and click OK. This gives us a nice random texture whilst at the same time retaining the lines.

4 The pattern is a little too harsh at the moment. We'll soften the effect using a light blur. Go to Filter > Blur > Gaussian Blur. Setting a value of around 0.5 pixels works well for this size of image. We don't want to add too much of an effect, we just need to take away some of the sharpness.

In step 5 it's necessary to zoom out to be able to see the entire area of the Free Transform box. To do this press *ctrl* – ⌘ – until you have enough space around the document. If you are using Elements' tabbed window display mode this is all you need to do. If however, you're using floating windows, the default setting is to scale the window down as you zoom, so you have to then stretch the window frame back out again. To change this, go to the Zoom tool **Z** and uncheck Resize Windows To Fit. Now when you zoom out, the window frame will remain the same size, allowing you to see the area around the document.

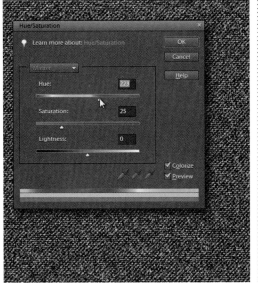

5 Enter Free Transform using *ctrl* *alt* *T* ⌘ ⌥ *T*; this mode automatically creates a new layer with the result. Hold *Shift* to rotate in 15° steps. Rotate the layer to 45°. Next, holding *alt* ⌥ use a corner handle to scale the layer up so it covers the whole image. Press *Enter* to commit.

6 We're almost there. Go to the Layers panel and set the top layer's blend mode to Multiply. Now press *ctrl* *E* ⌘ *E* to merge the layers. Open the Hue/Saturation dialog *ctrl* *U* ⌘ *U*. Check the Colorize box. Now use the Hue slider to change the color to the familiar denim blue.

SHORTCUTS
MAC WIN BOTH

The jean genie part 2

ON THE PREVIOUS PAGES we created a
denim cloth effect. Continuing on with
the project, we'll now add a pocket to give the
impression we are looking at a pair of jeans or
a shirt.

We'll use layers and layer styles, along with
some crafty shading using the Dodge and Burn
tools to create the hem around the edge and
give the the illusion of depth.

1 Grab the Polygonal Lasso. Starting at the edge of the
document, mark out the shape of a pocket. As this
is a close-up, we've only drawn a part of it. We do need
to continue on right around the outside of the image to
complete the shape, otherwise it will auto-join diagonally.

2 Our shape is too sharp and angular. We need to soften
it down a little. Go to Select > Refine Edge. Push the
Smooth slider up to 100. Now add a feather of around 1
pixel. Leave Contract/Expand at 0. We can see here that the
sharp corners are nicely rounded off. Click OK to apply.

3 Next we'll add some depth. Create a new layer. Fill the selection with 50% Gray. Deselect with *ctrl* **D** ⌘ **D**. Go to the Effects panel. Switch to Layer Styles and select the Bevels presets. We'll use the Simple Inner preset here. Double-click its icon to apply the style.

4 We need to adjust the bevel size. Double-click the layer's *fx* icon to open the Style Settings. Reduce the Bevel Size to 10 pixels. We'll also add a drop shadow: check its entry to enable it. Lower its size to around 5 pixels and its distance to around 4 pixels. Click OK to accept the changes.

5 If we change the layer's blend mode from Normal to Hard Light, the effect begins to take shape. The pocket now stands out. We need to hide the bevel edges at the top and left of the pocket. Switch to the Move tool **V**. Use the cursor keys to nudge them just out of the frame.

6 Now we'll create the raised hem. Grab the Dodge tool **O**. Set the Range to Highlights and the Exposure to around 50%. Using a small soft brush, paint along the edge, just inside the bevel. Switch to the Burn tool by holding *alt* ⌥. Now paint the darker area just inside the highlight.

HOT TIP

If you're using a version of Elements prior to 6 and don't have the Refine Edge tool, you can use the Smooth command found under Select > Modify. Be aware that the value we've used here will be too large in the individual command. A value of around 30 pixels will give us a similar result.

SHORTCUTS

The jean genie part 3

I N THIS, THE FINAL PART of our denim jeans
project, we'll be creating the stitching around
the pocket. This really does add the finishing
touch and gives us a very realistic image.

We'll be using one of Elements 10's new
features, the Text on Selection tool. With this
we can create a selection, or use an exisiting
one, as we'll be doing here, to define the path
the text follows. We won't be using words here,
of course, instead we'll use a series of minus
signs to create our stitches.

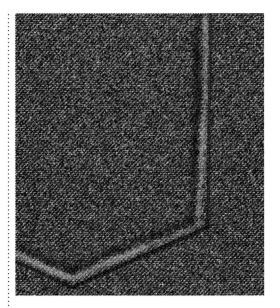

1 Make sure the pocket layer is active by clicking its
thumbnail in the Layers panel. Now hold *ctrl* ⌘ and
click its thumbnail again to load its selection. We'll need to
soften the selection again, so open the Refine Edge dialog.
Set the Smooth value to 100. Click OK to apply.

2 Select the Text on Selection tool **T**. Click anywhere
inside the selected area. Now press *Enter* to convert
the selection to a path. We can now set the typeface in the
Options bar. We'll use a clean font; Arial is good. Set the size
to 24pt. Don't worry about the color for now.

3 Hover the cursor over the path; you'll see its appearance
change to the one displayed in the inset. Click the
mouse to create a new text layer. Now press and hold the
minus key on the keyboard to create the line of dashes for
the stitching.

4 Press *ctrl* *Enter* *⌘* *Enter* to commit the text. Next, load the text layer's selection. Open Refine Edge again. Set the smoothing to 10 pixels. This gives us a more rounded lozenge shape. Now create a new layer. Fill the selection with a light yellow color. Leave the selection active for now.

5 Hide the original text layer. Enter Free Transform. Scale the the stitches down inside the hem. Because the text was cut off at the edges we can see where it starts to wrap around. Hold *ctrl* *⌘* for distort mode. Use the corner handles to make the adjustments. Press *Enter* to commit.

6 Create another layer. Fill the selection with 50% Gray. Go to Filter > Noise > Add Noise. Set an Amount of around 60%. Select Uniform and Monochromatic. Click OK. Now go to Filter > Blur > Motion Blur. Set an Angle of around 16°. Set the Distance to about 4 pixels. Click OK.

7 Press *ctrl* *D* *⌘* *D* to deselect. Set the top layer's blend mode to Hard Light. The stitching now has a cotton-like texture. To complete the effect, we'll add a small bevel and drop shadow. Finally, press *ctrl* *E* *⌘* *E* to merge the texture layer with the stitching's color layer.

HOT TIP

To make the overall effect even more realistic we can use the Dodge and Burn tools to add some random shading on the pocket and other areas of the image. This breaks up some of the flatness and gives the material a more natural appearance. We can also go one step further and use the Liquify filter to distort the pocket's edges slightly. To demonstrate, we've applied these techniques to the intro image at the beginning of this project.

SHORTCUTS

Making notepaper

USING PAPER IN A DESIGN can add that all-important handmade feel to it. This might be a piece of rich parchment declaring a special occasion or just a simple Post-it note to draw attention to a particular area of the artwork.

In this tutorial we'll create a piece of ruled notepaper using layers and selections. A key point to consider when creating objects from scratch is to give them some texture, in this case by adding some Gaussian Noise. This helps them to blend into a montage more convincingly – real life is never as pure as a digitally produced image.

1 Start by creating a new layer. Use the Rectangular Marquee to mark out the shape of your paper. Fill this with white. You can't see any difference, of course, as it is displaying against white. You can either hide the background layer or fill it to make it easier to work on the image.

2 Lock the paper layer's pixels with the icon in the Layers panel or by pressing [/]. This prevents the transparent areas from being affected. Select Add Noise from the Filter menu. Check the Monochromatic and Gaussian options. You don't need much, just enough to give a little texture.

3 Create another new layer. Draw a new rectangular selection positioning the bottom edge where the first line on the page will be. The rest of the box needs to extend outside the area of the paper. Select Stroke from the Edit menu. Set the Width and Color for the desired effect.

4 We need to remove the excess part of the box. Hold `ctrl` `⌘`. Click the paper layer's thumbnail to load its selection. Inverse the selection `ctrl` `Shift` `I` `⌘` `Shift` `I`. Now remove the unwanted area by pressing `Backspace`. This leaves us with a single line trimmed to fit.

5 Load the line's selection. Select the Move tool `V`. Press and hold `alt` `Shift` `⌥` `Shift`. Tap the down arrow key once. This duplicates the line. Hold `Shift` on its own. Nudge the line down a couple more times to create the spacing. Now repeat the process to fill the page.

6 Create the vertical margin using the same method as the horizontal line. I've chosen a different color here. By lowering the opacity we can control the faintness of the lines. When you're happy with the result press `ctrl` `E` `⌘` `E` to merge the ruled layer with the page.

7 To create the punched holes, draw a small circle using the Elliptical Marquee. Press `Backspace` to clear the pixels. Click and hold inside the selection. Hold `Shift` to constrain the movement. Drag the selection down into position. Delete the pixels again.

HOT TIP

Creating a selection before using the Move tool to duplicate parts of your artwork results in the copied area staying on the same layer. This is particularly useful when creating repeating patterns as we have here. Without doing so, we would end up with too many unnecessary layers.

SHORTCUTS
MAC WIN BOTH

The art of paper tearing

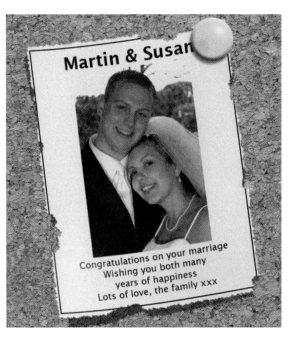

COMPONENTS OF YOUR ARTWORK often need a more handmade appearance, rather than the clean, precise lines of a selection or crop. Images such as the newspaper clipping above look far more realistic with a roughly torn edge.

As you'll see in the following project, it only takes a few quick steps to achieve the desired effect. The technique is also highly versatile and is easily adapted to suit a variety of styles. You might, for example, want to create an old treasure map or a background of notepaper for a web page.

1 Here we have a scan of some crumpled paper. It's already been placed on its own layer. We've changed the background to a more contrasting color, as this makes it easier to see how the effect is progressing than if it was against the default white.

2 We'll be creating the effect using a mask. Begin by loading the paper layer's selection by holding `ctrl` `⌘` and clicking its thumbnail. Now click the Add Layer Mask icon. The mask's shape is automatically defined from the layer's selection.

HOT TIP

As with the example, it's often necessary to combine different filters to achieve the desired effect. This is made simple by using the Filter Browser's effects layers. You can try different combinations and compare the result without the need to apply them first.

3 Let's begin by making the edges of the paper a little less straight, as though it has been torn from a larger piece. Grab a hard-edged brush. Set the color to black. Now paint out random areas around the edges. This is only affecting the mask, of course. The paper image remains intact.

4 Go to Filter > Brush Strokes > Spatter. Zoom in to an area to make it easier to see the effect. We can use the Spray Radius and Smoothness controls to fine-tune the appearance of the rough edge. Don't click OK yet as we are going to add another filter effect on top.

5 Click the New Effect Layer icon at the bottom of the dialog. Initially this duplicates the current effect so go back to the menu and choose Torn Edges. Again, we can finesse the effect using the slider controls. Once we're happy with the result, we can click OK.

6 Here's the final image. The mask has hidden the areas of the paper giving us a great rough torn edge. Because the image itself is not directly affected, we can always go back and edit the mask. We now have the basis for many different effects, such as the newspaper clipping in the intro.

SHORTCUTS
MAC WIN BOTH

223

Creating old paper

SO FAR WE'VE SEEN HOW TO MAKE crisp notepad paper and produce the appearance of fairly carefully torn edges. We're going to turn the clock back a little farther now and create the effect of old, battered parchment.

This simple yet very effective technique is quick to use and can easily be incorporated into your artwork. It is, of course, particularly useful for making old maps – as with the above image – medieval style letters, and anything else that needs to appear to have withstood the ravages of time.

1 Create a new document *ctrl* N ⌘ N and duplicate the background layer *ctrl* J ⌘ J. Grab the Freehand Lasso **L**. Set the Feather value to 1 pixel; this prevents a harsh edge. Draw a ragged outline to define the edge of the paper. Now fill the selection with a sandy brown color.

2 Press *ctrl* J ⌘ J to duplicate the layer again. Go to Filter > Render > Difference Clouds. Although we haven't constrained the effect, it only affects the area of the previous layer's pixels. The colors look a little strange but this is only temporary.

3 Set the layer's blend mode to Soft Light; this gives us a nice spread of tones. Depending on the effect you require, you can lower the opacity to make it less harsh. When you're happy with the result, press `ctrl` `G` `⌘` `G` to group the layers, then `ctrl` `E` `⌘` `E` to merge them.

4 We have our mottled effect but it still looks too clean. We need to give it an earthier appearance: open the Film Grain filter located under the Artistic menu. Use very low settings to create a subtle, gritty effect across the surface of the paper.

In step 3 we took the unusual action of creating a clipping group before merging the layers together. If we hadn't, it would have resulted in a thin dark edge appearing around our paper; this is due to combining layers which have been feathered. This can, of course, work in our favour if we wanted to have a slightly heavier border.

Once finished, you can add artwork such as maps or line-art using the Multiply blend mode. These can then be grouped so the missing areas are hidden on the image overlay as well.

5 To complete the effect we'll add some dark patches around the edge: select the Burn tool `O`, set its mode to Midtones, and paint over random areas all around the perimeter. This gives the effect of the paper having been handled and battered over time.

6 As an optional step you can create some holes in the paper to enhance the effect even more. Use the Magic Wand `W` to select the darker patches of the paper, feather the selection, then hit `Backspace` to delete the areas. You can also darken the edges as in the last step.

Ageing a photo in minutes

THERE ARE MANY WAYS to restore old, damaged photographs. You'll find a technique in almost every digital imaging how-to book. In this tutorial, however, we're going to do the exact opposite. By taking a perfectly good picture and applying a variety of effects we'll create the impression that it has been less than well cared for.

Although this might seem a little perverse, it serves as an extreme example of what can be achieved by combining and blending existing textures with a photo. In this case, we'll use the reverse side of an old, battered book cover. The dents, folds and creases provide an excellent basis for the effect.

1 Open the image. We've placed the battered book cover image beneath the girl's layer. Click the cover's thumbnail. Press *ctrl* J ⌘ J to duplicate it. Drag the copy layer above the girl's and hide it for now by clicking its visibility (eyeball) icon.

2 Click the girl's layer in the Layers panel. Now press *ctrl* G ⌘ G to group it with the book layer. Only the areas that correspond to the layer beneath are visible, so the edges of the photo now follow the rough outline of the crumpled cover.

It's a good idea to maintain a separate library of textures such as the book cover. Create a folder in the place where you create your projects or store your photos. Each time you scan or find a useful texture, place it there for easy access.

3 Set the girl layer's blend mode to Hard Light. This allows the texture beneath to show through. Create a Hue/Saturation Adjustment Layer above the girl. Make sure Colorize is checked. Drag the Hue slider across to create a sepia-like coloring.

4 Make the copy of the cover visible and click its thumbnail to make it the active layer. Press *ctrl* *Shift* *U* *⌘* *Shift* *U* to desaturate it. Set the layer's blend mode to Hard Light. Combined with the base layer, this really helps to bring out the crumpled texture.

5 The image has become a little washed out due to the white of the book layer. Press *ctrl* *L* *⌘* *L* to open the Levels dialog. Drag the Shadows slider across to the right to increase the contrast. This also brings out grainy areas, which really adds to the aged effect.

6 Click the photo layer's thumbnail to make it active. Load up either of the texture layers' selections. Go to Select > Modify > Contract. A value of 15 pixels works well. Click OK. Now add a mask by clicking the icon at the base of the Layers panel. This hides part of the photo, creating a border.

A quick repair job

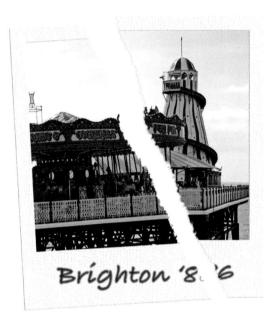

WHILST WE'RE ON THE SUBJECT of damaged photos, it appears that this seaside Polaroid has seen better days (actually, it was torn using the technique from earlier in the chapter). We're not going to spend hours retouching the image, though; instead, after crudely placing the pieces together, we'll create some strips of old, worn Scotch tape to make it look as good as new, well almost.

This is a slightly over the top example to illustrate the technique. You could, of course, use the effect in your scrapbook projects or to stick virtual photos up in your web gallery. With a bit of customizing, it could easily become solid electrical tape or even sticking-plasters.

1 We'll begin by putting the two halves together. They're on separate layers so we can use Free Transform to place them together. If it were a single layer, you could use the Lasso tools to select the pieces first. We want it to look botched so you'll want to leave some overlapping areas.

2 Add a new layer above the photo. Grab the Lasso tool **L** and draw a jagged selection. Press *alt* and release the mouse to switch to Polygonal mode. Drag out a side. Click and hold to switch back to freehand. Add the other ragged end. Join it up with another straight line.

3 Press *Shift* *Backspace* to open the Fill dialog. Select 50% gray as the Content. The hue of a neutral color can always be altered. Scotch tape is semi-opaque (even when aged) so set the Opacity to 50%. Finally, press *ctrl* *D* *⌘* *D* to deselect.

4 Select either the Dodge or Burn tool *O*. Choose a soft brush set to Highlights. Create some light and dark shading to give the appearance of the tape lifting. You can switch between Dodge and Burn modes by holding *alt* *⌥* whilst painting. Keep the effect subtle for the best results.

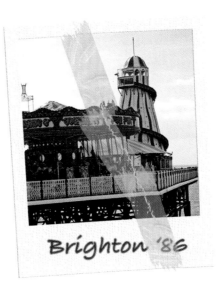

5 To give our tape a really authentic appearance we've used the Plastic Wrap filter (from the Artistic sub-menu). This is supposed to be old tape: we need to add some discoloration. A Hue/Saturation adjustment is good. You can control the effect from one dialog.

6 Press *ctrl* *T* *⌘* *T*. Reposition the tape. Rotate it to follow the tear. You could draw additional pieces from scratch. A quicker way is to press *⌘* *⌥* *T* *⌘* *⌥* *T*. This creates a new copy on the same layer. You can flip and distort them enough to appear sufficiently different.

229

Letting the dust settle

DUST IS USUALLY SOMETHING we don't like seeing. As with many things, there are exceptions, wine being one. Cellars often have bottles which have rested undisturbed for many years as they reach maturity and, as a result, have accumulated a thick layer of dust.

If, however, you're not a connoisseur and need a picture in a hurry, you can create the desired effect in a few easy steps. We'll be using a bottle for the project but the technique could just as easily be applied to many different subjects: items in an attic, perhaps. You could even consider using it in promotional material, for a cleaning company, perhaps – a before and after shot, for example.

1 Here's our bottle. It's been isolated and placed on its own layer. Begin by grabbing the Selection Brush **A**. Set the Mode to Mask. Now use a soft tip to paint in the areas where you want the dust to be. Don't worry too much about spilling over the edges; they'll be tidied up.

2 Switch back to Selection mode. Press `ctrl` `Shift` `I` `⌘` `Shift` `I` to inverse the selected areas. Hold `ctrl` `alt` `Shift` `⌘` `⌥` `Shift`. Click the bottle layer's thumbnail; the keypress forces the selection to intersect mode. Anything outside of the bottle's edge is discarded.

3 Even a thin layer of dust has depth. We need to create some extra space for the effect to sit outside of the bottle's edge. Choose Modify > Expand from the Select menu. I've used a value of 1 pixel here. You could, of course, use different values to produce thicker layers.

4 Create a new layer above the bottle. Open the Fill dialog *Shift* *Backspace*. Set the Contents to 50% Gray. Choose Dissolve for the blend mode. Now lower the opacity a little; in this case to 75%. Dissolve uses the opacity value to determine the visibility of the layer's pixels.

5 The result is not too bad; it's a little uniform, though. Press *ctrl* *D* *⌘ D* to deselect. Add some Noise to give a more random texture. Follow this with a very small amount of Gaussian Blur; you just need to take the harshness away from the effect.

6 Almost done. Select the Burn tool *O*. Set the Range to Highlights. Using the edge of a large, soft brush, darken down the sides of the dust layer. Use the shape of the bottle as a guide. Now hold *alt* *⌥* to temporarily switch to Dodge mode. Lighten up the front area a little.

HOT TIP

For extra realism, you may want to create some areas where the dust has been disturbed. This can be achieved by using a soft Eraser set to a low opacity. Parts of the layer can be progressively thinned out; great for creating fingermarks where the object has been handled.

SHORTCUTS
MAC WIN BOTH

231

You spin me round

WE CAN ALSO ADAPT NOISE for other types of effect. Here we'll be using it to create the dusty groove of a well-worn vinyl record; you remember those, don't you?

We'll be creating the whole thing from scratch – if you'll pardon the pun – using just layers, filters and blurs. The result is exceptionally realistic and can be used as the basis for a musically based website banner or perhaps a personalized birthday card for the aspiring rock star in the family.

1 Create a new document *ctrl* **N** **⌘ N**. Now create a new layer. Grab the Elliptical Marquee tool **M**. Hold *Shift* to constrain the proportions and draw out a large circular selection. Press **D** to select the default palette. Now press *alt* *Backspace* **⌥** *Backspace* to fill it with black.

2 Go to Select > Transform Selection. Hold *alt* **⌥** to force the scaling from the center. Reduce the selection down to roughly the size of the hole in the center of the record. Press *Enter* to commit, then press *Backspace* to delete the pixels. Press *ctrl* **D** **⌘ D** to deselect.

3 Before we add the surface texture we need to leave space for the lead-in. Duplicate the base layer *ctrl* **J** **⌘ J**. Load its selection by pressing *ctrl* **⌘** and clicking its thumbnail. Now go to Select > Modify > Contract. A value of around 6 pixels works well on this size of image.

4 Go to Filter > Noise > Add Noise. Set an Amount of 400%, the Distribution to Uniform and check Monochromatic.

5 Now select Filter > Blur > Radial Blur. Set an Amount of 100. Set the Method to Spin and set the Quality to Best.

6 The result is is too light. Open the Levels dialog *ctrl* *L* *⌘* *L*. Drag the Shadows slider to the left edge of the histogram, then drag the Highlights slider to the right edge of the histogram. Lower the opacity of the layer to blend it in. Leave the selection active.

7 Now we'll add the blank lead-out area. Create a new layer and fill it with black. Deselect *ctrl* *D* *⌘* *D*. Now use Free Transform with *alt* *⌥* to scale the circle down around the center. This should be somewhere around 60% of the original layer size.

8 Create a new layer. Grab the Brush tool *B*. Select a medium-sized soft tip. Press *X* to set the foreground to white. Create a few vertical stripes by holding *Shift* while you paint downward. Don't worry about going over the edges. Remember to release *Shift* after each one.

9 Go to Filter > Distort > Polar Coordinates. Select Rectangular to Polar and click OK. Press *ctrl* *alt* *T* *⌘* *⌥* *T*. This enters Free Transform and will duplicate the layer. Go to Image > Rotate. Flip the layer horizontally then vertically. Drag the new version to the top. Press *Enter*.

HOT TIP

In step 2 we use the Transform Selection command. If you're using a version of Elements prior to 8, you won't have this. Instead, you can duplicate the base layer and scale it down to size. Load its selection then switch to the original base layer and press *Backspace* to create the hole. You can discard the duplicate layer after that.

10 Press *ctrl* *E* *⌘* *E* to merge the two layers. Lower the opacity to around 30%. Now hold *ctrl* *⌘* and click the base layer's thumbnail. Press *ctrl* *Shift* *I* *⌘* *Shift* *I* to inverse the selection. Press *Backspace* to delete the excess area outside. Finally, deselect.

11 Finally, we'll create a blank label ready to have text added (check Chapter 6 for details on how to do this). Create a new layer. Load the lead-out layer's selection. Fill this with 50% gray and deselect. Finally, use Free Transform to scale it down slightly inside the lead-in.

SHORTCUTS
MAC | WIN | BOTH

A little light relief

PREVIOUSLY, WE SAW how the use of subtle shading can create the illusion of depth, changing a simple flat object into a three-dimensional one. The same is true for creating raised surfaces.

In this example, we'll create a traditional wax seal using a black and white logo as the basis for the effect. The edge of the artwork has been created purposely uneven to enhance the effect, giving the appearance of the hot wax spreading as the template stamp is pressed into it.

1 Here's our black and white artwork on its own layer. Grab the Magic Wand. Uncheck the Contiguous option. This tells the tool to select every instance of the specified color in the image. Click anywhere in the black area. Now press *ctrl* *C* *⌘* *C* to copy the selection to the clipboard.

2 Press *ctrl* *D* *⌘* *D* to deselect. Create a mask by clicking the icon at the base of the Layers panel. Hold *alt* ⌥ and click the mask thumbnail. Press *D* to restore the default colors. Now apply the Clouds filter. The reason for using the mask will become evident later.

3 The default effect is much too harsh; we don't want any hard edges. We'll soften it down with Gaussian Blur. Set it to a fairly high pixel radius: around 15 worked well here. We want to achieve a smooth tonal blend similar to the above image.

4 Press *ctrl* *V* *⌘* *V* to paste the previously saved selection then deselect. Press *ctrl* *alt* *F* *⌘* *⌥* *F* to open up the Gaussian Blur dialog again. This time, set a much lower value. We need to soften the edges but keep the detail visible. A value of around 3 pixels is used here.

5 Hold `ctrl` `⌘` and click the mask's thumbnail to load up the selection. Only a few small areas will appear; this is OK. The boundary only shows on areas that have more than 50% opacity. Choose Save Selection from the Select menu. Give it a name and click OK. Press `ctrl` `D` `⌘` `D` to deselect.

6 Hold `Shift` and click on the mask to hide it. Now click the artwork's thumbnail to exit Mask Edit mode. Re-enable the Magic Wand's Contiguous option. Select the area outside the artwork. Press `ctrl` `Shift` `I` `⌘` `Shift` `I` to inverse the selection. Create a new layer. Fill this with white.

7 Go to Filter > Render > Lighting Effects. Begin by loading the selection we saved earlier from the Texture Channel menu at the bottom of the dialog. Uncheck White is high. Increase the height to 90. Choose the Omni light type. Drag its circle out to the edges of the artwork.

8 The default settings are not good at all; we can hardly see the artwork. Lower the Intensity to around 7; this gives us a nice even lighting. We can also alter the properties. Increase the Gloss setting to 100. Set the Material to -100. This will give us a good result so click OK.

9 The result is OK but a little matt. Sealing wax has a mixture of flat areas and shiny highlights. The Plastic Wrap filter is perfect for this. It can be found under the Artistic section of the Filter menu. Use the sliders to bring out the detail and give it a more moulded appearance.

10 Finally, deselect then open the Hue/Saturation adjustment dialog. Click the Colorize box. Now adjust the sliders to add some color. We decided on the archetypal deep red. We finished up by adjusting the contrast with Levels to give a richer effect.

Stamp duty

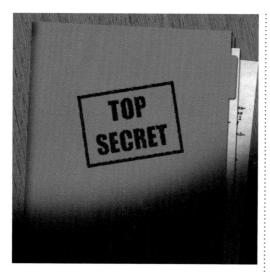

THERE WILL BE OCCASIONS where we want to use a piece of artwork or effect again in our projects. We obviously wouldn't want to keep recreating it each time. We could, of course, save it in the conventional way then import it into a document when it's needed, but there is a better way – creating our own brush preset. This has several benefits: we can save them, either individually or as sets to create libraries; they are non-destructively scaleable and can be resized far more quickly than the usual transformation method; they also take up relatively little disk space and, because they are self-contained files, they can easily be shared between other Elements and Photoshop users.

When creating a brush, it's important to know how they work. In essence, they are very similar to a mask, using grayscale to determine their opacity. Pure black appears 100% solid, becoming more transparent the closer it gets to white, where it disappears completely. We'll see this in action here by creating a simple rubber stamp effect. We could create a brush from any piece of artwork, of course, even photographs.

1 Let's start with a new blank document. Select the Type tool **T**. We want a bold font for this project: Impact is a good one. Set the text alignment to Center. Click the document to start a new text layer and type Top Secret, with a carriage return (**Enter**) in between the two words.

2 Create a new layer. Select the Rectangular Marquee **M**. Holding *alt* ⌥ click and drag the boundary out from the center of the document – remember to leave enough space around the text for our border. We can reposition the selection by additonally holding the Spacebar.

3 Select Stroke (Outline) Selection from the Edit menu. We need a strong border so a Width of 20 pixels is good for this size image. Set the Color to black and the Location to Inside – this gives us sharp-edged corners. If we'd used Center or Outside, the corners would be more rounded.

4 We could create our brush at this point. Rubber stamps wear down after a while and stop transferring the ink completely. We can give our artwork a worn look but we'll need it to be on a single layer so we can apply the filter. Press `ctrl` `Shift` `E` `⌘` `Shift` `E` to merge the layers together.

5 Press `D` to reset to the default color palette. Go to Filter > Distort > Glass. Choose the Frosted texture. Experiment with the Distortion and Smoothness settings to roughen the edges a little; it only needs to be a subtle effect. Click OK to apply.

Although flattening the layers in step 4 goes against our principles of always keeping the original artwork layers, in this instance it's a very simple image and easy to recreate. If we were working on something more complex, we could merge it to a new layer using `ctrl` `alt` `Shift` `E` `⌘` `⌥` `Shift` `E` then hide the original layers to avoid confusion.

6 Now we can go ahead and create our brush. Use the Magic Wand to select the artwork; hold `Shift` to add the individual parts. Go to Edit > Define Brush from Selection. It's important to give it a meaningful name as this will make it easier to find amongst the other presets.

7 Grab the Brush tool `B` if it's not selected. Our brush will appear as the last entry in the currently selected brush presets. Although it will be stored automatically, we'll save it, as a precaution. Click the brush, then open the fly-out menu and click Save Brushes. Name the file and click OK.

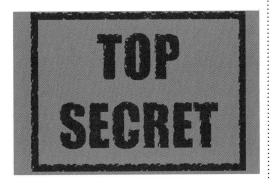

8 Save or discard the original artwork document and create a new blank one. Here we can see the outline of the brush. Just like a mask, the original white areas are hidden, leaving only the slightly uneven black areas where we applied the filter.

9 We've filled the background with color to demonstrate the effect. Being a brush, we can quickly scale it up or down using the left and right square bracket keys `[` `]`. We can also change its color simply by setting a new foreground color – we've chosen red, of course!

Finger-friendly stained glass

STAINED GLASS HAS BEEN AN ARTFORM for centuries. From the huge ornate windows of churches and cathedrals to the understated adornment of an urban door, people love its radiance and color.

You may have discovered the Stained Glass filter in Elements; its results are passable but tend to resemble a mosaic more than the traditional effect. In this tutorial, we'll go back to basics and create some of our effect by hand, using a photo as a template for tracing the outline, then applying filters and layer styles to achieve our result.

This technique can be used for all kinds of projects. On its own it's a great effect for greetings cards. It could also be used as an ornate border for framing a photo. You could, of course, use this technique as a basis for designing the real thing.

1 Create a new layer. Set the foreground to mid-gray. Use a small, hard-tipped brush **B** to trace the outline of the bird. It needn't be perfect as long as we get the shape.

2 Select the entire document by pressing *ctrl* **A** ⌘ **A**. Choose Stroke Selection from the Edit menu. Set the same color and width as the brush. Use Inside as the location.

3 The background needs to be divided up into panels. Draw a few lines between the border and the bird's outline. Use some of the contrasting areas of detail as a guide.

4 Now divide up the bird itself. Again, use the prominent details to make up the panels. Remember that each section must be completely enclosed and connected by the leading.

5 We need a separate layer for the individual colors. Press and hold *ctrl* ⌘. Click the New Layer icon in the Layers panel. This creates a new layer beneath the current one.

6 Reselect the outline layer by clicking its thumbnail. Grab the Magic Wand **W**. Click an area of the bird to select that section. The top of the head is a good place to start.

7 We need to ensure there will be no gaps between the leading and the glass. Expand the selection (Select > Modify). A value half the width of the leading is fine.

8 Click the layer you created in step 5. Open the Fill dialog *Shift* *Backspace*. Set the contents to color. Use the Eye-dropper to pick a suitable shade from the photo.

9 Press *ctrl* *D* *⌘* *D* to deselect. Color the rest of the panels by repeating the process from step 6 onwards. I've also painted the center of the eye with a small black brush.

10 Add a new layer between the color and the outline. Press *D* to restore the default foreground and background colors. Fill the layer with the Clouds filter.

11 Open the Glass filter (under Distort). Set the Texture to Frosted. A Smoothness value of around 2–3 gives a good stipple effect. Raise the distortion level to blur the texture.

12 Change the layer's blend mode to Multiply. This filters out the lighter areas of the glass, allowing the color to show through, but still retains the effect.

HOT TIP

As well as the four presets, you can also load custom textures into the glass filter to use as a basis for its distortion effect. Click the fly-out menu to the right of the Textures menu to access the file dialog. You can use any image saved in Photoshop (.psd) format.

13 Make the outline layer active. Select the Wow Chrome layer styles set from the Effects panel. Apply the Beveled Edge setting. It may look a little odd at this stage.

14 Double-click the style icon to the right of the layer's thumbnail. Lower the drop shadow's distance. Adjust the Bevel size. Around 6 pixels works for this size of image.

15 Here's our completed image. Adjusting the layer style has made all the difference. You may want to make the glass layer a little lighter using Levels or Brightness/Contrast.

SHORTCUTS
MAC WIN BOTH

Blueprint for design

KIDS HAVE WONDERFUL imaginations and can come up with all kinds of fantastic inventions – such as this idea for a failsafe alarm clock involving boiling water, melting ice cubes and a tipping glass at the end of the process.

The trouble is, these designs are always sketched on whatever materials come to hand – in this case, a page torn from a spiral-bound notebook. We're going to see how to turn this sketch into an official-looking blueprint, but first, we need to find a way to get rid of the lines in the background of this ruled paper.

1 Begin by opening the Brightness/Contrast adjustment. Drag both sliders all the way to the right to set both Brightness and Contrast at their maximum values. This will make the rules fainter, but won't get rid of them altogether (unless your rules are gray, rather than black).

2 Now desaturate the image ctrl Shift U ⌘ Shift U. This will knock out all the extra colors that crept in during the previous step. Use the Threshold adjustment to turn it to pure black and white. You may need to erase a few stray pieces of line; paint them out with a white brush.

3 With the image fully cleaned up, we're ready to start turning it into a blueprint. Choose Invert to turn the image from black on white to white on black. If any of the ruled lines still show up, paint over them in black to hide them.

4 Now for the blue background. If the original artwork is still your background layer, double-click its thumbnail to turn it into a regular layer, then set the mode of this layer to Screen. You won't see any difference until you make a new layer behind it, filled with blue.

5 The white of the original layer is a little stark, so let's give it a touch of blue. Open the Hue/Saturation dialog and press Colorize. Reduce the Lightness slightly and change the Hue slider to get a pale blue; you may want to increase the Saturation a little as well.

6 Finally, let's place a graph paper grid behind the image. This grid is white on black, and we've set the opacity to just 20% to make a faint background. It's a bit of a fiddle to draw graph paper from scratch, so we've provided this for you as a layer on the original image.

HOT TIP

The hardest part of this job is cleaning up the original drawing. It would be better, of course, if kids could be persuaded to use clean, unlined paper – but when inspiration strikes, we use whatever's to hand. This is an extreme example, with solid, dark rules; most clean-up processes won't be as complex as this one. But the combination of Brightness/ Contrast and the Threshold adjustment usually does the trick.

SHORTCUTS
MAC | WIN | BOTH

Unfinished illustration

YOU'VE PROBABLY SEEN THIS STYLE of illustration many times, where only parts of the image, generally the main detail, are in color and the rest is left as a sketch or given a lighter wash of paint. It's used a lot in children's books and architectural projects but is also an artform in its own right.

We're going to explore a variety of techniques here in order to create our illustrative style image. Starting with a photo, we'll first convert it to a sketch, then use filters to create a painterly effect, then combine the two, and finally use a layer mask to add or remove portions of the image. The use of layers and masks makes the technique very versatile, allowing us to decide how much of the color we show. We could, of course, simply leave it as a line drawing or decide to go for the full color picture instead.

1 The first stage of the process is creating our ink outline. Duplicate the background layer by pressing *ctrl* *J* ⌘ *J*. Now press *ctrl* *Shift* *U* ⌘ *Shift* *U* to desaturate (remove the color from) the image. Make a copy of this layer. Press *ctrl* *I* ⌘ *I* to invert it.

2 Change the blend mode to Linear Dodge. The document will go white; this is normal. Open the Gaussian Blur filter. Set the Radius to 0. Now drag to the right; we'll see the effect emerge. Stop when there is a visible outline – around a 2-3 pixel radius works well for this image.

3 Now we'll make the outline bolder. Merge the layers together *ctrl* *E* ⌘ *E*. Open the Levels dialog *ctrl* *L* ⌘ *L*. Drag the Shadows slider to the right so it meets the left edge of the histogram. Now adjust the midtones and highlights to fade out the grayer areas of the image.

4 We're finished with the outline for now so hide the layer by clicking its eyeball icon. The next step in the process is to create the painted on canvas effect. Select the background layer again by clicking its layer thumbnail and create another duplicate.

5 Open the Filter Gallery from the Filter menu. Select Paint Daubs from the drop-down menu. We used a Brush Size of 7 and a Sharpness of 4 with a Wide Blurry brush type. This gives us a great painterly effect. Don't click OK yet as we're going to add another filter.

6 Click the New Effect Layer icon at the bottom right of the window. Now select Underpainting from the drop-down. Here we've used a Brush Size of 4, Texture Coverage of 2 with the Texture set to Canvas, and a Relief of 4. Finally, set the Light to Top Left and click OK to apply.

7 The image looks a little blotchy and formless at the moment. Make the outline layer visible again. Now set its blend mode to Multiply. This hides the white area of the layer, leaving just the outline so it overlays our painted effect. This really brings the image to life. We're almost done.

8 Only parts of the image have a canvas texture. Create a new layer beneath the painted layer. Fill this with white. Select Filter > Texture > Texturizer. Set the attributes to match those we used in the Underpainting filter and apply it. Finally, set the painted layer's blend mode to Multiply.

9 Create a layer mask on the painted effect layer. Press *ctrl I* ⌘ *I* to invert the mask. This hides the content. Now, using a white brush – some of the Wet Media brush presets work really well – we can start to paint over the mask, bringing back those parts of the image.

243

Finding images for free

MOST OF THE TIME, you'll be using your own images for the project you're working on – you won't find a more inexpensive source than that. There will be situations, however, when you'll need a photo of an object you don't have the time or resources to take. It may be completely impractical because it's not something you normally find in your home town or even the country you live in; a famous building or indigenous animal, for example. Whilst you could improvise by altering the project or modifying an image of something similar, there is a much better way of tracking down that elusive picture: the World Wide Web.

In recent years, as more people have switched to digital cameras and fast internet connections become more commonplace, huge online stock photography sites have sprung up, containing hundreds of thousands of images. Sites such as **stock.xchng** (www.sxc.hu) and the curiously named **Morguefile.com** (traditionally a publishing term given to reference libraries of old images and cuttings) provide categorized and searchable libraries of people, places and objects from all around the world. Because they are submitted by the public for the public, the quality is not always superb; it does mean, however, that you have a good chance of finding something bizarre which would not make it past the strict scrutiny of the commercial libraries. The biggest benefit, of course, is that they are completely free. The sites are kept running solely on advertising and the good will of public donations. This, of course, is great news for the montage artist on a tight or nonexistent budget.

The exact terms of use vary from site to site. Most, however, allow unlimited use for both private and commercial projects, providing it's not detrimental to either the photographer, their subject or the site itself. When you download an image, it's usually anonymously; the photographer may like to know how their photo has been used but it's rarely mandatory. Stock.Xchng allow the contributors to set their own requirements: some require you to apply for explicit permission, depending on the content – generally, and understandably, when there are recognizable faces. It's one thing to allow someone to post photos of you but quite another to find yourself placed in an image of questionable content.

In addition to the dedicated libraries, there are also community sites such as **Flickr.com** and more recently, **Wikipedia Commons** (commons.wikipedia.org). These operate under the new Creative Commons license – a system devised for intellectual rights management on the internet. Under this license, photographers can determine what can and can't be done with their images. This ranges from complete free rein to total copyright protection; the latter is very often negotiable through polite communication with the person concerned. Another site worth checking out, if you're looking for images to use in fantasy scenes, is **DeviantArt.com**; there is a dedicated stock section where members post their images. Do check their individual rules, however, as some images are not to be used outside of the site. Be warned, some of the content is not for the faint-hearted!

It's also worth noting the governmental public domain libraries. These offer more specific images: military, political figures and, of course, there is **NASA.gov** which holds a wealth of scientific, aeronautical and astronomical photos. Again, these images are all free to use for private projects but commercial use carries some regulations; these can be found in the site's terms and conditions.

If all else fails, you can always try a search through **Google** or **Yahoo**. Both have offshoots of their sites devoted to images. Great care must be taken here. Grabbing images from web searches puts you right in the middle of the copyright minefield. If you're using the pictures at a purely personal level, making backgrounds for your computer desktop and so on, you'll be OK – surveillance techniques haven't infringed the home, just yet. If, however, you intend to publish these images as part of your website or as a printed design, make sure you obtain permission from the owner of the site or photo. There's usually an address to write to. If you are in any doubt as to the copyright status, don't risk it; at the very least, you'll receive an irate email asking for removal of the image, and at worst, you may find yourself in court.

As long as you respect the rules and guidelines, there is a wealth of useful content to be found. Browsing the sites can also be a good source of inspiration; something you find by accident can often spark a whole new project idea.

The camera never lies, we're told. But sometimes we wish it would be less scrupulously honest. The photo above is a charming shot of two people who love each other, but how much nicer it would be for them if some of the ravages of time were washed away. And perhaps they could be in a better location, as well.

People and animals

THE LATE, GREAT W. C. FIELDS told us never to work with children or animals. Sound advice, for sure. But we photograph people and pets more than just about any other subject, so we need to know how to work with them in Elements.

In this chapter we'll look at how to fix blemishes, how to reverse the ageing process, and how to make people look slimmer. We'll also explore several other everyday tasks to enhance our images – as well as some tasks, such as swapping heads, that are far from commonplace. Whether you're making a birthday card for a friend, or simply enhancing a family photo, we've got the solutions to make the job easier.

Heads on bodies

ONE OF THE MOST IMPRESSIVE tricks we can play in Elements is to place a celebrity's head on the body of a family member. It's easy enough to come across suitable celebrities on the internet: one of the best places is Wikipedia, which includes thousands of images of celebrities that are free to use in its Wikimedia Commons department.

The trick to making this technique work lies in choosing a head shot at the right angle to work with your image. Don't worry about the size and the color, as we can easily fix that later; all that matters for now is that the orientation is as close as you can find to the head in the original photograph.

1 We found this picture of Arnold Schwarzenegger on the Wikipedia website. It's just the right angle to fit on the body of the dad in our family shot. The first step is to cut it out from its background, using any of the techniques described in Chapter 1.

2 Drag the cut-out head into the image where you want it to appear. To make it roughly the right size, it helps if you position it next to the target head, rather than on top: by being able to see both at the same time, we can be sure to get the size right.

3 Rotate and further scale the head as necessary using Free Transform, and place it on top of the original head. Take your time with this step, as it's the key to making the montage work. Here, we've rotated the head anticlockwise slightly for a more appealing look.

4 Although we got the size and angle right in the previous step, Arnie's coloring didn't match the rest of the photograph. The best way to adjust the color of the new head is to use the Levels adjustment, which also allows us to correct the contrast.

5 There's a hard line under Arnie's chin that needs to be dealt with. The simplest way of removing this is to use a small, soft-edged Eraser **E** to smooth out the join; for more control, however, use a layer mask – see Chapter 4 for more details on how to do this.

6 Finally, we need to remove the pieces of the original head that are still visible behind Arnie. On the background layer, use the Clone Stamp tool to sample pieces of the background and paint them in to cover up the original ear and other features that stick out.

SHORTCUTS
MAC WIN BOTH

Photomerge: faces

O N THE PREVIOUS PAGES we looked at how to place a head on a different body. Elements 6 brought us a new technology, Photomerge, which automates the process.

Unlike the previous method, Photomerge doesn't require us to cut out the original head first: it can recognize a head shape within an image, even against a background as complicated as the one behind Ronald Reagan in this example.

The technology isn't perfect and it can be a little tricky to control: but it's a quick way of moving heads between images and can be a lot of fun to play around with.

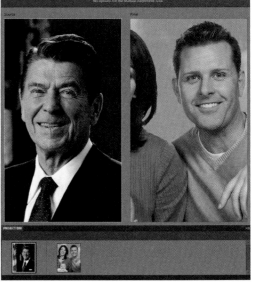

1 To begin, make sure the head you want to copy into the mix is on the left in the Panel Bin – drag it there if it isn't in place already. Now choose New > Photomerge Faces. You'll be prompted to drag the final image into the space on the right.

2 Now click on the Alignment tool within the Photomerge dialog and three numbered crosshairs will appear. Drag these onto the first image – one for each of the eyes and one for the mouth. Accurate placement of these markers is essential to making this technique work, so zoom in first.

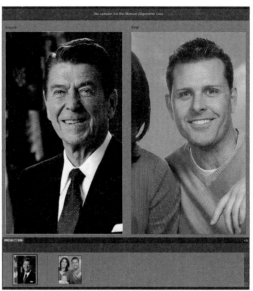

3 Now place the markers on the second face in corresponding positions and click the Align Photos button. As we can see, this has produced a rather distorted shot of Reagan in the first frame; we need to adjust the positions of the markers to correct this.

4 Move the markers on either image and press Align Photos again to correct the distortion. It can take a few tries to get it right: you need to move the markers in the opposite direction to what you'd expect in order to undistort the face.

5 Now for the fun part. Grab the Pencil tool and draw over Reagan's face. In a couple of seconds, the face will appear superimposed over the family photograph. As we can see, though, it's also darkened up the sky behind the figure and Reagan's ear overlaps the original ear.

6 We can't do much more editing here, but pressing Done will produce a new document with two layers – the original family shot and the family with Reagan placed over the top. Erase parts of this layer or use a layer mask to make a better fit.

HOT TIP

If you find that too much of the image has been copied into the picture, use the Eraser tool within the Photomerge dialog to remove some of the drawn pencil line. Experiment with erasing and redrawing pencil lines until you get a result that works well.

251

Cosmetic surgery: healing

HERE'S A GRUMPY TEENAGER. So what else is new? Well, this teenager has a reason to be grumpy: she's about to go on a hot date and her face is covered in acne spots. (To be fair to the original model, we should point out that we added these blemishes ourselves.)

A two-week course of antibiotics could clear this up – but we have a quicker method. Using the Healing Brush and the Spot Healing Brush – how appropriate – we can lose those ugly spots with just a few clicks.

Using this innovative tool isn't always plain sailing, however, as we'll see here: when the blemishes are close to an edge, unwanted effects can occur. This tutorial explains the best way to prevent those errors.

1 Choose the Spot Healing Brush (shortcut: **J**) and make sure it's set to use a hard-edged brush. This seems contradictory: you'd expect a soft brush to blend in better. But that's not how this one works. Paint roughly over the spot on the forehead and you'll see where you've painted.

2 As soon as you release the mouse button, the Spot Healing Brush does something extraordinary: it samples the texture around the place you painted and blends that texture in perfectly with the surroundings. Our first spot disappears instantly.

3 We can carry on in the same manner, painting over each spot in turn on the girl's right cheek. Paint just enough area to cover the spot, and no more, for the tool to perform at its best.

4 When we paint over the spot on her left cheek, however, something goes wrong. The tool has inadvertently sampled the edge of her face, producing what looks like an ugly scar. There are occasions when the Spot Healing Brush doesn't have a clear enough region from which to sample.

5 Undo that last step and, instead, switch to the regular Healing Brush. This works in a slightly different way: first, we hold *alt* ⌥ and click a point from which to sample the texture – the forehead works well – and then paint over the spot. Now, it disappears as we wish it to.

6 The spot above the lip presents a different problem. The spot is just too close to the mouth. Before healing, make a selection that includes the spot, but which stops at the top of the mouth. Now, when we use the tool, it won't act outside that area – and so the mouth is left intact.

HOT TIP

The Healing Brush is a hugely powerful tool. Use it to remove birds from the sky, beetles from a rock, or even commonly unwanted picture elements such as telegraph wires and signposts. The really clever thing about it is that you don't need to match the lighting or even the color: only the texture is sampled and is blended in perfectly with the background.

SHORTCUTS

253

Cosmetic surgery: weight loss

THIS IS THE WEIGHT LOSS PROGRAM the world's been waiting for: no diets, no exercise, just a ten-minute workout with the Liquify filter.

In order to make this procedure work properly, you'll need to cut out your image from its background. Otherwise, the existing background will be too distorted to look realistic.

We'll use this image of a woman who, while not obese, would perhaps value the opportunity to shed a few pounds.

1 Use Filter > Distort > Liquify to enter the Liquify dialog. The default tool is Warp: use this to push the waist in, as we start to slim our model. Use a large brush size: small brushes will simply create additional wrinkles and that's the very thing we want to get rid of.

2 It's easy to distort the hands by accident when smearing them with Liquify. The solution is to stick with a large brush size and to click and drag directly on the hand. With luck, the entire hand should move as one; switch to a smaller brush to clean up if necessary.

3 Push the bottom and the tops of the legs into the center to make them appear slimmer. Again, be careful not to distort the hands.

4 Don't forget such details as slimming the ankles – again, by pushing in from either side. It's details like this that make all the difference between a convincing montage and one that looks fake. But be careful not to get carried away if you want a realistic result.

5 The face is trickier. With a smaller brush size, push the chin and neck inwards. Switch to the Bloat tool and press on the eyes to make them slightly larger: this accentuates the features and makes the whole face look less chubby.

255

Age and youth

HOW OFTEN HAVE YOU TAKEN a photograph of an elderly relative, only for them to complain that they look much older than they expected? We all have an idea of how we appear to others, and the image in our minds is often several years younger than we really are.

If only there were a way to take the years off without resorting to expensive and painful surgery. Well, there is: we can harness the power of Elements to darken hair, remove wrinkles, tighten that sagging chin and present an altogether more youthful appearance.

We've taken the approach to extremes in this tutorial; generally, you'd only want to remove a few lines and creases. And perhaps fix that chin. Oh, and you may as well darken the hair a little while you're at it...

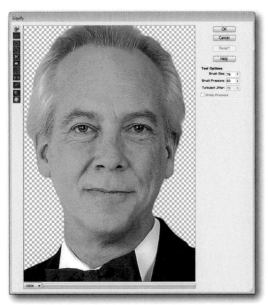

1 The first thing to do is to tighten that sagging chin. Go to Filter > Distort > Liquify and use the default tool to push the chin up and in. Start with a large brush: you can use the **[** and **]** keys to make the brush size smaller and larger.

2 Select the hair with the Lasso tool and apply a 5 pixel feather to it (*ctrl* *alt* *D* ⌘ ⌥ *F*) to soften the edge. Make this into a new layer with *ctrl* *J* ⌘ *J* and open the Levels dialog. Drag the middle gray triangle to the right to darken the hair.

3 Use the Spot Healing Brush **J** to paint out the lines on the forehead. It will sample texture from around the area you paint, patching the lines perfectly. Because there's so much clear forehead texture around the wrinkles, the tool works well here.

4 The Spot Healing Brush would have trouble with wrinkles close to facial features. Instead, switch to the regular Healing Brush and **alt** **⌥** click on the center of the forehead to set the source point. Now when you paint over the wrinkles they'll heal perfectly.

5 Let's address the hair loss that our unfortunate senior citizen has suffered. Rebuilding hair is tricky, but here's a simple solution. Select the top half of the hair and use **ctrl** **J** **⌘** **J** to make a new layer from it. Drag it down using the Move tool or Free Transform so it covers more of the forehead.

6 Switch to the Smudge tool **R** and choose a soft-edged brush – or one of the star-shaped custom brushes. With a pressure of around 70%, smudge the new hair both up into the original and down onto the forehead. This tool makes it easy to blend the new hair in with the old. Our rejuvenated favorite uncle is now complete.

SHORTCUTS
MAC WIN BOTH

Adding people to the scene

THE SCENE IS AN ENGAGEMENT PARTY: the blushing bride-to-be shares a glass of champagne with her future husband. Such a shame her father couldn't be there to enjoy the occasion... but, thanks to Elements, he can be. Adding people to a scene is just one of the techniques every Elements montage artist should be familiar with.

1 We'll start by cutting the bride's father out from his original background (we've already done this for you in the project image file). Once he's been moved into the engagement photo, the first step is to use Free Transform to make him the right size. Again, we've done this for you. Next, we need to place him behind the happy couple. Although we could do this with the Eraser tool, it's far easier, not to mention less destructive, using a layer mask – once we have added the mask we can paint on that layer to hide him behind the couple.

2 After a lot of painting in and out, pressing **X** to swap between foreground and background colors, we're able to tuck Dad firmly behind the couple. Since they're both holding glasses, though, we need to make them slightly transparent: and this is how it's done. Still working on the layer mask, set the foreground color to white (to paint the figure back in) and set the Opacity to just 20%. Now, when we paint over the glasses area with a hard-edged brush, we reveal a hint of Dad's shirt pattern as seen through the champagne glasses.

3 The final problem is one of coloring. The photo of Dad was too blue in comparison with the bride and groom photo. So switch to Dad's layer and open the Levels adjustment dialog. Begin with the Blue channel (*ctrl* 3 ⌘ 3), dragging the middle gray slider to the right to reduce the amount of blue in the image. Then switch to the composite RGB channel and drag the same slider to the right to reduce the brightness overall. Finally, switch to the Red channel (*ctrl* 1 ⌘ 1) and this time drag the slider slightly to the left to increase the amount of red a little.

SHORTCUTS
MAC WIN BOTH

Eyes wide shut

W E MAY HAVE the ability to take as many pictures as we want with our digital cameras, but unfortunately we still can't guarantee they'll be great shots every time, as is the case with our example. While the kids obliged us with a lovely pose for the portrait, one of them blinked at precisely the wrong moment.

All is not lost, however: using another picture (shown in the inset) of the girl in which her eyes are open, we can copy them from one image to the other and blend them in seamlessly, rescuing our photo from the delete pile.

1 The second image has been brought into the document as a new layer, and we've lowered the opacity to enable us to see the original image below. The girl is facing slightly to the right in the first photo but to the left in the second, so we need to flip the layer horizontally. We can now use Free Transform to scale, position and rotate the layer, matching it as closely as possible. Don't spend too much time trying to get it perfect first time; we can make finer adjustments later.

2 Now we have the layer in place we can bring its opacity back up to 100%. At this point we could use the Eraser to remove the excess from the image; there is a far better way, however. Grab the Selection Brush **A** and choose a large, soft tip. Paint in a loose, mask-like selection over and around the eyes; now press *ctrl* J ⌘ J to create a copy of the eyes on a new layer. We can hide or discard the previous image as it's no longer needed.

3 With just the eyes overlaid on our original photo we can see that, whilst it's a very close match, we still need to do a little fine-tuning. Enter Free Transform mode again; because we're now working on a smaller area, we can make more accurate adjustments. In this case all that's needed is a very slight rotation and a nudge upward. These changes can make all the difference. Our brains are trained to read faces and any anomalies can be glaringly obvious.

4 We're almost done – there's just a bit of tidying up to be carried out. Because the second image has slightly different lighting, some areas are too bright for the original photo. Select a medium-size, soft Eraser **E**, lower its opacity and use its edge to feather out the area around the periphery of the eyes to bring back some of the original shadowing. As she has such a nice smile in the other photo, we've added that in the same way to finish the image off.

SHORTCUTS
MAC WIN BOTH

Warhol-style pop-art

THE ICONIC IMAGE OF MARILYN MONROE is one of Andy Warhol's most famous works. He used the screen-printing process to transfer photographs to canvas which were then overlaid with blocks of heavy, garish color, giving them the now familiar impressionistic style. The aim was to streamline the process to enable the images to be mass-produced whilst each would be slightly different to the last.

We can recreate the effect surprisingly easily: by simplifying the photo to purely black and white we can then build up the image using individual layers of color – a digital version of screen-printing, as it were. Because we're using Adjustment Layers we can, of course, edit the image time after time, changing its colors or altering the level of detail.

1 Start by isolating the woman from the background; the best choice for this image is the Magic Wand **W**. Disable the Contiguous option to select all the black areas at once; tidy any stray areas on the face with the Selection Brush **A**. Inverse the selection and copy to a new layer.

2 Add a Threshold Adjustment Layer above the new layer. The initial result is too strong and we've lost a lot of the detail. Slowly drag the slider to the left until all but the main features are visible — make sure the eyes are fairly well defined. Press *ctrl* **G** ⌘ **G** to create a clipping group.

3 Create a Solid Color Adjustment Layer above the Threshold layer. Select a suitable color for the skintone and set the blend mode to Darken. Now click the layer's mask thumbnail and fill it with black to hide the effect. Using a hard brush, paint in white to reveal the areas of color.

4 Add another color layer the same as before but select a yellow for the hair. Again, paint over the mask to reveal the color. Now add a white layer for the eyes and teeth: this time set the mode to Overlay. The order of the layers can be important as the blend modes affect surrounding layers too.

HOT TIP

Holding *alt* ⌥ whilst selecting an Adjustment Layer from the menu in the Layers panel forces its Option dialog to appear. From here you can rename it, choose to create it as a clipping mask, and set the blend mode during the creation process.

5 Create a red layer for the lips; this will need to be set to Lighten. Paint in the eyeshadow and the necklace. If you're finding it tricky to see which parts should be a certain color, hold *alt* ⌥ and click the original photo's visibility icon; this toggles the effect on and off by hiding the layers.

6 Duplicate the head layer and place it at the top of the stack. Set its blend mode to Color Burn and lower the opacity to 50%. Create a new Threshold adjustment and this time drag the slider to the right to increase the black detail. Add a plain, colored background to complete the effect.

263

Hollywood glamor

1 We'll start, as ever, by duplicating our background layer by pressing `ctrl J` `⌘ J`. From the Enhance menu, select Convert to Black and White. This opens a dialog showing the before and after image along with presets and fine-tuning controls. We'll use the Portrait preset.

CONTINUING ON THE THEME of iconic portraiture, we're going to take a look at the photographic style of the 1940s and 50s; in particular, images of the film stars of the day. These were often shot in high contrast black and white but with a selective soft focus effect. This smoothed out the skin, giving the subject a glowing, dreamlike appearance.

2 This preset levels out the tones of the image, which looks OK, but we want a more high-contrast style. Drag the Contrast slider to the right – a value of around +40 works well. For other images it may be necessary to try different presets or alter the individual color settings.

3 We'll blur the image to smooth out the model's skin. Duplicate the black and white layer. Now open the Gaussian Blur filter. We'll need a fairly heavy effect so set a radius of around 8 pixels. Change the layer's blend mode to Overlay. This enhances the contrast and softens the skin.

4 Create a duplicate of the blurred layer. Go to Filters > Distort > Diffuse Glow. Set a moderate amount of Graininess. The Glow should enhance the highlights but not overpower the image. Finally, set a high Clear Amount. This controls the amount of diffusion, similar to opacity.

5 We can see the effect is far too strong. Set the blend mode to Hard Light. Now lower the opacity – around 45% here. Merge the two layers *ctrl* **E** ⌘ **E**. Now grab the Eraser **E** and using a small, soft brush, go over the eyes, lips and eyebrows to reveal the lighter, sharper image below.

6 Use a larger brush size to bring back the detail in her hair and the fur she's wearing; be careful not to go over her hand. Finally, open the Correct Camera Distortion Filter dialog. Drag the Vignette slider all the way to the left. Now lower the midpoint a little to finish off the effect.

SHORTCUTS
MAC WIN BOTH

265

Bobblehead caricature

TYPICALLY, CARICATURES FOCUS on one or more of the subject's features which are then drawn greatly exaggerated. Bobbleheads, on the other hand, have huge versions of the person's head atop a ludicrously small body. The head and body are usually connected by a spring, which, when tapped, causes the head to bob about – hence the name. These collectable models generally depict sporting personalities but some movie stars also have their own jittering counterparts.

As we'll see in the following example, we can, of course, create our own digital versions. This simple yet effective technique can be used to make great humorous greetings cards or gifts for friends and relatives.

1 Our singer is already on a separate layer so begin by loading up his selection. Select the Freehand Lasso tool, holding `alt` `Shift` `⌥` `Shift` and carefully draw a line starting from his ear and down around his jawline. Close this off with a loosely drawn area around the rest of his head.

2 Copy the head to a new layer with `ctrl` `J` `⌘` `J`. Click the original body layer's thumbnail and use Free Transform to scale it down to a suitably comical size; we want to emphasize the face whilst retaining the body detail. You may also want to tilt the head slightly to the left.

3 We need to make him look more like a a model: open the Smart Blur filter and leave the Quality set to Low. Adjust the Radius and Threshold to smooth out the detail but retain a suitable amount of clarity to the features. Switch to the body and reapply the effect by pressing *ctrl* *F* ⌘ *F*.

4 Now we've toned down his features we can give him a real plastic appearance with the Plastic Wrap filter. Experiment with the slider adjustments until you have the desired effect; we want to keep it fairly subtle. As before, apply this to the body layer as well.

HOT TIP

The results from the Plastic Wrap filter can vary immensely depending on the lighting and quality of the source image. If you are having difficulty producing a balanced effect, try duplicating the layer(s) before applying the filter. Doing this enables you to fine-tune the result by altering the opacity and blend mode to produce a more subtle effect.

5 We need to have the hand with the microphone in front of his head. Hide the head layer for now and make sure the body layer is active. Draw a selection around the hand using the Lasso, copy it to a new layer and move it above the head in the Layers panel by dragging its thumbnail.

6 Here's our finished image. We've increased the saturation a little and added some shading under his head with the Burn tool; this helps to bond the image together. We've also given him a shadow to place him properly – see Chapter 7 for more on how to do this.

SHORTCUTS
MAC WIN BOTH

267

All in the mind

WHAT'S ON A YOUNG GIRL'S MIND? Hard to say with any certainty – but we can make a safe bet that it would include teddy bears, ponies and candy. We're going to show these interests graphically, by lifting the top of her head and placing all these items inside.

The only thing we have to concern ourselves with here is the correct order of the layers in the stack. In order to place everything inside the head, we need to position the objects between the face and the interior – which means splitting that rim into two, so the front half will remain in front.

1 The first step is to draw the inside of the head, as an ellipse. We'll use the Elliptical Marquee tool to mark out a selection – remembering to hold **Shift** to draw a perfect circle – on a new layer. Here, we've filled it with blue and set it to Multiply so we can see through it.

2 Use **ctrl T** **⌘ T** to enter Free Transform, and rotate and squeeze the circle so it becomes an ellipse at the right angle. Don't stretch it all the way out to the right: remember, her head is actually some distance inside all that hair.

3 Fill the ellipse with a flesh color sampled from her skin and change its mode back to Normal. With the ellipse selected, move to the girl's layer and press *Backspace* to delete her head from this area; then deselect. Use the Eraser *E* to remove the top part of the head above the ellipse.

4 Load up the ellipse selection by holding *ctrl* *⌘* and clicking on its thumbnail in the Layers panel. Use Select > Modify > Contract to make the selection around 8 pixels smaller; then, using the Burn tool, darken the interior so that it looks hollow.

All the elements inside this head are behind the head layer. If we wanted the horse's nose, for instance, to poke in front of the head, then we'd need to select the nose and use *ctrl* *J* *⌘* *J* to make a new layer from it. When we bring this to the top of the layer stack, we can move the horse and its nose together, and position them as we wish.

5 Don't deselect. Instead, inverse the selection using *ctrl* *Shift* *I* *⌘* *Shift* *I*, so that just the pink rim is selected. Hold *alt* *Shift* *⌥* *Shift* as you trace a loop around the front half of the rim with the Freehand Lasso; press *ctrl* *J* *⌘* *J* to make a new layer and bring it to the front.

6 Send the head interior to the bottom of the layer stack, so that it's placed behind the head. We can now add all our objects as we like, behind the head layer, and they'll appear to be inside it. Add a little shading, on a new layer, to complete the effect.

Dog in a basket

H AIR AND FUR are among the trickiest materials to cut out in Elements. Take this photograph of a dog, for instance: we can see its wispy, shaggy fur well enough, but how on earth are we supposed to cut it away from all that grass?

The solution, as ever, is to cheat. Rather than even attempting to use one of the many selection methods to trace around the fur, we'll do a smooth cut-out and then redraw the fur using the Smudge tool.

We're going to practice our technique with a dog's fur here, but we can use the same method on people: it's far easier to recreate the effect of flyaway hair using the Smudge tool than it is to try to cut it from a complex background.

1 Begin by cutting out the dog from the background, using the Lasso or Selection Brush, or any of the selection tools described in Chapter 1. No need to be too accurate here – you don't need to trace over every strand of hair; but cut inside the hair rather than outside it, so that no grass is included in the selection.

2 We've placed our dog in this basket, just because it looks cute. To make this work, we've copied the front half of the basket to a new layer: with this section in front of the dog and the original behind, it's easy to manipulate the two so that it looks as if the dog's sitting inside.

3 Switch to the Smudge tool **R**, set to a pressure of around 80%. The key to making this easier lies in choosing the correct brush for this tool: a Spatter brush, which is one of the default Elements brushes, is perfect. Drag out clumps of fur around the edge of the dog, following the direction in which it would naturally grow.

4 Continue all the way around the dog, pulling out clumps of fur with the Smudge tool. Refer to the original photo if you like, but it's just as easy (and just as convincing) to guess at what the fur will look like. If you find 80% pressure is too great, reduce it for a smaller effect.

HOT TIP

This technique works best if you have a pressure-sensitive graphics tablet: it's far easier to tweak out the fur if you can vary the pressure, rather than relying on the uniform pressure provided by a mouse alone.

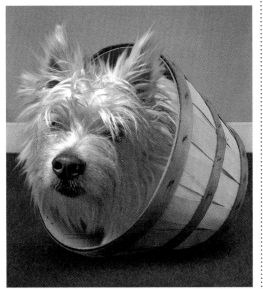

5 We now need to tweak out a few individual strands of fur for added realism. Still using the Smudge tool, choose a small, soft brush – around 3 pixels in diameter – and pull out the strands one at a time. This greatly increases the realism of the fur.

6 The technique works well enough against a white background, but it really comes into its own when we place the entire assembly into a real room. Paint in shadows beneath the basket and inside it, under the dog, for a more realistic appearance.

SHORTCUTS
MAC WIN BOTH

TIFFs, JPEGs and the rest

ONE OF THE MOST BAFFLING issues facing the Elements user is the Save As dialog. It should be straightforward: after all, all you want to do is save your file. So why are there so many options? Here are all the main file types you'll see listed, with an explanation of what they're used for.

The formats you'll need

Photoshop (.psd) is the full file you're working on, containing all the layers, styles, effects, Adjustment Layers, and so on. Save in this format when you want to carry on working on your image.

JPEG (.jpg) stands for Joint Photographic Experts Group, and is a highly compressed format that's good for delivering images over the internet. There's a trade-off between high quality and small file sizes: the higher the JPEG value, the more faithful the image will be to the original, but the bigger the file.

TIFF (.tif) stands for Tagged Image File Format, and this was the file format of choice before JPEGs came along. It's not lossy, as JPEGs are, and the resulting files are much bigger; unlike JPEGs, it can contain both layers and selection channels, so is good for exporting images for use in other applications.

JPEG 2000 (.jpf, .jp2) is a newer version of JPEGs that offers better quality and also supports selection channels. Most web browsers can't read this format, though, so it's no good for internet delivery. Sadly, Adobe dropped support for this format in Elements 8 and files in this format will no longer open by default. All is not lost, however: a fully-functional third-party plugin is available from the following website: http://www.fnordware.com/j2k/. With this installed you will be able to use the dedicated JPEG2000 sites: http://www.thefullmontage. com and http://www.absolutvision.com.

Compuserve GIF (.gif) stands for Graphics Interchange Format, and is a format introduced in 1987 and used primarily for web delivery. It includes only a very limited range of colors, so images will look very rough; on the plus side, it can contain multiple frames of an animation.

PNG (.png) stands for Portable Network Graphics, and is a more recent format intended for internet delivery. It's not that commonly used, although it does support transparency and so is useful for web designers.

Photoshop Raw (.raw) is the high-end, high bandwidth version of images captured by professional-quality digital cameras. Many professional photographers prefer this format for its extended tonal range.

Photoshop PDF (.pdf) stands for Portable Document Format, which was developed so that one complex file including text and graphics could be viewed identically on multiple computer platforms. The Photoshop Elements version is there to provide compatability.

The formats you won't need, but may as well know about

BMP, or 'Bitmap' (.bmp) is a format designed for use internally by MS-DOS and, later, Windows. It's hugely wasteful, resulting in enormous file sizes.

Photoshop EPS (.eps) stands for Encapsulated PostScript, and is the format images used to be converted into for color printing. It's now rarely used, except for jobs in unusual color spaces – such as those to be printed in CMYK plus a special Pantone color.

Scitex CT (.sct) was a high-end reprographic format in the early days of desktop publishing. CT stands for 'continuous tone'.

Targa (.tga) was a graphics format used on graphics cards for IBM compatible PCs. Many games still create screenshots in Targa format; the online game 'Second Life' accepts textures in this format, which supports transparency.

The formats you don't even need to know about

PICT (.pct) and **PCX (.pcx)** were internal formats used by early Mac and DOS computers respectively. Along with Photo Creation Format and Pixar, they're only provided as options in case you want to open graphics files created many years ago on ancient computer systems.

Two images of a car on an airport runway. It's the identical car in both photographs, but in the top image it looks false and out of place, whereas in the bottom one it belongs in the scene. The difference is that in the top picture the car is too high for the perspective of the scene; in the bottom one, the perspective is correct.

11
The third dimension

ALMOST EVERY PHOTOGRAPH WE TAKE captures a scene in three dimensions. When we want to add, edit, or adjust objects in the scene, we need to pay close attention to the perspective in the original scene if we're going to achieve anything like a convincing montage.

There are complex rules governing how perspective works, and these have been refined ever since they were first formulated by the Persian philosopher Alhazen in the 11th century. Since we're dealing with photographed images, rather than a blank canvas, we can read the existing perspective out of the scene: in this way, by using our eye and drawing vanishing point lines, we can guarantee that any new picture elements we add are consistent with the scene we started with.

Lifting the lid 1

DESPITE THE HUGE AMOUNT OF IMAGES available through stock photography sites, there will come a time where you cannot find exactly the right one for your project. This is not always a problem, as we'll see in the following tutorial.

The image of the wooden box is perfect except it's closed and we want it open. Unlike the real thing we cannot simply remove its lid: the rear sides of the box don't exist. With a few selections and transformations we'll create the missing areas using copies of the remaining sections.

1 Our first task is to isolate the lid from the rest of the box. The Polygonal Lasso **L** is perfect for this. Create a selection around the whole of the lid. Press *ctrl* *Shift* *J* ⌘ *Shift* *J* to cut it away from the rest of the image. Hiding the layer shows the problem: we only have half a box.

2 Make the lid visible again. Change the layer order so the lid is behind the box. Enter Free Transform *ctrl* *T* ⌘ *T*. Start by lowering the lid so its front corner lines up with the existing sides of the box. Hold *ctrl* ⌘. Now distort the outer corners to match.

3 Next we'll cut a hole in the top. This serves two purposes: we can use the edges as a guide for the missing sides. It will also give them substance. Create a selection following the perimeter of the lid but a few pixels inside the edge. Press *Backspace*.

4 Make sure the box layer is active. Create a selection around the front side of the box. Press *ctrl J* *⌘ J* to create a copy. Move this layer down the stack so it's behind the rest. Now reposition and distort it into place as the back side of the box.

5 Repeat the last step to create the remaining side; remember to switch back to the box layer first. Switch to the back side layer. Make another copy. Again, move it to the bottom of the layer stack. Distort this to create the floor of the box.

6 All that remains is to add some shading inside the box. Grab the Burn tool ⬤. Set the mode to Highlights. Use a large, soft brush to paint in some shadows; you'll need to switch between the layers. We only need a few subtle areas in this instance as the original lighting works quite well.

HOT TIP

It can be helpful to have a guide to follow when distorting in perspective. Sometimes you'll be able to use other areas of the original image. You can also create your own reference. This could form part of the object, as with the rim of the box. You can also use layers to create an overlay which can be turned on and off during the creation process.

SHORTCUTS
MAC **WIN** **BOTH**

277

Lifting the lid 2

ON THE PRECEDING PAGES we opened a box by removing its lid completely. You may, however, decide that you want to keep it in the image, opening as though it were hinged.

This is not difficult to achieve. We can't, of course, simply pivot the lid to open it. This is two-dimensional artwork after all. Instead we'll use geometry in our favor. By flipping and rotating the lid, its angle is mirrored against the box. Once in place, we can use a variation on the previous technique to create the hollowed-out effect.

1 To avoid unnecessary steps in creating the open box we'll use the completed image from the last technique. The original lid has been selected and placed on a separate layer. The first thing to do is flip the layer. Do this by selecting Flip Layer Vertically under Image > Rotate.

2 Use Free Transform to move and rotate the lid into place at the rear of the box. You'll notice it doesn't quite fit: it's too wide. Use the corner handles to squash the lid up a little so it meets the corners of the box. Make sure it meets the edge; you may need to rotate it a little more.

3 We could leave it at this stage. That lid looks a little heavy, though. Use the Polygonal Lasso to create a selection a few pixels within the edge of the lid's panel. Press *ctrl* *Shift* *J* ⌘ *Shift* *J* to remove the area and place it on its own layer. Drop it behind the lid in the Layers panel.

4 Use the Move tool *V* to push the panel toward the rear of the lid. This creates a recessed area. Don't place it too far back, we need to give the illusion that it has thickness. Again we can see the problem. The rear and side panels are missing.

5 Click the lid layer's thumbnail to make it active. Select the top edge of the lid. Press *ctrl* *J* ⌘ *J* to copy it to a new layer. Drop this new layer behind the lid and panel layers in the stack. Use Free Transform to distort it into position. Repeat to create the missing right-hand side panel.

6 Select the Burn tool *O*. Set the mode to Highlights. Choose a large, soft-edged tip. Paint in some areas of shadow on the inside of the lid, particularly at the top and in the corners where less light would reach. You may also want to darken the inside of the box itself.

HOT TIP

Whilst this is a very efficient method of opening a lid, your composition may require it at a different angle. To do this you'll first need to break the lid down into separate layers comprising its component parts. These can be maneuvered into the correct position individually to produce the desired effect. A similar technique is used to create a complex reflection in Chapter 8.

SHORTCUTS
MAC WIN BOTH

279

Tiling the floor

THERE'S NOTHING LIKE A SPOT of redecorating to brighten things up. The old wooden floor of the changing room in this photo could certainly do with renewing. Let's replace it with something a little more lavish: a nice marble checker to complement the border on the wall, perhaps?

The effect is not as difficult to produce as it might seem. We'll create the pattern on a layer, using the Clouds filter to add the marbling effect. We already have the existing perspective to use as a guide so it's simply a matter of distorting the new floor into position.

You can, of course, use any pattern or texture with this technique. Perhaps use it to visualize ideas for decorating your room before you commit to a particular design.

1 Create a new layer. Grab the Rectangular Marquee **M**. Draw a selection holding *Shift* to keep it square. Fill this with black. Holding *ctrl* *alt* ⌘ ⌥, click and drag the selection to create a copy. Place it next to the last square. Fill this with white. Repeat this twice more to finish the pattern.

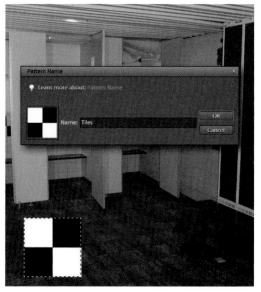

2 Hold *Shift* to keep the selection square. Now select the whole tile. It's worth starting a pixel or two inside to avoid any gaps.. Select Define Pattern from Selection from the Edit menu. Give it a name for later reference and click OK. We can delete the layer as it's no longer needed.

3 Create a new layer at the top of the stack. Press *Shift* *Backspace* to open the Fill dialog. Choose Pattern for the Contents from the drop-down menu. Select the tile pattern from the panel. Clicking OK will fill the whole layer with our new pattern.

4 Add another new layer. Fill this with the Clouds filter. Apply the Find Edges filter from the Stylize menu. This gives us a nice marble-like texture. Set the blend mode to Difference. Lower the opacity slightly to reduce the contrast. Press *ctrl* *E* *⌘* *E* to merge the layers together.

5 Now we have our new floor we need to distort it into position. Enter Free Transform. Hold *ctrl* *⌘* and distort the corner points to match the floor in the photo. You'll need to zoom out to be able to maneuver the left-hand side of the new floor into position.

6 We need to mask out the areas around the bench and the cubicles. This can be achieved by using the original floor as a clipping mask (see Chapter 4). A Hue/Saturation adjustment adds a slight color cast and darkens the floor down. Some shading is added to complete the effect.

HOT TIP

It can be tricky to get the perspective right when you don't have the whole area to match up to. Try to find as many points of reference as possible. In this image we have the lines of the original floor. The problem is they are hidden beneath the new layer. You can, of course, lower the opacity; a better solution here, however, is to change the tile layer's blend mode to Multiply or Screen. This will hide the white or black squares respectively, allowing us to accurately match up the visible edges.

SHORTCUTS
MAC WIN BOTH

Opening doors

ONE OF THE NEATEST TRICKS we can play in Elements is to open a closed door. It's impressive to see it done, but here's the real trick: it's very easy to do.

The procedure makes use of the Free Transform tool, which performs perspective distortions with ease – and without us even asking anything of it. Distort a corner handle or two and the object in question will do its best to fill the space in a true three-dimensional manner.

In this tutorial we'll concentrate on opening the door and giving it some thickness so it looks real. The view through the door we'll leave as a gaping black hole; overleaf, we'll see how to fill this hole with a convincing view.

1 Use the Polygonal Lasso to trace the shape of the door, then use `ctrl` `J` `⌘` `J` to make a new layer from it. Load the door region by `ctrl` `⌘`-clicking on its thumbnail, then make a new layer behind it, filled with black. The three layers are shown here offset to show the stacking order.

2 Enter Free Transform on the door layer using `ctrl` `T` `⌘` `T` and drag the center-left handle to the right in order to flip the door so it's facing the other way. It would be a little difficult to open otherwise.

3 Now for some perspective. Hold `ctrl` `Shift` `⌘` `Shift` as you drag the top-right corner handle up; repeat this for the bottom-right handle, until the door looks like it fits the space.

4 To give the door some thickness, we'll need to add a side. Make a rectangular selection with the Marquee tool from the door itself and make a new layer from it; move it to the side.

5 We can distort this new piece of door in a similar way to how we distorted the door itself, using Free Transform to adjust not only the width, but the height. The edge where the side touches the door should be slightly higher than the edge away from the door.

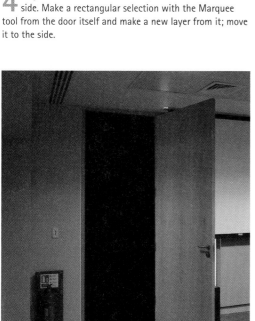

6 Brighten up this door side a little using Levels or the Brightness/Contrast adjustment – whichever you prefer. Here, we've also drawn in a lock mechanism, just for the sake of completeness: a rectangular selection was filled with a color sampled from the door handle.

7 Now, that all-important shadow. It's only a tiny amount of shadow, painted on a new layer beneath the door layer, but it makes all the difference to the realism of the scene. And how about copying the original room, grouped with the black layer, to make the view through the door?

HOT TIP

Getting the perspective on the open door exactly right is the only tricky part of this exercise. There's no simple way to describe precisely how this should be done, but if it looks right, then it probably is. In step 5, we distort the side of the door to match the opened door. It can be hard to do this accurately in Free Transform, so here's a simple solution: make the side higher than you need, then remove the top and bottom with the Lasso, or even a hard-edged Eraser, to fit the door.

SHORTCUTS
MAC WIN BOTH

283

Using perspective

PERPSECTIVE IS ONE of the trickiest techniques to master in Elements. It's the factor that distinguishes convincing montages from those that just don't feel quite right. But, by following a few straightforward rules, it's possible to make perspective work for you, rather than against you.

The key to reading perspective in a photograph lies in using horizontal lines in the original image to calculate where the vanishing point of the image lies: once we've established this, anything we draw will naturally fit the scene.

1 In this photograph of an office hallway, we're going to remove the elevator and replace it with a corridor. At first glance, the task looks daunting. While there are plenty of horizontals here that are parallel to the wall facing us, there are very few at right angles to it. But we're fortunate in having that side wall, containing the doors, just in view: using these, we can read the perspective for the scene, which is enough to give us our vanishing point.

2 We'll begin by making a new layer. Then choose the Line tool **U**. Draw two lines that follow the strongest horizontals in the left-hand wall: in this case, the bottom of the doors and the very top of the wall. Where these lines converge, over on the far right of the image, is the vanishing point. Next, on another layer, draw a selection that matches the face of the elevator opening – going right down to floor level – and fill this with black.

3 We can now draw two new perspective lines, to give us the top and bottom of our hallway. Start from the left corners and finish at the vanishing point. It's now possible to draw our first wall by using the Polygonal Lasso tool to follow these persepective lines, then filling the selection with a color to match the other walls. Group this wall layer with the black base layer we made in the previous step, so it only shows up where the two overlap.

4 We can now recolor the black layer to make a suitably colored ceiling. It's behind the wall layer, so the wall still shows up. To make the carpet, copy a section of the existing carpet and paste it in place, grouped with the ceiling layer but behind the wall layer. You may need to distort it to fit.

5 After drawing in the end wall, finishing off the scene is simply a matter of copying the elements we want from elsewhere in the picture. Here, we've taken a copy of the door on the far left and distorted it to match the perspective of the hallway.

A section of skirting board, taken from the far left of the facing wall, is copied and then stretched to run along the base of the new wall, and another small copy bent around the end wall. Finally, we made a new layer and added some shading to it with a large, soft-edged brush, to give the impression of the corridor darkening as it recedes into the distance. This final touch accentuates the sense of the corridor as a real space, adding extra realism to the scene.

SHORTCUTS
MAC WIN BOTH

Make your own jigsaws

WITH ALL THE MULTITUDE OF FILTERS in Elements, it's perhaps surprising that, hidden among the stained glass and other effects, there isn't one for creating jigsaws.

Here's a technique that makes use of a custom shape that we've included for you to download from the website. Instructions for installing these shapes, as well as the other custom files, are in the root of the Goodies folder.

1 Choose the shape Jigsaw Portrait from the Cheat section of the Shapes dialog. Once the shape is selected, use the Shapes tool to drag from corner to corner within your image, so that the entire space is filled with the jigsaw pattern. You'll see it appear as faint lines as you do so.

2 Once you release the mouse button, the shape layer will be filled with the default color – generally blue. We'll only be using this as a template, so there's no need to change the color of the layer: it won't appear in the final illustration.

3 Load up the shape layer's pixel area by holding *ctrl* ⌘ and clicking on its thumbnail in the Layers panel. Then return to the image layer and use *ctrl* *J* ⌘ *J* to make a new layer from that selection. Hide the shape layer to see the image made up of jigsaw pieces.

4 To give the pieces some depth, add a Simple Inner bevel Layer Style. Open the Style Settings dialog and reduce the size of the Bevel to about 5 pixels; add a slight drop shadow to make the pieces look more three-dimensional. You can play around with the Bevel settings until it looks right.

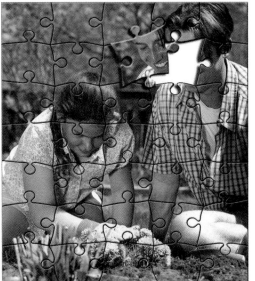

5 Now let's make the dividing lines clearer. Load up the selection of the shape layer again, then inverse the selection using *ctrl* *Shift* *I* ⌘ *Shift* *I*; now everything except the pieces is selected. Make a new layer and fill the selection with black to make the lines between the pieces.

6 To take one piece out of the jigsaw, go to the lines layer we just created and click in one of the pieces with the Magic Wand. Return to the image layer and use *ctrl* *Shift* *J* ⌘ *Shift* *J* to cut the selection to a new layer. Move it to the top of the layer stack and move and rotate it as you like.

HOT TIP

We've included two versions of the jigsaw shape – one in portrait (vertical) orientation, the other in a landscape (horizontal) shape. Choose whichever one is most appropriate for the shape of the image you're working on.

SHORTCUTS
MAC WIN BOTH

287

Out of bounds

1 Here's our original painting. The format – one girl helping another down from a wall – is perfect for our purposes.

2 The first step is to select and copy the figures to a new layer, using a combination of your favorite selection tools.

THE 'OUT OF BOUNDS' TECHNIQUE is a popular one with Elements artists and it's not hard to see why: breaking a picture out of its frame makes for an arresting image.

The process can be as simple or as complex as you want to make it. Here, we'll look at a rather more detailed version of the trick, using not a photograph but a painting – *Little Thieves* or *Petites Maraudeuses*, by William-Adolphe Bougeuereau.

3 Now place the picture frame between the two layers, distorting it using Free Transform until it follows the angle of the wall in the painting.

4 Let's now add our own wall. Make a rectangular selection on a new layer filled with solid color; the skirting board is easily painted at the bottom.

5 Now enter Free Transform and, holding *ctrl Shift* ⌘ *Shift*, drag the bottom-right corner down until it matches the painting's perspective.

6 The carpet is added on a new layer: solid color, Gaussian Noise, then Gaussian Blur. We've also deleted the section of wall behind the painting.

7 Use Shadows/Highlights to brighten that dark skirt and the Dodge tool to lighten the legs; then clone out the foliage on the skirt.

8 The shadows behind the girls give them some distance from the wall: use the techniques outlined in Chapter 7.

9 We've added a chair to give a sense of the room continuing out of the frame and to make that plain wall look a little less bare.

10 Finally, add shadows for the chair and picture frame. And while we're at it, we may as well include a plaque to the painter.

RGB or CMYK?

PICTURE THE SCENE: you've spent hours creating the perfect birthday card in Elements. It features a lovingly crafted cut-out image against a bright green background, a dazzlingly bright red headline, and a contrasting blue caption. But when you print it out on your inkjet printer, the text looks dull and lifeless, and the background is far darker than it looked on the screen – despite having used the best quality glossy photo paper. What can have gone wrong?

The problem is the fundamental difference between what you see on the screen and what can be printed on paper. And it all comes down to two acronyms: RGB and CMYK.

RGB stands for red, green and blue, and refers to the colors used by computer monitors. In standard 8-bit mode, each pixel on your screen can display each of these three colors in 256 different levels of brightness. 256 is 2^8, or 2 multiplied by itself 8 times – which is what 8-bit means. By combining these three basic colors, each pixel can display 2^8 x 2^8 x 2^8 different colors – over 16 million in total.

We start with a black screen and the more color we throw on it, the brighter it becomes. These are known as 'additive' colors for this reason: we're adding light to blackness. When we add the maximum value of each of the three primary colors, we get white.

Printing ink on paper, however, works in precisely the opposite way. Rather than using red, green and blue, printers use cyan, magenta and yellow. But when we print, we start off with white paper; the more colors we add, the darker the result (just as you find when you mix paints together). These are known as 'subtractive' colors. If we add 100% of cyan, magenta and yellow together, we get black. Or rather, we don't; we get a muddy brown. That's why printers use an additional color, black, to deepen the shadows and strengthen the printed image. The four colors combined give us CMYK. Surprisingly, no one seems to know precisely what the 'K' stands for. Most claim it means 'key', although that seems a poor substitute for 'black'.

When you mix the primary colors together, either on screen or on paper, you get some surprising results. On screen, mixing red and green makes yellow, red and blue make magenta, and green and blue make cyan. Do those colors sound familiar? They should do – they're the primary colors of printing inks. And, when printing, mixing magenta and yellow produces red, magenta and cyan make blue, and yellow and cyan make green.

So what does this have to do with poor quality printing? The trouble is that while your monitor is capable of displaying a huge range of colors, CMYK is capable of reproducing only a very limited part of that color 'gamut', as it's known. That's the reason why commercial printers use additional Pantone colors, chosen from swatch books similar to those you'd use to choose household paints. If you want a color that can't be achieved with CMYK, you need to use additional inks.

Some inkjet printers try to get around this problem by using six colors, rather than four. And this does expand the range slightly, but the unfortunate fact remains that not everything you see on your monitor is capable of being reproduced on paper.

What's the solution, then? Can't we just convert our images to CMYK before we print them and see what the difference is? Not in Elements, although we can in its big brother Photoshop. The ability to prepare print-ready artwork is one of the reasons Photoshop costs nearly ten times as much.

Avoid 100% green or blue, as these are the colors least likely to reproduce well; dazzling pinks are also problematic, although 100% magenta and solid red will work well. If a color combination on your monitor looks larger than life, then that's probably a good indication that you won't be able to print it. Ultimately, though, it comes down to experience: seasoned users get to know which colors will work and which won't. If in doubt, sample colors from your photographs rather than creating them from the Color Picker – you're much more likely to get printable colors that way.

■ Two versions of
the same vacation
scene. The top one,
as a Photoshop
Elements file, takes
up just over 4Mb
of disk space. The
bottom one is
saved as a low
quality JPEG file,
takes up just 78K.
Can't spot the
difference? That's
because Elements'
Save for Web
feature can make
huge size savings
with minimal loss
of quality.

12

Advanced techniques

CREATING FANTASTIC IMAGES in Elements is one thing. Getting them off your computer screen is another matter entirely. As with most techniques, there are right and wrong ways of doing the job.

In this chapter we'll explain how to save files for speedy internet delivery, both for single images and for animations. (We'll also look at how to create eye-catching animations directly in Elements.)

We'll also show a useful technique for creating standard artwork into which you can drop any background photo, and an ingenious way of isolating tricky objects from their backgrounds.

Catching the drops

WE OFTEN NEED TO CHANGE the background in a photo; whether we just want a more appealing image or to move the subject to a different scene entirely, we need to be able to make a good selection and one that comprises all the required details.

In our example, the fountain's background is hardly inspiring, so we'd like to cut it away and replace it with something more fitting. The problem we have is all the little splashes of water: we need to keep them because the image would look static and unrealistic without them but it's too much for the Magic Wand to cope with. Zooming in and selecting each one by hand would be far too time-consuming. As we'll see, if we apply a little lateral thinking, we can make fairly short work of the task.

1 We'll begin by selecting as much of the fountain and water as possible. The Quick Selection tool is perfect and makes short work of this. For earlier versions of Elements, we could use the Magic Selection Brush or a combination of the Magic Wand and the normal Selection Brush.

2 With the basis of our selection complete, we'll store it for later: go to the Select menu, choose Save Selection and give it a name and click OK. Now deselect *ctrl* **D** ⌘ **D**. In preparation for the next part of the technique, we'll duplicate the background layer *ctrl* **J** ⌘ **J**.

3 Select the Threshold adjustment from the Filters menu. This converts the light and dark areas to pure black or white. Now we can clearly see where the water drops are. Making slight adjustments to the level gives us some fine-tuning. This is a good balance so we'll apply it.

4 There are a lot of areas that we don't want: we can paint these out using a hard-edged black brush **B**. The fountain is saved so we don't have to be too careful around it, as long as we leave the splashes intact. We can erase the area at the top where it meets the windows, for example.

5 Grab the Magic Wand **W** and uncheck Contiguous in the Options bar. Clicking in one area of white will select them all. Open the Save Selection dialog. Choose our previously saved one from the list and click Add to Selection. Finally, click OK. We can hide or discard this layer now.

6 Make the background layer active and load the saved selection. Apply a 1 pixel Feather to soften the edges, then press *ctrl* *J* ⌘ *J* to make a copy. Shown against black, we can see how good the result is. We can add a more suitable background, of course, as our intro image shows.

HOT TIP

As an additional step, we could separate the main water spurt from the rest of the image by selecting with the Rectangular Marquee and cutting it to a new layer *ctrl* *Shift* *J* ⌘ *Shift* *J*. We can desaturate it to remove any unwanted color casts and also lower its opacity a little to make it slightly translucent.

SHORTCUTS
MAC WIN BOTH

Reusable images

PEOPLE ENJOY GETTING PERSONALIZED items and Elements is a great way of doing this. It can, however, be a very time-consuming job to create an image from scratch each time. This is where working with layers and masks comes into its own. We can create and save image templates that can be used over and over again. These can be used for almost anything: wedding album covers, birthday cards, invitations; the list goes on.

The trick is to make sure the subject image is quick and easy to replace. In this instance we'll add a photograph to our example image so it appears under all the components of the scene. Initially this takes quite a bit time for the selection work, but once this has been done all we ever need to do is change the photo; a task which takes seconds to complete.

1 First we need to make a selection of the box, glass and flowers. A combination of the Quick Selection tool and the Selection Brush works well. We'll ignore the shadows and we only need to include enough in the selection to be able to slot a variety of photo sizes under the objects.

2 Press *ctrl* J ⌘ J to create a copy on a new layer. Click the background layer's thumbnail in the Layers panel. Go to File > Place and select *Wedding.jpg*. The image will be sandwiched between the two layers. Hold *ctrl* ⌘ and drag the corners to position the image.

3 We have a problem with the glass: we should be able to see through it. Make the cutaway layer active and add a layer mask. Grab the Brush tool **B** and select mid-gray for the foreground color. Paint over the base and stem of the glass to make it translucent.

4 Create a layer below the cutaway layer. Set the blend mode to Multiply. Select a soft brush. Set the color to black. Now begin to paint in some shadows around the box, glass and flowers. Lower the opacity to match the existing shadows on the rest of the image.

5 To add to the effect, create a new layer above the photo layer. Now hold *ctrl* ⌘ and click the photo layer's thumbnail to load its selection. Select Edit > Stroke (outline) Selection. Set the Width to about 10 pixels. Set white as the color. Make sure the Location is Inside and click OK.

6 Finally, we've added a small drop shadow to the photo to add a little more depth. We can now save the image as a .psd file, which keeps the layers intact. To reuse the template we simply open it and place a new photo using the existing one as a guide, as we have in the intro image.

HOT TIP

Our example image is fairly complex and selections won't always be as tricky as they are here. It is, however, worth spending the time making the cut-out as perfect as possible as it only needs to be done the once. To make the file a little more lean, we can merge the cut-out and shadow layers together (*ctrl* E ⌘ E). The opacity and translucency are retained in the single layer.

SHORTCUTS
MAC WIN BOTH

297

Saving files for the internet

W E ALL WANT to share our photographs and montages with others, and the internet provides a simple, easy way to do just that. But rather than just taking your Elements file and uploading it to a website, you first need to save it in a format that web browsers will understand.

JPEG, GIF and PNG are the three most common file types. Elements provides a useful way to save images for web delivery: it's called Save for Web and you'll find it under the File menu.

Here, we'll look at what each of the three formats has to offer and see how to use the Save for Web dialog to get the best possible results from your digital images.

1 Here's a detail of our original photograph, enlarged so we can see the detail – but at 313K, it's far too big for internet delivery.

3 Reducing the number of colors in this GIF file to 64 reduces the file size to 168K, but we can clearly see the 'dither pattern' in the skin tones.

5 As a JPEG file with a quality of 50, this is very close to the original, but its size has been reduced to just 73K – fine for the internet.

7 For the sake of comparison, here's the file at a JPEG setting of 0. The image is just about unusable, but takes up just 19K of space.

2 As a 256-color GIF image, we can see a little blockiness appearing in the white of the teeth: this image is a hefty 264K in size.

4 As an 8-color GIF, the file size comes down to 72K: it's now acquired the appearance of a poorly photocopied sepia print.

6 Taking the JPEG quality down to 20 produces some marked 'blockiness' and reduces the file size to 38K.

8 A 24-bit PNG file produces the best results, but at a cost: this file is a massive 604K – nearly twice the size of the original.

The first step in Save for Web is to choose the file type. JPEG is best for photographs and GIF is best for areas with a lot of flat color, such as buttons and badges. PNG supports transparency, unlike JPEGs, and produces good quality – but at the cost of increased file size.

Unless you're creating page furniture for web pages, it's best to stick to JPEG format, as this will give you the best results. There's a trade-off between file size and quality: the better the quality, the larger the file will be, so the longer it will take people to download.

A JPEG setting of 50 or more will produce an image that's almost indistinguishable from the original file. The more complex an image, the larger the file will be: so a shot of a cloudy sky will produce a much larger file if there's an intricate fence in front of it.

As you drag the Quality slider, you can see the results of the JPEG compression in the right-hand pane (the left one always shows the original image). If it's not showing an area you want to concentrate on, drag within the window to move it and both images will pan together. You can also zoom in using the Magnifying Glass tool at the top left to see an area of interest in detail.

JPEG files can be set to 'progressive', which means that they will load in stages, each pass producing a more detailed version of the image. This was an issue when most people had slow modems, but is now rarely used.

Beneath each image is a readout showing the file type, the size the resulting file will be, and the time taken to download it. Click the tiny arrow at the top right of the images to change the speed of download: the default 28K applies to old-fashioned modems, which are hardly relevant in the era of high speed broadband.

You can also choose to reduce the physical image size as well, using the New Size section (center right). This will, of course, reduce the file size as well, but you need to be sure of the dimensions you want to end up with before playing with these numbers.

If you have a favorite combination that works well for your images, you can save it as a preset and then apply it to each image that passes through the Save for Web dialog. You can also choose to include ICC profiles, which aim to maintain consistent color: unless your computer has been calibrated to do this, it's best avoided.

The Matte box is used for saving GIF and PNG images with transparency: if you want to place images on a colored background in a web page, specify that color here and the transparent pixels will be blended with it. This is necessary because GIFs and 8-bit PNG files only support one level of transparency – on or off.

When you've chosen your settings, press OK and the standard file Save dialog will open. Be sure to specify a different name for your file to avoid overwriting the existing image.

299

Animated GIFs

MOVEMENT IS ONE of the characteristics that most distinguishes the internet from printed books. We can create short animations right inside Elements, using the Save for Web feature.

In this example, we've made a simple montage containing just five layers: the background, with the road and sky; the clouds; the car; the crate on the back of the car; and the shadow beneath it.

By moving each of these layers around and making a new composite copy as a separate layer, we can create our animation as a series of separate Elements layers. It's then an easy matter to string these together to make a moving image.

We can't show our finished animation in this book, of course, but it is available to download from the website if you want to see how it looks when it's moving. Details on this can be found at the end of the book.

1 Begin with Select All (*ctrl* *A* / *⌘* *A*) then Merged Copy (*ctrl* *Shift* *C* / *⌘* *Shift* *C*). This makes a copy of everything in the artwork. Now choose Paste (*ctrl* *V* / *⌘* *V*) and move that copy to the top of the pile, as shown in the Layers panel (right).

2 That's frame 1 done. To make frame 2, first hide the first merged copy, then drag the clouds layer to the left a little way. Move the car up a fraction and rotate the crate to give the impression of them jiggling around as they move.

3 Repeat the Select All, Merged Copy, Paste procedure as before, to create another new layer – and, once again, make sure it's at the top of the layer stack. Each of these new composite layers will form a single frame in our animation.

4 The same process once more: move the clouds and jiggle the car and the crate, then Select All, Merged Copy, and Paste. Remember to hide the previous composite copy by clicking its Eye icon in the Layers panel before you attempt to move anything. When moving the clouds, hold the *Shift* key to make sure you're moving them horizontally.

5 When we get the big cloud over to the far left (frame 4 in our animation), we need to make a copy of this cloud layer and drag it over to the right, so the small cloud is just creeping in from that side. This will allow us to make the animation run for ever.

6 For frame 5 and for subsequent frames, we need to move both the original clouds layer and its copy. In Elements 5 and later you can select both layers together in the Layers panel, but it's just as easy to use *ctrl* **E** ⌘ **E** to merge the two layers together, so you can move them as one.

7 You can make as many frames as you like in your animation: we're using just six. In this final frame, the small cloud, which has been sliding in from the right, is now approaching its original position, and we can see the copy of the big cloud starting to make an appearance too. By duplicating the cloud layers in this way we're able to create an animation which appears to run seamlessly for ever.

8 Here's how your Layers panel will look (below) after all six frames have been completed. We now need to delete all the original layers – including the background – leaving just the six composite frames of the animation.

9 Now's a good time to save your document. But rather than overwriting the original, choose Save As and give it a different name: we don't want to lose all those individual layers that we've had to delete in the previous step.

Choose File > Save for Web to open the dialog, which will look exactly as it did on the previous pages. This time, though, check the Animate box near the top of the dialog window.

The number of frames in the animation is set by the number of layers in the document – one for each layer. But we can specify the time each

frame is to last for, as well as whether the animation will run just once or will loop for ever. This is the option we'll choose here: that's why we wrapped the clouds around in that way.

Adjust the Dither and number of colors, if you like, to reduce the size of the file; our example weighs in at over 600K, larger than a standard web animation would normally be.

Click the Preview button at the bottom to see how your animation will look in a browser: this is the first time you'll be able to see it moving. When you're happy with the timing, press OK to save the animation as a GIF file.

HOT TIP

Although we've gone to some lengths to wrap the background clouds around so that the animation will loop convincingly, you don't need to do this with every animation. However you choose to animate your constructions, do be sure to save a copy before deleting all the original layers: Elements can only work with one layer equalling one frame of animation and you don't want to accidentally lose all your hard work.

SHORTCUTS
MAC WIN BOTH

Actual size

Displaying the image on screen so that one pixel in the image exactly matches one pixel on the monitor. This is not the same as print size, which is determined by the resolution of the image.

Adjustment Layer

Special layers that perform non-destructive tonal and color adjustments to all or part of the artwork; they can be turned on or off and altered as required.

Aliasing

The opposite of anti-aliasing: no attempt is made at blending elements of the artwork to avoid jagged edges. This does have its uses: it can be used with very small fonts to avoid them becoming unreadable.

Alignment

A set of tools on the Options bar to force multiple layers to line up with each other using edges or centers.

Alpha channel

An area used to store a layer's selection information. This can be loaded and saved whilst the document is open; some file types can store alpha channels permanently with the image information.

Anti-aliasing

The method of creating a smooth transition between contrasting colors to avoid harsh, jagged lines.

Background layer

By default, this is the base layer upon which all others are added. Most operations can be performed on this apart from moving and applying styles.

Bitmap

The method of creating an image by adding individual pixels of a specific color in a two-dimensional grid. Most images produced in Elements use this process.

Blend mode

Used to combine the content of two or more layers by blending the upper layer with the layer beneath in different ways to produce a variety of effects.

Brightness/Contrast

An adjustment method used for enhancing the strength of layers and images.

Channel

The area that holds the color information of an image. In Elements there are three channels: red, green, and blue, that are mixed together in varying amounts to define all the colors.

Clipping group

Hiding areas of the artwork by grouping two or more layers: the base layer acts as a mask template, its pixels defining what is visible on the layers above.

CMYK

Abbreviation for cyan, magenta, yellow, and black – the colors used for reproducing images in printed materials.

Color settings

A section of Elements' Preferences that set whether images are displayed for on-screen viewing or optimized for printing.

Compression

The method of reducing image file sizes using complex algorithms. There are two types: lossless, which does not affect the quality of the image, and lossy, which sacrifices some quality in favor of smaller files.

Constrain

Forcing the direction of movement when using a particular tool, usually adhering to 45° angles. This is often used to ensure layers remain aligned when they are moved around the artwork.

Constrain Proportions

When enabled this function maintains the dimensions when resizing an image, shape, or bounding box. When used with the Marquee tools it ensures a perfectly circular or square selection.

Contiguous

This is an option for tools such as the Magic Wand. When enabled only the local area around the cursor will be affected; otherwise instances will be selected from the entire document.

Cropping

Reducing the frame around an image to focus on an area of interest.

Depth of field

This is the area of the image that remains in sharp focus whilst the rest is left softer. The technique is often used to draw attention to a point of interest in the picture.

Desaturate

Removing the color information of an image leaving only grayscale tones describing the shadows, midtones, and highlights.

Dingbat

A font style that uses monotone images in place of standard letter characters. These can be anything from a simple symbol to a famous person's face. Being text, all the same effects can be applied as you would normally.

Displacement

A method of distorting an image according to the brightness values in an associated grayscale image file.

Distribute

A method of arranging layers to produce equal spacing between their centers or edges.

Dithering

The method of making an image appear to have more colors than it actually has by creating a patterned transition with a mixture of the available colors.

Dots per inch (DPI)

A measure of the output resolution of an image. On-screen images are typically displayed at 72 or 96 dpi whilst professional-quality prints are 300 dpi or sometimes more.

Feathering

The method of smoothing and blending a selection to avoid jagged edges. This differs from anti-aliasing as the edge is blurred against the destination rather than bridging using a gradient.

Filter Gallery

The dialog that lets you browse and apply individual filters or stack several filters together as layers to achieve different effects. These can be previewed prior to committing them to the image.

Gaussian Blur

A filter that uses a bell-shaped curve to give the impression of soft focus.

Gaussian Noise

A filter that adds random pixels in black and white (or in color) to create the effect of tight texture.

GIF

A lossy file format used in the early days of the internet. Today, GIF images are used for creating animations, a feature not possible with most other file formats.

Graphics tablet

A device connected to the computer that allows you to control the cursor with a pen-shaped stylus instead of a mouse. Many are pressure-sensitive, allowing much more accurate control of the tools.

Grayscale

An image composed of black, white and shades of gray, with no color component.

Hard Light

A blend mode in which midtone gray is invisible, leaving just the highlights and shadows on view.

Hue/Saturation

An adjustment method used for changing the color of layers and images.

Interpolation

This is the method of resizing up or down by adding or removing pixels. When upsizing, an algorithm works out the average between adjacent pixels and places new ones in between.

JPEG

A method of compressing images to take up less space on disk. JPEG files can have a variety of settings, offering smaller file sizes at the expense of some quality.

Layer

All images in Elements consist of at least one layer: they are equivalent to laying sheets of acetate on top of each other to build up areas of the artwork.

Layer linking

Layers can be linked together, allowing them to be moved and transformed as a single item. This is useful if you need to uniformly reposition or scale multiple sections of the artwork

Layer mask

Masks are used to selectively hide parts of the artwork by painting in shades of gray: black hides the area, white reveals it, and anything in between makes it transparent.

Glossary

Layer style

These add effects to a layer without permanently affecting the artwork. Examples include: drop shadows, bevels and glows. These can be combined and their attributes adjusted to suit the image.

Leading

The adjustable spacing between lines of text. The term originates from the early days of printing when lead blocks were placed to keep the type separated.

Levels

An adjustment dialog for correcting and enhancing the shadows, midtones and highlights of a photo. They can be applied to the image as a whole or to the individual color channels for finer control.

Liquify

A powerful self-contained filter with which you can distort an image as though it were oil floating on water. This is very useful for flowing, organic substances and also for retouching photos.

Magic Wand

A selection tool that finds areas of an image of a similar color to the area in which the tool is clicked. Commonly used for selecting and removing backgrounds.

Marquee

This is the outline that defines a selection. It's often called the 'marching ants' because of its continuously moving dotted line.

Merge

The Merge Down command will combine one layer with the layer directly beneath it. Merge Visible will produce a single layer from all visible layers in the artwork.

Modifier keys

The keys ctrl, shift and alt that provide additional functions when held down in conjunction with certain tools, usually serving as shortcuts for switching between the tool's modes.

Non-destructive

A term used to describe an effect which does not permanently alter the image and remains editable, even after the image is saved and reopened.

Opacity

Determines how transparent the content of a layer appears: 0% is completely invisible, 100% is solid. Adjusting this value can be used for blending components of the artwork or for creating special effects.

Options bar

The contextual toolbar that sits across the top of the Elements window. This provides specific options and controls for the currently selected tool.

Out-of-bounds

A framing technique where parts of the image extend outside of the frame's boundaries; often used to emphasize the action of a photo.

Painting tools

Any tool such as the Brush, Clone tool, Smudge tool, and so on, that affects the area of an image over which it is dragged.

Palette

An area in the workspace containing sets of items such as styles, brushes or layers. These can be collapsed or hidden away when not in use.

Photoshop CS5

The 'big brother' of Elements, which offers superior controls and a range of additional features.

Pixel

A loose abbreviation of 'picture element'. The individual dots which make up a digital image; each can be one of the millions of colors available.

Pixelation

Visible degradation often caused by scaling the image larger than its original size. This is also used to describe the stepping effect when anti-aliasing is disabled.

Preset Manager

A dialog with which you can load, save and organize any brushes, gradients, color swatches and patterns you may have downloaded or created, along with the program's built-in presets.

Print size

A viewing mode in which an image is displayed at approximately the size it will print, using the current resolution settings.

RAM

Random Access Memory: the part of the computer that holds running programs and their data; for Elements this would be open images and the undo history.

Raster image

An image that is formed of individually colored dots (pixels). This is the most commonly used format for digital painting and photo editing.

Resolution

The method of describing the quality of a digital image by the number of individual pixels it contains. The higher the resolution, the more defined the areas of the picture can be.

RGB

Abbreviation for red, green, blue – the colors used by a computer monitor for displaying images.

Saturation

The depth and intensity of the colors in an image.

Scratch disk

A special area of the computer's hard drive reserved for temporary data storage when system RAM is running low.

Scrubby slider

An alternative method of increasing and decreasing the value of a particular attribute in some dialogs by positioning the cursor over the value and dragging right or left.

Shadows/Highlights

An adjustment method for recovering image data from the darkest and brightest parts of an image without affecting the midtones.

Simplify

Also referred to as rasterizing. The method of converting a shape or text layer to a regular bitmap layer; this can also be applied to layer styles to make them permanent.

Smart Fix

A simple method of automatically enhancing images that requires minimal technical knowledge on the part of the user.

sRGB

A color space devised to make graphic elements look better on computer screens. sRGB is a limited space that's best avoided for printing purposes.

Swatches

A collection of favorite colors and gradients stored in an easily selectable panel.

TIFF

A lossless image file format (see JPEG). Some digital cameras have the option of saving images in TIFF format.

Tolerance

This setting determines the precision of the associated tool. The higher the value, the larger the area of similar tones affected and vice versa.

Unsharp Mask

An adjustment that attempts to make the image appear crisper by enhancing the contrasting edges. The 'mask' element allows the area of the effect to be fine-tuned by means of a tolerance-like setting.

Vanishing point

Used when working or drawing in perspective: these mark the position on the horizon where two or more lines converge, for example as when looking down a straight road or railway tracks.

Vector graphics

A way of creating images using interconnected points, lines and curves generated by mathematical formulae. Unlike pixel-based artwork they can be scaled to any size without losing definition.

Visibility (layer styles)

Similar to changing a layer's opacity except it only affects the pixels of the layer, leaving the style itself untouched. The three modes, Show, Hide and Ghosted, turn the pixels on and off or render them semi-transparent.

Accessing the online content

This edition of the book is the first to have its content on the accompanying website, rather than on a CD or DVD supplied with the book itself, as has been the case in the past. To access this content, you'll first need to go to the following web address:

http://www.howtocheatinphotoshopelements.com/resources/

You will then be asked for a username and password. The username is **htcie**. The password is **takemethere**; these both need to be in lower case. Once you have entered these, a new page will open containing links to all the available content, as well as the necessary installation guides.

Project files

This symbol indicates that you'll find an Elements file on the website to accompany the tutorial. They're available to download in batches based on each chapter. Each one includes the starting point for each workthrough. The project files are named with both the page numbers and the title of the project to make them easy to find.

This symbol means that there's also a movie available on the website that shows the tutorial played out in real time. Sometimes it's easier to understand a concept when you see it acted out live, rather than just by reading about it. You can choose to watch the movies on the website or download them to watch straight from your computer. To view them, you'll need the free QuickTime player from www.apple.com/quicktime, if you don't already have it installed.

Previous editions

Times change and Elements has not been left behind. Throughout the *How to Cheat in Photoshop Elements* series, we have done our best to keep the projects compatible with all versions of the program. Sadly, we cannot keep every spread in the book so we've moved them to the website in PDF format, along with their supporting files.

Shapes

The custom jigsaw pattern shapes, as described on page 286 are also available to download. We've also included a small selection of stars so you can make your own starbursts to place behind text announcements.

To use them, download them from the Goodies section of the website; there are instructions on where to place the files on the hard drive depending on which operating system you are using (Windows and Mac OS X).

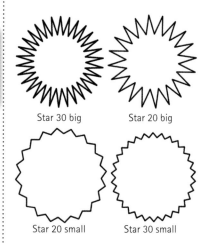

Star 30 big   Star 20 big

Star 20 small   Star 30 small

Above:
Jigsaw
Landscape

Left:
Jigsaw
Portrait

Layer styles

We've included a range of useful layer styles to complement those already present. As well as the neon text effects used in the book, we've added a range of inner shadows, some metallic styles and two new types of inner and outer glow, the difference being their blend mode is set to Multiply; this can be useful for creating shadows which are centrally placed, rather than offset to one side. The files and installation instructions can be found in the Goodies section of the website.

Smart brushes

Smart Brush presets for the project on page 122 can also be found here. Refer to the information on the website for details on how to install them.

Gold paint

Silver paint

Metallic paint

Diamond paint

Inner shadow big soft

Inner shadow big softer

Inner shadow small

Inner shadow big hard

Inner shadow edge

Inner shadow small soft

Neon blue

Neon blue 2

Neon pink

Neon green

Neon red

Neon yellow

Metal bling

Metal chunky gold

Metal chunky chrome

Metal rust

Metal chunky gold 2

Metal chunky chrome 2

Inner stroke

Center stroke

Outer stroke

Inner glow multiply

Outer glow multiply

Bevel and shadow